How Long Will South Africa Survive?

How Long Will
South Africa Survive?

RW Johnson

HURST & COMPANY, LONDON

In memory of Lawrie Schlemmer (1936–2011)
A friend, a colleague and a great South African.

First published in South Africa by Jonathan Ball, 2015.

Published in the United Kingdom in hardback in 2015 by
C. Hurst & Co. (Publishers) Ltd.,
41 Great Russell Street, London, WC1B 3PL
© RW Johnson, 2015

Second impression, 2015

Printed in the United Kingdom by Bell and Bain Ltd, Glasgow

Distributed in the United States, Canada and Latin America
by Oxford University Press, 198 Madison Avenue, New York,
NY 10016, United States of America.

A Cataloguing-in-Publication data record for this book
is available from the British Library.

ISBN: 978-1-84904-559-9

www.hurstpublishers.com

This book is printed on paper from registered sustainable
and managed sources.

Contents

Abbreviations and Acronyms

Acsa	Airports Company South Africa
Amcu	Association of Mineworkers and Construction Union
APDP	Automotive Production and Development Programme
CIS	Commonwealth of Independent States
Codesa	Convention for a Democratic South Africa
Contralesa	Congress of Traditional Leaders of South Africa
Cope	Congress of the People
Cosatu	Congress of South African Trade Unions
CRA	Contingency Reserve Arrangement
DA	Democratic Alliance
DRC	Democratic Republic of Congo
EFF	Economic Freedom Fighters
FDI	foreign direct investment
FLN	Algerian Front de Libération Nationale
GEM	Global Emerging Markets
ICBC	Industrial and Commercial Bank of China
ICT	Information and Computer Technology
ICT	Imperial Crown Trading [ch 2]
IPID	Independent Police Investigative Directorate
MAF	Mazibuye African Forum
MK	Umkhonto we Sizwe

MKMVA	Military Veterans Association
MPRDA	Mineral and Petroleum Resources Development Act
MRDI	Masibambisane Rural Development Initiative
NAM	Non-Aligned Movement
NDB	Brics New Development Bank
NDP	National Development Plan
NDR	National Democratic Revolution
NEC	National Executive Committee
Nepad	New Partnership for Africa's Development
NFP	National Freedom Party
NHI	National Health Insurance system
NIA	National Intelligence Agency
NIC	Natal Indian Congress
NPA	National Prosecution Authority
NUM	National Union of Mineworkers
Numsa	National Union of Metalworkers of South Africa
PAMDC	Pan African Mineral Development Company
PBOC	People's Bank of China
PIC	Public Investment Corporation
RDP	Reconstruction and Development Programme
SAA	South African Airways
SABC	South African Broadcasting Corporation
Sactwu	SA Clothing and Textile Workers Union
SADF	South African Defence Force
Sadtu	South African Democratic Teachers Union
SAIRR	SA Institute for Race Relations
SANDF	South African National Defence Force
Sanef	SA National Editors' Forum
SAPS	South African Police Service
Sassa	State Social Security Agency
SDRs	Special Drawing Rights
SOE	state-owned enterprise
Unctad	United Nations Conference on Trade and Development
WGC	World Gold Council

Preface

I t feels strange for me to be writing about South Africa in the era of Jacob Zuma. Once he sat in my classes.

Jacob Zuma never expected to be president. Migrating to Durban from a bone-poor rural background (his mother a domestic, his father a policeman who died young), Jacob worked at whatever he could get. 'I used to polish the verandah, you know, jobs like that,' he told me. I remember the Durban of those days, the Zulu 'house-boys' wearing white calico uniforms trimmed with red on their sleeves and shorts. They were men-boys and they used to congregate on the grass verges to chat in the evenings, calling out to the Zulu maids who passed by. The men were in shorts and bare feet in the warm Durban evenings, the maids still in their domestic uniforms, having finished their work for the day and often giving rather tart answers to the men. But the chances were that they would all end up in some *khaya* (servants' quarters) behind the white household, flirting and drinking while playing raucous Zulu music on a record player. It was the sort of music you heard on the Zulu programme, which was a half-hour slot at 9.30 am every day on the main SABC English radio – the fact that Zulus merited just half an hour a day in a province where they constituted 85 per cent of the population telling you all you needed to know about how apartheid worked. Often, as a boy, I would step outside at night and hear those sounds and feel that that music was the best of it, as good as anything else I could listen to.

The very existence of such a group of men as these Zulu house-boys bespoke the humiliation of the Zulu nation. Once they would all have been young warriors. Now they were infantilised as 'boys', well into manhood, basically men who did whatever they could to get by, usually working in white households, occasionally for schools or companies. Many white households felt that a Zulu man was intrinsically a bit more threatening than a Zulu woman, so to keep their jobs they had to prove how harmless they were and become expert in all the dissembling acts known in the Deep South, the deliberate stupidities, the rolling eyes, the avoidable mistakes and so on. In a word, playing up to being merely a boy even though a full-grown man. Jacob was perfectly typical of this group in having virtually no education at all – the white missionaries had never been so numerous in the Zulu heartland as they had been among the Xhosas of the Eastern Cape, so the Zulus were always handicapped that way. Jacob was only to learn to read and write in English as a prisoner on Robben Island, taught by his cell-mate, Harry Gwala, a Zulu schoolteacher who had become a hardline communist.

Jacob Zuma was full of bounce and life, always a very jovial man, and also politically aware. He enthusiastically joined the African National Congress, which was natural enough – Albert Luthuli, a Zulu chief, was its leader and for Zuma, with his rural Zulu background, that mattered a lot. But with the effective take-over of the ANC by the Communist Party (the SACP) in the late 1950s, everything moved to the left just as the ANC moved towards confrontation with the Verwoerd government. For those of us who supported the ANC – which, as a young white radical, I did – it was made clear that Mandela was the radical leader of the new epoch and that Luthuli was somewhat *dépassé*. I remember a Mandela rally held in Commercial Street, Durban in the early 1960s – Zuma was doubtless there too in the large crowd. Mandela spoke in his usual wooden way, to huge enthusiasm, but at a certain point someone bobbed towards him to whisper in his ear and he looked up and said: 'We must go,' and bolted from the platform. The meeting broke up in disorder as the police arrived in force to close the meeting down. We all fled. My sister Francesca and I were two of only a handful of whites in the crowd and the Special Branch naturally followed us home in order to ascertain who we were.

A year or two later, after the Sharpeville massacre had led to the declaration of a State of Emergency and the banning of the ANC, my great friend and mentor, Rowley Arenstein, was trying hard to keep the left alive in Durban. Rowley and his wife Jackie were both banned communists and under house arrest and therefore unable to address any meeting of more than two people. But Rowley had organised lectures on Marxism-Leninism to be given in Lakhani Chambers, down in Grey Street, the heart of Durban's Indian area, and I, as a (then) young Marxist, got volunteered to lecture on his behalf. I didn't know much more than *The Communist Manifesto* but what I had to say was enthusiastically received by a room full of young Zulu men, most of them rather older than me. It was only many years later that I learned that Jacob Zuma had been in my audience, and he and I all but fell upon one another's shoulders as we realised this, for we both held extremely positive memories of Rowley. 'He was our leader in those days,' Jacob said, without any trace of exaggeration. For Rowley was one of a small band of Jewish communists who played an absolutely cardinal role in shaping South Africa's future. Rowley ended up supporting Inkatha while I reverted to my earlier liberalism, but both Jacob Zuma and I still think with great warmth about the part that Rowley played.

Many people have helped me in the writing of the book. Most directly, I relied on the assistance of Melissa Sutherland and Carol van Vuuren, who were invaluable. As always I owe a great deal to Irina Filatova for an incessant exchange of ideas. Hermann Giliomee and Charles van Onselen also provided a continuous stimulus as well as their friendship. But I owe the Van Onselen family more than that for, increasingly, I have found stimulus in the perceptive writing of Charles's son, Gareth. I am also grateful to Professor Jannie Rossouw and his colleagues and to Paul Trewhela, Rian Malan and Omry Makgoale for their continuous and penetrating insights into recent South African history.

The only person to whom I owe as much as I do to Irina is Lawrie Schlemmer, a truly irreplaceable man whose death I still mourn. He was my dear friend and no one taught me as much. Lawrie made the under-standing of South Africa's complex politics, economy and sociology his life's work and nobody whom I have ever met knew anything like as much as he did. South Africa enjoys a somewhat arid intellectual climate and Lawrie was, for political reasons, never given the appreciation or recogni-tion that he deserved. We both knew how ridiculous this was and often laughed at it together. Truth-telling has never been a popular profes-sion. Ironically, South African universities now implicitly recognise this through their bizarre practice of giving out posthumous honorary degrees. The whole point of this is to give belated recognition to people that the university would never have been brave enough to have honoured in their own time. Should this absurd practice continue, perhaps even Lawrie will get a posthumous degree some day. I can hear him laugh at the thought.

This book is also part of a personal journey. I had written *How Long Will South Africa Survive?* in 1977 as an Oxford don but as the pace of change quickened I determined to come back to South Africa. Partly, hav-ing been an anti-apartheid activist and ANC supporter back in the 1960s, I just wanted to see how the story ended. My faith in the ANC had long since eroded and I had no illusions about likely outcomes – indeed, I have been neither surprised nor disappointed by anything that has happened since. But I decided that the most valuable thing I could do was to chroni-cle this unparalleled experiment in which a Third World nationalism came to power in a (relatively) developed country. Nothing like that had ever happened before. The important thing was to try to tell the unvarnished truth. This was more difficult than it sounds, because political correctness in the new South Africa forbade many things to be said out loud, no mat-ter how true. I decided to ignore all that. This did not, of course, make for popularity.

Clearly, the first democratic election would be a landmark and so, together with Lawrie Schlemmer, I produced *Launching Democracy. South Africa's First Open Election, April 1994* (1996).

Since I am a liberal I was much concerned at the fate of liberalism in the new South Africa that it had done so much to create and in 1998, with David Welsh, I produced *Ironic Victory: Liberalism in Post-Liberation South Africa*. I then tried to situate modern events against the whole canvas of

South African history in *The First Man, The Last Nation* (2004). But I wanted to do a big book about the ANC in power and this I finally produced in the shape of *South Africa's Brave New World: The Beloved Country Since the End of Apartheid* (2009). This was one of my best-selling books, but happily I was excused from all the normal promotional activities since its publication coincided with an accident in which I lost a leg and, indeed, was given only an 11 per cent chance of survival. It was nice to read reviews of the book in the intensive care unit. Once I got out of hospital I returned to my academic concerns with *The African University? The Critical Case of South Africa and the Tragedy at UKZN* (2012).

Thus, despite various diversions, I have managed to carry out my intention to chronicle the Great Change. The current volume should be seen as a further instalment in this long-term commitment. For the result of 20 years of ANC rule has been to make the question in my title relevant all over again. I love South Africa and, happily, I believe in its resilience.

RW Johnson

CHAPTER ONE

Then and Now

I n 1977 I published *How Long Will South Africa Survive?* – shorthand for how long it would be before the then ruling white establishment encoun-tered a regime crisis. The general expectation at the time was that such a crisis could be expected almost at any moment – in the wake of the 1976 Soweto uprising there were many predictions and declarations of immi-nent revolution – and the assumption was widely held that the country would then sink into a protracted race war. I thought both assumptions were wrong. It seemed to me that white power was far stronger and better entrenched than many of its opponents seemed to realise or, indeed, were willing to admit. And secondly, it seemed to me that, in common with many other parallel colonial situations – Indochina, Algeria, Kenya – the point would simply come where the game was up, which essentially meant when the metropolitan power (France in Indochina and Algeria, Britain in Kenya) decided that the status quo could not be sustained there would be a complete regime change, after which a new and different country would emerge. And contrary to predictions of endless racial strife in Indochina, Algeria and Kenya, this had not actually occurred and even those whites who remained quickly adjusted to life in the now decolonised country.

South Africans, more than any other people on earth, are prone to speculate about the future of their country, for it has always seemed to be a case of the irresistible force and the immovable object. Once the great change of 1990–94 took place there was a general loss of interest in South Africa in the world at large because it was assumed, crudely speaking, that 'the problem has been solved, they've democratised, end of story'. Journalists operating from South Africa suddenly found that editors in London, New York or Paris were now far less interested in stories from Johannesburg than they had been while the great drama of apartheid was still being played out. But domestically no one ever stopped asking the question 'What on earth is going to happen in our country?' – as this book bears witness.

Because South Africa exists at the tip of a continent with which it interacts little, its society has a strong tendency to insularity, even parochialism. This is why such antique ideologies as apartheid and communism could linger on when elsewhere in the world they had faded away. Similarly, most discussions of South Africa's quandaries assume that they will be decided solely by the balance of forces on the domestic scene. Throughout the apartheid period this meant seeing the situation through the simple optic of white oppression and black resistance. This was, of course, the way in which the exiled ANC tended to see things and its 'struggle narrative' was both compelling and influential. However, the key point behind *How Long Will South Africa Survive?* was to show that this narrative was far too simple and that a great variety of other factors were involved. (Because this book shares the same title, I shall hereafter refer to the 1977 edition as *How Long* (1977).) Below I will briefly summarise what I had to say in 1977 and what was wrong about it.

South Africa in the international order

South Africa, for all its sense of isolation, is and was deeply integrated into an international political economy which was decisively capitalist in nature. What this meant was that a good deal of its fate was likely to be decided through the mechanisms of that political economy. And the deeper the integration of the country into that system, the more important external factors were. Moreover, the main significance even of many internal events lay in their impact abroad. *How Long* (1977) was written in the shadow of the Soweto uprising and I pointed out that 'just as at Sharpeville, the African demonstrators showed that they wielded power in the world money markets, even if there was not much they could do against the brute force of the police'.

What interested me most was the complex interplay between these multiple factors. Crudely put, it seemed to me that the white establishment had sufficient strength to stave off internal challenges almost indefinitely but that the concatenation of external factors would probably see that establishment topple by the early-to-middle 1990s. This was a controversial conclusion, since those who held to the 'struggle narrative' were prone to predict a successful internal revolution long before that date.

South Africa had been moving at some speed, I pointed out, from being still in large part a colonial economy dominated by its relationship with a single metropole to one which was much more widely integrated into more diverse international markets. Thus in 1955–66 the UK still provided 31.7 per cent of all South Africa's imports, with another 18.9 per cent from the USA. Similarly, the UK and the USA accounted for 44.6 per cent of all South Africa's exports in that period, with 20.9 per cent of exports going to 'other Africa', most of this being trade with British subsidiaries in Anglophone Africa. By the 1960s, however, this picture had changed fundamentally, with an ever-increasing share of trade being done with Germany, France and other Western European countries as well as Japan and the East.

This was changing so fast because South Africa under white rule had an extremely dynamic economy. Thus during 1945–64, GDP growth averaged no less than 8.3 per cent per annum across this whole 20-year period, while the manufacturing sector grew even faster, at 10.6 per cent per year. These figures have never been equalled in any other period of South Africa's history and even though growth slowed down after 1964, in the whole decade of 1960–70 it was to average 5.9 per cent. This headlong growth brought major new investment flows into the country, particularly from Europe and especially from Germany. British and American investment continued to be predominant but this was the result mainly of the re-investment of profits made within South Africa rather than fresh new investment from abroad.

The result of this impressive growth was not only to strengthen the position of the white establishment; it also brought new factors into play. France, which practised a forward if idiosyncratic policy throughout Africa, became critically important, not only because of its investment and trade, but because it rapidly became South Africa's main arms supplier. And finally, the decision by President Charles de Gaulle to challenge the hegemony of the dollar in the world's money markets was to have crucial significance for South Africa.

The post-war rise of West European capitalism meant that by the 1960s Europe was able to mount a response to the *défi Américain*. This counter-challenge was most clearly expressed by de Gaulle's decision to push as much as possible of French monetary reserves out of the dollar and into gold, for he and his monetary adviser, Jacques Rueff, were believers in the role of gold as a permanent store of value. This view had long been ridiculed by Keynesians as a 'barbaric' remnant of times gone past. There was, after all, no real reason why a country's financial strength should be measured by how many ingots of gold (or any other metal) it had stored in some dungeon. Nonetheless, gold has always had its followers in every country in the world and they were (and are) sufficiently numerous to make a difference. As de Gaulle bought more and more gold, so the Americans were increasingly embarrassed by having to sell their ingots to him at the prevailing price of $35 per ounce.

This valuation of gold had been fixed by President Franklin Roosevelt before World War II and it had suited the USA to keep it stuck at that level. De Gaulle, on the other hand, believed that the gold price was being artificially held down by the political fact of dollar dominance. Thus his aim was to force a large-scale devaluation of the dollar against gold. This move was naturally resisted strongly by the US Treasury.

The need to break out

This campaign against the hegemony of the dollar was of critical importance to South Africa. Its economy depended increasingly on the large-scale import of advanced technology from the West. On its own it simply could not build the jet engines and other high tech that was becoming central to modern life. In order to pay for these vital imports, the National Party government had launched a policy of opening up towards black Africa, hoping that a political détente with its new leaders would see South African exports surge into the rest of the continent.

This policy failed almost completely, however. Partly this was because the old imperial powers like France and Britain were still attempting to hang on to their dominant trading position in their former colonies, but far more important was the fact of the anti-apartheid trade boycott which meant that most of black Africa was either wholly unwilling to trade with South Africa or was determined to keep that trade to a minimum. The failure of Pretoria's outward initiative left the country in a parlous position. From 1963 to 1971 imports had increased by 226 per cent to R4 144 million while at the same time, exports (excluding gold) had risen by only 119 per cent to R2 178 million. The gap between these two figures was widening alarmingly and it was a matter of desperate urgency to the whole white establishment that the gap be closed. The alternative would be an enormous economic crisis which would also make it impossible to afford the arms imports on which white power depended. The only way that relief could come would be via a dramatically higher gold price – and this was exactly what de Gaulle and his successors managed to achieve. By 1971 the first cracks in the American defence opened up and the gold price rose to $65 per ounce by mid-1972. Then the oil crisis of late 1973 pushed it up further to well above $100 per ounce. South Africa, which was then producing something like three quarters of the world's gold, benefited enormously.

It was thus not surprising that when that master of *realpolitik*, Henry Kissinger, first emerged as Nixon's key national security adviser, one of his earliest acts was to draw up a security assessment of Southern Africa, NSC 69,[1] which stated flatly that 'the whites are here to stay and the only way that constructive change can come about is through them. There is no hope for the blacks to gain the political rights they seek through violence, which will only lead to chaos and increased opportunities for the Communists.' Kissinger advised President Nixon that although he should 'maintain public opposition to racial oppression' he should also 'relax political isolation and economic restrictions on the white states' (that is, South Africa, Ian Smith's Rhodesia, South West Africa and the Portuguese colonies). Thus the critical factor for white South Africa was that while the Cold War lasted, it could rely on the implicit backing of America and much of the West if it seemed likely that the overthrow of apartheid would create a favourable situation for the large communist presence within the ANC.

Hence the main theme of *How Long* (1977) – that whatever the merits of the ANC's 'struggle' narrative, it was also essential to reason from South Africa's integration into the international capitalist order and to study how the shifts within that order were also a key determinant of South Africa's fate. There were many facets to these influences. Thus American power was being battered through the 1960s both by the Vietcong in Vietnam and by the French offensive in the gold market. Naturally, as the gold price began to rise, the French example of increasing its gold reserves was copied not only by South Africa but by an increasing number of European countries. This culminated in the effective overthrow of the old dollar supremacy, with the Watergate crisis of 1973 providing the final straw. Nixon was forced out of office by August 1974 and by the end of that year the gold price had risen to no less than $197.50 per ounce. This meant that South Africa was now getting five and a half times as much for its gold as it had previously.

The result was a bonanza for the white establishment. The value of South Africa's gold output soared from R775 million in 1967 to R1 161 million in 1972, R1 770 million in 1973 and R2 560 million in 1974. The rand was upwardly re-valued to $1.49. Thus, while the world slumped into recession after the 1973 oil crisis, South Africa's economy grew at no less than 8 per cent in 1974. Pretoria was now able to spend all it liked on infrastructure, defence and an increasing attempt at self-sufficiency. Against all previous predictions of doom, South Africa's white establishment had come through stronger than ever.

However, other shifts in the world capitalist order were a great deal less favourable to South Africa. Two factors were of particular significance. First, the oil crisis of 1973 had seen the rise not only of OPEC, but also of an Afro-Arab bloc within the United Nations General Assembly which flexed its muscles in several different directions, demanding a whole New International Economic Order and a far greater place in the sun for Third World nations in general. Opposition to apartheid South Africa was a point of consensus within the whole of that bloc and its rise was severely threatening to Pretoria.

Second, the British decision to enter the European Economic Community was a disaster for South Africa. Once again, Pretoria had greatly benefited from French intransigence. Thanks to de Gaulle, Britain's bid to join the EEC was turned down twice in the 1960s but the arrival in power of President Georges Pompidou in 1969 spelt trouble for Pretoria, for Pompidou was far less averse to the British bid than de Gaulle had been. The result was that Britain entered the EEC at last in 1973.

This hurt South Africa in several different ways. First, British trade policy had to be remodelled away from its old Commonwealth partners and towards its new European partners. Second, the EEC had provided for extensive and favourable trading arrangements with most of Africa under the Lomé Trade Agreement, but South Africa and the other white-ruled states now found themselves as the only parts of Africa not allowed to benefit from these new trade arrangements.

Finally, British entry to the EEC meant that Portugal, for whom Britain was both oldest ally and principal trading partner, had little option but to apply for EEC entry too. Yet it was impossible for the fragile Portuguese state to face the blast of competition from its European neighbours and simultaneously maintain its African empire. The denouement came quickly with the Portuguese revolution of April 1974, which brought radical regimes to power in Guinea-Bissau, Mozambique and Angola. This was a tremendous blow to the white South. Not only had white Rhodesia and South Africa lost their northern tier of defence against the encroachment of the African nationalist tide, but the example of the victorious liberation movements in Mozambique and Angola had a profound effect on South Africa's black population. Until then black South Africans had found it hard to believe that white power could ever be overthrown. Now this disbelief vanished overnight. Thus the seeds of the 1976 Soweto uprising were sown.

As a challenge to white power the Soweto uprising failed completely and was firmly repressed. However, as I pointed out in *How Long* (1977), it had a huge effect in international markets, causing a collapse of investor confidence in South Africa. This came, moreover, at the same time that a gradual resurgence of American power had been reflected in a falling gold price. These two factors, plus the general collapse of commodity prices after 1973, hit South Africa very hard and 1977 was one of the country's toughest years since the depression of the 1930s.

Soweto changes the game

Moreover, after the Soweto uprising nothing was ever quite the same again domestically. The temperature of the entire black resistance movement had risen and stayed at its new level, prompting a series of disconnected acts of resistance and a growing mood of confidence about the demise of white power. The murder of Steve Biko in 1977 was a crucial watershed in that it led President Valéry Giscard d'Estaing to decide that France would join the UN ban on arms sales to South Africa. Having depended heavily on France for Mirage fighters, Alouette helicopters and a wide range of other defence equipment, the white establishment searched desperately for new international partners to help it through this difficult period. An effective alliance with Israel was born and for some time Pretoria dreamed that it might be able to replace the Mirages with Israeli Kfir fighters. But the problem was that the Kfir used General Electric J79 engines and the US would never agree to their onward export to South Africa. Pretoria also sought an alliance with the Shah's Iran and got most of its oil from Tehran.

President PW Botha even attempted to make alliances with Paraguay and Uruguay. Most fantastic of all, the National Party government dreamed of establishing relations with communist China. Jan Marais, the Afrikaner head of Trust Bank and a pillar of the National Party, announced that 'I would vote with both hands for good ties with Red China' while Connie Mulder, the minister of information, began to punctuate his routine denunciations of communism with the qualification 'I mean Moscow by that, not Peking'. Ultimately, all these initiatives led nowhere. None of these new partners really had the power or the willingness to alleviate South

8

Africa's problems. In the end the fact was that South Africa was reliant on the Western bloc, particularly Britain and America, and that was what it would have to deal with.

Indeed, 1976 saw a critical juncture at which Kissinger badly wanted to provide President Gerald Ford with a diplomatic success before the November election. He determined to push South Africa's premier, John Vorster, into pressuring Ian Smith to concede the principle of majority rule in Rhodesia – an essential step towards ending the Rhodesian crisis. To this end the USA exerted heavy downward pressure on the gold price through staging IMF gold sales and also US Treasury gold sales. This squeezed the South African economy until the pips squeaked. Vorster did as Kissinger wanted, Smith made the necessary concession – and lo! the gold price suddenly recovered as US pressure eased. The episode badly rattled Vorster, who campaigned flat out against American influence in the 1977 election, but the point was thoroughly made: when the chips were down the apartheid regime could not stand against concerted Western pressure. This fundamental point was to become increasingly salient in the 1980s as more and more Western countries joined the financial and economic boycott of South Africa. In the end there was no escape from that.

Colony and metropole

Trying to think about how apartheid would come to an end and how regime change would at last take place in South Africa, I argued in *How Long* (1977) that the key paradigm was that of the colony and the metropole.

In the rest of Africa and, indeed, further afield as well, colonial and white minority regimes had been overthrown as a result of a complex struggle in which the metropolitan power had played the final and decisive role. It was important to understand that those who fought against colonial oppression did not actually need to win. Thus for example, the guerrilla fighters of the Algerian Front de Libération Nationale (FLN) did not actually need to defeat the French army – a task considerably beyond them. All they needed to do was to create a situation in which their low-intensity war against the French presence in their country made the situation humanly and financially untenable for the metropolitan power. In the end that power (France) would intervene to impose a solution – and no solution would work unless it was acceptable to the FLN. That is to say, most colonial wars against settler minorities were not settled by the complete overthrow of the metropolitan power or even of the ruling white minority. All that had to be achieved was to make the price too high for the other side to continue to fight.

This was so for the simple reason that whereas the fighters of the FLN had nowhere else to go and would thus fight to the bitter end, the white minority did, in the last analysis, have somewhere else to go. Moreover, as long as Algeria (or Kenya, or Rhodesia or the Portuguese African territories) retained their colonial status, the metropole always retained the power to impose change. This had been true even in the really tough case of Indochina, where the Vietminh had defeated a French army at Dien Bien Phu in 1954. The French could easily have reinforced their army and continued the war – the Americans were even offering them nuclear weapons – but they had seen the writing on the wall. Despite the anguished pleas of French settlers and planters throughout Laos, Cambodia and Vietnam, the French decided to end the war by imposing a settlement acceptable to the Vietminh.

When it came to South Africa, I argued in *How Long* (1977), the problem was that it lacked a true metropole – it had been an independent state since 1910. So there would have to be a solution which was at least to some extent internally generated. However, what would drive that change was movements in international capital and money markets and in South Africa's relationships with the rest of the capitalist world. Under the stress of those pressures, South Africa would have to negotiate its future with the virtual metropole of 'the West'.

Up until that point I had resisted the ANC's 'struggle narrative'. I had been an ANC supporter myself until I had been utterly horrified by what I had seen of the movement in exile. I also knew that the ANC's guerrilla army, Umkhonto we Sizwe (MK), was the worst led and most ineffective of all Africa's liberation movements. So I was well aware even in 1977 that MK offered no sort of threat to the South African Defence Force at all. Nonetheless, while all the analysis above still stands up, it was here that I made my greatest mistake in *How Long* (1977). I simply could not imagine that MK would remain as ineffective as it then was. I was mindful of the way in which the once tiny forces of the MPLA (Angola), Frelimo (Mozambique), PAIGC (Guinea-Bissau) and Zanla (Zimbabwe) had all developed into formidable guerrilla movements once they had a foreign sanctuary to rely on.

In the scenario which I envisaged, MK, thanks to its sanctuaries in Mozambique, Zambia and elsewhere, would constitute a growing threat and this would trigger major South African strikes against those neighbouring countries. This in turn would generate international pressure for a 'solution', which would in turn cause the collective metropole of the West to impose terms on South Africa. I was sure that the whites were strong enough to stand against the onslaught through the 1980s, but at some point after that they would have to give in.

My assumption that MK would become a growing threat to white power turned out to be wrong. It is true that it exerted some pressure on the whites, but Western sanctions were always more important. I should have stuck to my initial assessment that MK was essentially impotent. It wasn't just that it was badly led. It was that it was wrong in its whole conception, just as my old communist mentor, Rowley Arenstein, had always told me. The point was, as Rowley argued, that the National Party regime was extremely conservative, indeed reactionary, but it was not fascist. Accordingly, incremental, reformist change was possible. And in the end reformist change was what triumphed.

The iron law again

How that occurred is nonetheless instructive. Continuing internal unrest led to the Rubicon crisis of 1985 when President Botha promised major reforms and then famously decided on a U-turn. In the ensuing crisis of confidence international banks led by Chase Manhattan fled the country, followed by foreign investors in general. This was the crucial moment, although Botha resisted for another five years. When, inevitably, regime change followed in 1990, this was merely like a cash register ringing up what was already in the till.

That change occurred in this way was because the actors involved were sophisticated enough to understand the laws of anticipated reactions. That is to say, President FW de Klerk knew well enough that the SADF had hardly been tested, that MK was on its knees, and that his forces could guarantee white supremacy for many years ahead. But he also knew that the South African economy simply could not cope indefinitely with the growing Western economic sanctions. In addition, the end of the Cold War had resulted in a huge step-up in diplomatic pressure from all sides – and had also given him an opportunity for a settlement which would not result in a communist take-over. And there was a lot to be said for a settlement born of his own decision. Further delay would not only weaken his hand but might rob him of the initiative.

The ANC, for its part, had recently re-assessed the condition of MK and concluded that it was in no position to step up the conflict. Behind the scenes the USSR was also pressing it towards negotiation. Moreover, the USSR was getting out of Eastern Europe, the Wall had gone down and communist states were collapsing in front of its eyes – including, ultimately, the mighty Soviet Union itself. This was bound to mean an enormous weakening of the ANC over time, for the Soviet bloc had always been its main backer and provider. But as yet that change had not fully kicked in and meanwhile it was aware that overwhelming Western pressure for a settlement had provided it with an opportunity too.

Thus neither side wanted to go all the way down to the wire and both were well able to imagine the costs of doing so – and could see an opportunity in front of them. But the crux of the matter lay with De Klerk: if he released Mandela, unbanned the exiled organisations and offered negotiations for a democracy, the ANC could not really refuse and its backers would, in any case, never tolerate such a refusal. Later on there was to be much euphoric talk of a 'South African miracle' but really none existed – or, at least, to the extent it existed it lay simply in the fact of the President's rational calculation. De Klerk put the situation at its plainest when he declared simply that 'we just can't go on in this way'. He had seen PW Botha keep the lid on for the last five years to no avail; the period had been a strange autumn of the patriarch in which all progress was frozen, and meanwhile the international pressures against South Africa had steadily mounted. There was no point at all in seeking to continue this Canute-like policy.

Yet again the iron law of South African history reasserted itself. What was fascinating and somewhat unexpected was that as the moment for change neared so South Africa redeveloped something like the old colony–metropole relationship of the past. That is to say that the De Klerk government, recognising the true nature of the crisis, negotiated its terms of surrender mainly with the Thatcher and Bush administrations. In effect Britain and America were made referees because they had the power to restore capital flows and therefore a settlement acceptable to them had to be reached. A close examination of the events of that time shows that Margaret Thatcher and her emissary Robin Renwick probably played the most important role of all. Indeed, Renwick behaved very much like an old British governor-general and was often referred to as the extra member of the South African cabinet. This re-negotiation of the old colony–metropole relationship happened because both sides wanted it. Thus De Klerk's famous speech of 2 February 1990 abandoning apartheid and welcoming back the ANC and other exiles in order to negotiate a democratic settlement had been cleared in advance with both the British and the Americans. Quite clearly, though, the Americans allowed the British to take the lead role, respecting the fact that South Africa had always been a British sphere of interest.

It is critical to understand that despite the rhetoric of both the ANC and the SACP about their 'revolution' in fact there was no South African revolution; this was not just a matter of the ultimate settlement being peaceful and of being sufficiently inclusive to satisfy all parties more or less. More to the point, there was no revolution because the black population of South Africa had never really wanted to destroy white South Africa. Instead they were more like spectators at Wimbledon watching the interplay of white politics over their heads, observing the relative luxury of white society and envying the superior schools, hospitals and other facilities enjoyed by whites. Inevitably what black people wanted was to be incorporated into that game on the basis of equality so that they too could enjoy a democratic political system and access or potential access to the desirable life which they saw whites living. This is indeed what actually happened, so that very quickly there were black millionaires, black cabinet ministers, black talk show hosts, black professors and so on and so forth. Black people simply moved into the structures which they inherited from the old white regime, most of which remained intact. It was no miracle that the transition was so largely peaceful. There was a great deal of black-on-black violence but very little black–white violence. Contrary to the dark predictions of a whole generation, there was no race war – because nobody wanted it.

It is true that on the left many dreamed of revolutionary change in the future, usually in the form of the ANC's proposed National Democratic Revolution. However, after 20 years of ANC rule there was little sign of this and even Communist Party spokesmen such as Jeremy Cronin and Ronnie Kasrils had begun to talk about where and when everything had gone wrong. Typically they thought there had been some sort of deal or compromise with white capitalism in the early years of ANC rule and this had blocked the revolutionary changes they would have liked to see. Yet there had been no such deal that anyone could point to. All that had happened was that a new constitution had been devised and a government of national unity had (briefly) been put in place. No one could point to any agreement beyond that. What was striking was that by 2014 both Cronin and Kasrils saw radical change as something which had definitively eluded the ANC regime and which could now not be achieved. The revolution was over before it had ever happened. This did not, of course, prevent a continuing torrent of revolutionary rhetoric.

One result of the flow of recent South African history was that a whole generation was brought up amidst the great struggles of the 1980s and then the ANC's triumph in the 1990s. This had the effect of shifting political perspectives steadily leftward so that a Marxist perspective was very widely shared amongst intellectuals of all races, and the general expectation was that further change would occur in a leftward direction. By 2014 however this seemed unlikely. All manner of things had begun to happen which were not in the ANC's script. Despite all its rhetoric and promises, it had presided over rising unemployment and de-industrialisation. The party itself was clearly beginning to lose support; it was massively corrupt and had entirely lost the moral high ground it once enjoyed. The Opposition was gaining apace – as was tribalism. The media, once subservient to the

ANC government, was now highly critical of it. It was quite evident that the ANC's early hopes of establishing a moral and political hegemony over society had vanished.

Understanding the past – and future

The key to understanding South Africa's development lies in its integration into a world capitalist political economy. This has been true at least since the 1880s with the development of deep-level mining. This sort of mining, although lucrative, required very large-scale capital investment. This could not all be provided from within South Africa. The country simply had too many very poor people to have a very high savings ratio and thus local capital available for investment was always limited. Accordingly the industry proceeded on the basis of a steady inflow of foreign investment. That inflow had to continue for the country to go forward. The iron law of South African history is that if this inflow is seriously threatened, not only can no government survive, but an interruption of this flow tends to produce a generalised regime crisis which is solved only by the installation of a new regime.

The twentieth century had seen four such crises:

❏ The Rand Revolt of 1922, essentially caused by a sharp fall in the gold price and thus of foreign direct investment (FDI) into the mining industry. It became clear that investment flows would only be resumed if labour costs were dramatically cut. The resulting revolt saw the crushing of the white workers, but since they were a key part of the white electorate and had to be placated, a new regime was installed, based on the industrial colour bar. Fredrickson, in his classic study, *White Supremacy*,[2] rightly picks out this moment as the point when South Africa began to head towards a regime of increasing racial and labour oppression.

❏ The Fusion Crisis of 1932. This was caused by a persistence with the gold standard which in turn made South African goods of all types too expensive and thus stifled FDI across the board. The result was a virtual insurrection of the white electorate and the creation of a Fusion government representing a 'new form of regime' in which both Afrikaner farming interests and the English-speaking mining and industrial interests were equally represented. The first move of the new regime was, of course, to take the country off the gold standard.

❑ The Sharpeville Crisis of 1960–61. Enormous volumes of foreign capital fled the country after the massacres at Sharpeville and Langa. South Africa's foreign reserves dwindled almost to nothing and the government was forced to slam on the brakes, bringing growth to a halt. Briefly it seemed likely that this too would result in a generalised regime crisis. Thus Paul Sauer, deputising for Verwoerd, made his famous speech about how 'the old book of South African history was closed at Sharpeville'. Had the investment strike continued, regime change would have been inevitable. Instead Verwoerd reasserted himself, saw the crisis out, intensified labour and political repression and watched FDI flow back in again.

❑ The Rubicon Crisis of 1985, as mentioned above, was really what brought apartheid down. When President Botha promised reform but didn't deliver it, there was a complete collapse in international investor confidence, leading to a withdrawal of loans and investment. Ironically, the anti-apartheid movement had never understood that financial sanctions were far more important than trade sanctions, so this investment strike occurred autonomously. In the end Pretoria was even locked out from access to Special Drawing Rights at the IMF. Afrikaner civil servants understood that the game was up and looting started in earnest after 1985. In the end regime change came in 1990. Thereafter the country was ruled by an NP–ANC duopoly which, from 1999 on, was followed by one-party ANC government.

After 1994 South Africa entered into a euphoric era – which slowly turned sour. For all its promises that it had learnt its lessons while in exile in independent Africa, the ANC in fact repeated all the classic mistakes of such regimes. There was a lot of misgovernance, but perhaps even more than that, there was simply no governance. For years the government was protected by a friendly international environment, by a long commodities boom and by growth which resulted simply from the opening up of the rest of Africa to South African trade and investment. After 20 years of almost complete fecklessness, an extremely serious situation had been reached by 2014. It is the contention of this book that South Africa is now heading fast for another investment crisis which will in turn end in another regime change, as such crises always have in the past.

CHAPTER TWO

KwaZulu-Natal, the World of Jacob Zuma

On 21 June 1998 Sergeant Craig van Zyl, together with his partner, Solly Shozi, was driving down the esplanade of Durban's Victoria Embankment towards Durban airport, where they were investigating a narcotics case. As they passed the imposing neo-Gothic building which houses the Durban High Court, Van Zyl noticed to his astonishment that five men just disgorged from a vehicle were armed with AK-47s and were moving towards the court. Van Zyl bravely challenged them, though he only had a handgun, and a shoot-out ensued, which was quickly joined by other members of the Durban police. Van Zyl himself was shot dead, as also were two bystanders, one of them an 80-year-old woman. Three of the attackers were arrested and another shot dead but two more escaped in a red BMW. Later, detectives found camera footage of the getaway car clearly showing that the driver was himself a policeman, Constable Sibusiso (S'bu) Mpisane.[1]

Enter Mandla Gcaba, JZ's nephew

Detectives quickly hypothesised that what they had interrupted was a murder attempt mounted by the notorious Umlazi taxi boss, Mandla Gcaba.[2] South Africa's black taxi business is one of the roughest in the world and those who rise to prominence within its frequent taxi wars are often passable imitations of Al Capone. Gcaba, one of the richest and most successful taxi bosses in the country, had a fearsome reputation as a man who relied on direct action and took few prisoners. To be fair, the black taxi business is often a kill-or-be-killed affair; Gcaba's father, Simon, had been murdered in a taxi war in 1996, and Gcaba's brother, Moses, met the same fate in 1997. Gcaba himself had stopped four bullets. The trial at the High Court in June 1998 concerned the men accused of Moses' murder and the police surmised that Gcaba had decided not to wait for the uncertain workings of the justice system but simply to take summary vengeance on the steps of the court itself.[4] In fact there had been an exact precedent on 2 August 1997 when Michael Phungula, one of the six men implicated in Moses' murder, was brought to the same court on the Victoria Embankment: as the police car he was in approached the court it came under fire, and in the ensuing melee Phungula was killed.[5]

This was all part of the taxi wars of the 1990s between the Gcaba and Sithole factions. Even back then, the police averred, 'every taxi boss has his own hitman', and assassinations of opposing bosses could cost anything between R100 000 and R1 million. Taxi bosses paid huge sums to the taxi associations and to the rank managers who ran the taxi ranks. 'Anyone who questions what taxi bosses do with the money (they get) gets shot,' the police said.[6]

On this occasion the getaway driver, Constable Mpisane, was arrested and agreed to make a statement in exchange for immunity from prosecution. He confirmed that he had been driving the getaway car and that he had had prior knowledge of the murder attempt. He said that Gcaba had ordered the attack and that he (Mpisane) had driven the two attackers he had rescued straight to Gcaba's home, a luxury mansion in the upmarket resort of Zimbali, where he lived amongst fellow-tycoons on the KwaZulu-Natal north coast. Gcaba and three others (including his brother, Royal

Roma Gcaba) were arrested and charged with the murder of Van Zyl and two others.

Those who knew Mandla Gcaba could hardly believe that he would be made answerable to a court, and so it turned out. Everything depended on Mpisane's testimony against Gcaba, but shortly before the trial Mpisane went missing and stayed missing. Even though the judge ordered a special delay in proceedings to enable the police to find him, this was fruitless. The court was left with no option but to acquit Gcaba and his friends. A year later Mpisane suddenly re-appeared at his old police job, claiming that he had been kidnapped, a story that was never verified. It suddenly emerged that – though still a humble constable in the Durban Metro police dog unit – he was now an immensely rich man. Even in Capone's Chicago this would undoubtedly have led to an investigation and disciplinary action by the Chicago police. In ANC-ruled Durban (eThekwini), to whose city council the Metro police are responsible, there was no such investigation and the city manager, the ANC ultra-apparatchik Mike Sutcliffe, refused all comment on this apparent cover-up.

Constable S'bu Mpisane and his wife, Shauwn – 'Durban's queen of bling' as the local press loved to call her – became fabled figures in the life of the city.[7] Though earning only R15 000 a month as a policeman, Mpisane bought a R17-million mansion in upmarket La Lucia; his wife also bought the house next door. Mpisane owned a Lamborghini and over 60 other cars and the couple exchanged Rolls-Royces as Christmas gifts to one another.[8] They held frequent glittering parties at which all of Durban's ANC notables were prominent guests, including Jacob Zuma's nephew, Edward, and Bheki Cele, the burly ANC and Communist Party boss who became national police commissioner and always arrived at the Mpisane parties dressed in white suits with a rakish gangster trilby. (I remember sitting opposite Cele at one party, though at a house far more modest than the Mpisanes'. His opening conversational gambit was: 'So what's your ideology, then?')

Shauwn Mpisane was a notable in her own right. Her mother, Florence Mkhize, had been a legendary ANC militant in Durban – I remember Jackie Arenstein, her comrade in struggle of many years, shuddering as she described just how tough Florence was. Once the ANC triumphed,

Florence became an ANC city councillor, chair of the municipal housing committee and, while she was still a councillor, founded the Zikhulise Cleaning, Maintenance and Transport Company which – of course – sought lucrative municipal contracts, for Florence was not a lady slow to cash in on the struggle.[9] She seems to have raised her children in a similar spirit of combative competitiveness. Shauwn inherited Zikhulise from her mother and proceeded to win a succession of multi-million tenders from both national and local government. Indeed, Durban City Council under Sutcliffe's direction acted as if the enrichment of the Mpisanes was a prime objective. This drew the attention of the local Durban newspaper, *The Mercury*, but it turned out that the Mpisanes did not welcome investigative journalism: before long its editor, Philani Makhanya, was laying complaints of intimidation against S'bu Mpisane. In the end Mpisane apologised.[10]

The cash-in-transit game

S'bu Mkhize (Shauwn's brother) was an infamous armed robber in the huge cash-in-transit heist business of the early 1990s. Over and over again, bank vehicles would be hijacked by formidably armed robbers who gunned down any guards and used explosives to open up the armoured transit vehicles. Such attackers invariably had inside information about exactly how much cash was to be transported where and at what time. S'bu Mkhize ultimately died in a shoot-out with the police after a heist too far.

No mention of the cash-in-transit heist business is complete without mention of Sifiso Nkabinde. The ANC's struggle was far more violent in KwaZulu-Natal than in any other province because there they met the entrenched strength of Chief Mangosuthu Buthelezi's Inkatha movement. From the 1980s on, Inkatha and the ANC (or, rather, the fore-running United Democratic Front) slugged it out with a regular casualty rate of some 200 deaths a week. It was, in effect, a Zulu civil war. Inevitably, leaders on both sides became warlords. Most famously, in the Natal Midlands, there was Harry Gwala, an ANC and communist leader who took no prisoners and who was notorious for killing anyone even within ANC ranks who he deemed to be an opponent. His opposite number in Inkatha was David Ntombela, who was equally lacking in squeamishness. I remember approaching Ntombela once as he got out of his car and opened its boot to reveal about 20 automatic rifles. Ntombela was a big tall chap, full of charm. Harry Gwala was quite different, a strange figure of only medium height and no charisma at all, a former schoolteacher with a paralysed left arm. He would give violent speeches at ANC meetings (I remember him at Curries' Fountain in particular) in a strangely undemonstrative way because he couldn't move his arm, but woe betide anyone who thought this a sign of real passivity: his nickname in the movement was 'the one-armed bandit'. I once interviewed a young Zulu boy who had been his assistant in the ANC: he had run away because 'Comrade Harry kills people all the time. If I had stayed he would have killed me.'

When Gwala died he was succeeded as ANC warlord of the Midlands by Sifiso Nkabinde. However, Nkabinde soon found himself in a dissident position *vis-à-vis* the ANC, though he continued to rule the Midlands by armed force against all-comers. Later, I interviewed a gunman hired by the ANC to deal with Nkabinde. He was full of admiration for him, for he had ordered his troops into battle (on motorbikes) by cell-phone using the classic old horns-of-the-bull Zulu formation. 'He was a bonny fighter,' he told me. 'We killed about a dozen of them before he realised that we understood that tactic. He lived to fight another day.'[11]

In the end Nkabinde ended up in jail, with all manner of charges against him. I was then running the Helen Suzman Foundation in Johannesburg and sent our researcher, Cheryl Goodenough, down to Pietermaritzburg to interview him in jail. Nkabinde told Cheryl what he told various others: that in his view the ANC in KwaZulu-Natal was an out-and-out criminal organisation, hardened by many years of warfare. He was, he said, quite certain that he would be murdered before he ever went to trial, to stop him from 'singing' – and he was right about that. But he also spoke very frankly about the cash-in-transit heist business. The point was, he said, that in 1994 the ANC had won power everywhere except in the Western Cape (where it didn't amount to much anyway) and in KwaZulu-Natal. In KwaZulu-Natal, the ANC had a huge sense of entitlement – it felt it 'ought' to have won the civil war there, though it hadn't. So although after 1994 the local ANC bosses were invited into coalition by Buthelezi, they lacked control over the main sources of patronage, for which they hungered. Thus, according to Nkabinde, they went into the cash-in-transit heist business – as did he. And this was why, above all else, he had to be prevented from 'singing'. As he duly was – he was assassinated.[12]

KwaZulu-Natal: theatre of struggle – and criminality

The point to be taken from all this is that although the ANC in power nationally was gradually to fall prey to the criminalisation of the state apparent in many African countries, this process was far more advanced in KwaZulu-Natal than elsewhere. Some would argue that the Zulu warrior past meant that the province was hard-wired for conflict and violence, but such impulses were clearly greatly hardened by the epochal struggle of the 1980s and 1990s between Inkatha and, first, the UDF, later the ANC. After 1990 gun-running into the province, both down from Mozambique and up from the Transkei, was endemic and guns were so cheap and common that I remember seeing a 12-year-old with an AK-47 in Wembezi township, near Estcourt. I frequently taught at the (then) University of Natal and one of my academic colleagues, Ian Phillips, a leading communist, almost clanked as he walked because he was packing so many weapons. (He explained to me that he and his comrades had to 'get their retaliation in first against Inkatha'. Ian was a heavy drinker and had previously had a reputation as an extreme right winger. Looking back, he was typical of the many psychologically marginal people who got involved with violence in those days. He died young of Aids.) Many otherwise normal people got used to a great deal of killing in that period, let alone lesser crimes against the law. Even when Zuma and Buthelezi began working together in earnest to try to restore peace to the battered province, violence often spiralled on because what had started as political violence had bedded down into local feuds in which one family or another always wanted to avenge the death of a brother or nephew.

This atmosphere of criminal violence had long since infused much of the ANC in KwaZulu-Natal. Many ANC activists in the province who had been involved in the violent struggle against Inkatha had simply got used to living with high levels of violence and to the notion that most crimes went unpunished. It was a recipe for warlordism.

Naturally, criminal bosses of every kind thrived in such an environment, often entering into coalitions of convenience with local political bosses. I remember covering the troubles of the early 1990s in the vast squatter camps of Inanda and Phoenix. Three-way fighting between the ANC, SACP and Inkatha had led to a major police presence to suppress the violence. But the local ANC was strongly committed to getting the police out of these townships. On investigation I found that the chief local industries were drug-running and the manufacture of pipe guns and that both these key economic activities were being prevented by the police presence. In effect the local ANC had made itself the ally of the drug dealers and arms manufacturers.

Zuma returns

This was the world that Jacob Zuma confronted when he returned from exile in February 1990. He was elected chairman of the ANC's Southern Natal region (which includes Durban), but the next year he was elected deputy secretary-general of the ANC, a post which could not be combined with any other, so he had to resign his local job, which went to Jeff Radebe instead. Zuma was not known to be a good administrator but the fact was that there were not enough Zulus in the senior ranks of the ANC, so his name was always likely to get mentioned, especially since Mandela was acutely conscious of the need for ethnic balance.

Harry Gwala, who dominated the Natal Midlands, was a major problem for the ANC in those days. Gwala had considerable support elsewhere as well and harboured ambitions to take over not only the leadership of the province but the chairmanship of the ANC nationally. Mandela had clashed with Gwala and Govan Mbeki on Robben Island – they were communist hardliners who had no time for Mandela's 'reformism'. As the 1994 election neared Mandela and ANC headquarters at Shell House (now Luthuli House) in Johannesburg were desperate to avoid having Gwala as head of the ANC list in KwaZulu-Natal, not only because that might help Buthelezi, but also because they had to prevent a known murderer like Gwala from rising higher in the ANC. So it was arranged for Zuma to take over the Northern Natal ANC and then just manage to beat Gwala for the nomination to head the ANC list in the province. Gwala, furious that his old cellmate had pipped him at the post, put out a contract on Zuma's head. This was too much even for the SACP, which suspended Gwala, partly on that charge of attempted murder.[13] Happily for almost everyone – and therefore a bit suspiciously – Gwala died soon afterwards. Zuma was elected to the Provincial Assembly and became minister for economics and tourism in a coalition government with the IFP.

This at least meant that Zuma had a proper salary at last. Previously he had had to rely on the somewhat meagre allowance paid to him as ANC deputy secretary-general and whatever he could borrow. With his large family of some 20 children, his needs were very great and his less than expert financial management did not help. He opened a bank account, ran up a very large overdraft and made no move to pay it off, despite increasingly irate demands from the bank.[14] Most of the rest of Zuma's income probably came from loans or gifts from Indian businessmen in Durban, particularly Schabir Shaik and the tycoon Vivian Reddy, though some may have come from Mandla Gcaba. Certainly, in Schabir Shaik's later trial it emerged that Zuma was often having to turn to Shaik for amounts as small as R10, R20 or R30 for parking fees, his children's pocket-money and so on. The really striking thing about Zuma in this period was that he 'blithely incurred large debts – for cars, property, loans, building his Nkandla homestead – without bothering to consider where the money would come from'.[15] His family and lifestyle required far more money than he could ever pay from his salary.

Allies across the ethnic divide

This pattern of sympathetic Indians subsidising Zulu politicians was almost traditional in KwaZulu-Natal. Ever since Gandhi founded the Natal Indian Congress there had been some degree of affinity and overlap between the

NIC and ANC, while apartheid increased the solidarity between the two groups. With the ANC's growing influence after 1945 there was also the possibility that helping key ANC figures might lead to commercial advantage later on. But beyond even that was the simple demography of Durban. Of South Africa's 1.1 million Indians almost two-thirds live in Durban, where they vastly outnumber whites. Indeed, if one used the pre-1994 municipal boundaries, Durban was primarily an Indian city. After 1994 the boundaries were extended to include the even larger African population round the city's periphery, also making Durban the largest single agglomeration of Zulus. Durban is thus quite unlike any other South African city and it is a world where Indians and Zulus continuously interact.

Gandhi's political career in Natal was constrained by the fact that while he continuously protested against anti-Indian discrimination of any sort, he also campaigned (in vain) for more Indians to be allowed to immigrate to Natal. This placed him in the position of bemoaning the plight of local Indians while simultaneously admitting that many more were keen to leave India in order to share that plight.[16] For the fact was that although the province's Indian population arrived as indentured labourers, owning nothing, they soon left the sugar cane fields to take advantage of the commercial opportunities they saw about them and quite quickly their standard of living overtook that of Indians still in India. Moreover, this continued whatever obstacles were put in their way. The Indians invested heavily in their own education and the result was a social transformation with ever-increasing numbers of Indian businessmen, traders and professionals. Right through apartheid, Indian per capita income improved every year. This was greatly resented by the surrounding Zulu population, a resentment which fed into the murderous anti-Indian riots of 1949. The riots made the hostility between the two communities unmistakably clear – and yet there were always counter-currents and nothing really stopped the ascent of the Indian community.

It was, indeed, as if the Indian community regarded the injustices and humiliations of apartheid as a challenge. Many Indian merchants found ingenious ways round the apartheid laws which, for example, forbade them to own property in 'white areas' like Durban's central business district, setting up prosperous businesses there using white front-men as the apparent owners and directors. Once apartheid was removed, the social ascent of the Indian community continued quite smoothly even as whites faltered. Indian families tended to be close and supportive and the Indian community was highly networked, so that everyone seemed to know everyone else. As both other Asian groups and Jews have shown, such factors can bring distinct advantages.

But while this meant that the social and political gap between Indians and Zulus grew – and most Indians supported the Opposition – the ANC's dominance of Durban, together with the NIC inheritance, ensured that a minority of Indians remained loyal to the ANC while many more were happy to work with the ANC if it was advantageous to do so. The fact that Indians were relatively well educated and commercially apt meant that typically, they provided the clerical and accounts department manpower for private companies and public bureaucracies alike. This had political ramifications too: in every town up and down the coast, Durban included, one would find Indians as deputy mayors, chief financial officers, accountants and clerks; often the people who made these ANC-ruled municipalities actually work. Inevitably, as with all ANC-run municipalities, there was a good deal of corruption, a sport in which both Indians and Africans shared. As usual, a critical field of play was in tenders and contracts allocated by the councils – and Durban alone had a total budget spend of over R23 billion in 2013–2014. I was down the KwaZulu-Natal South Coast in 2013 when I met the Indian treasurer of one local council. I put it to him that it was people such as himself who really drove the councils. 'Oh yes,' he replied, 'the Tamils control the entire coast.'

A factor which does much to facilitate corruption in Durban and its environs is the large 'black economy', much of which is transacted on a cash basis in order to avoid tax. This is notorious, for example, in the property market where commercial premises often change hands for sums which include large amounts of (undeclared) cash. This enables the purchase price to be set artificially low (which is advantageous for tax purposes) and also enables the buyer to get rid of large amounts of 'hot money' which has to remain invisible to the tax man. Both whites and Indians play this game.

Another factor which separates out the Durban world is that many Indian families now have relatives in Britain, Australia, Canada and elsewhere, and prosperous Muslim Indians in particular often have widespread international networks. And Durban is part of an Indian Ocean world, so that around the tables of Durban's Muslim merchants one may find traders from Dubai, Nairobi or Mumbai, bankers from Riyadh and so on, with Islam the common factor. Money is easily moved around such networks. The rise of Mauritius as a banking centre has been of critical importance to this group and already the island functions as Durban's offshore financial service centre.

The rise of Zuma

Thus the Durban world is richly textured and unlike anything one may encounter elsewhere in South Africa. And although Jacob Zuma remained a country boy at heart, always yearning to be in his native Nkandla with his wives and his cattle, Durban was inevitably the city he looked to and where he spent much of his time.

When Zuma was elected to the KwaZulu-Natal provincial legislature in 1994 it seemed that his political career was to end at this parochial level. However in the run-up to the ANC's national conference at Mafikeng in December 1997, events turned sharply in his direction. Mandela was intent on stepping down as president as soon as possible. With Thabo Mbeki's succession to the top job already settled, the chief question was who would become deputy president of the ANC and thus, inevitably, also deputy president of the country when Mandela stepped down in 1999. Mandela suggested Zuma, but Mbeki was not at all keen and tried hard to get the loyal and ineffectual Joel Netshitenzhe elected in his place. In the end Mandela insisted that it had to be Zuma. Deeply aware that the ANC had had three Xhosa leaders in a row – Tambo, himself and Mbeki – Mandela was always sensitive to the importance of tribal divisions and felt it would be folly to again disappoint the Zulus, South Africa's biggest ethnic group. Events were to bear him out. Later, however, as the Zuma presidency turned sour, critics tried to contrast his sleazy ANC with the golden age of Mandela as if there were no connection between the two. Yet the fact is that Zuma's ascendancy was the result of a very deliberate Mandela decision.[17]

Zuma served as deputy president from 1999 on, though he told me[18] that within months of his election he became aware that he was the subject of a police investigation – which he knew could not have happened without Mbeki's agreement. For, although the two men had been friends and collaborators in exile, Mbeki had a low opinion of Zuma.[19] In part this was just because Zuma was essentially a poorly educated peasant and a hopeless administrator, but it was also because Mbeki, who (on somewhat shaky grounds) considered himself an intellectual, had a simple disdain for Zuma. Mbeki also, as was typical of the younger ANC generation, thought Mandela's insistence on the importance of tribal divisions was completely outdated. This was to lead him to a fatal under-estimation both of Zuma and of the continuing power of ethnicity.

Mbeki tolerated Zuma at first: he was Mandela's hand-picked man and Mandela was still very much around. But once Mbeki was re-elected in 2004 he wanted Zuma out. In ANC politics, seniority counts for a great deal, so that Zuma was now increasingly seen as Mbeki's natural successor. When Mbeki's Aids denialism and support for Mugabe caused a collapse of confidence in his presidency, it became clear that Zuma might even be a preferred alternative. This was intolerable to Mbeki. And in any case, he was already thinking of how to circumvent the constitutional limit of a two-term presidency.

Typically, Mbeki began the pursuit with a patient stalking process. In 2001 Zuma's friend and patron Schabir Shaik was arrested and after lengthy investigation was finally sent to trial in 2004 for corrupt dealings with Jacob Zuma. For years it was clear that (the greatly discomfited) Zuma too was effectively on trial. Finally, on 14 June 2005 Mbeki sacked him as deputy president of both the ANC and the state. A virtual insurrection within the ANC saw Zuma reinstated to his party office – a warning signal which Mbeki refused to take. Mbeki's life had been in exile politics and there it had always been axiomatic that anyone who was expelled by the ANC's central leadership could never come back and that any attempt to resist that leadership was futile. What Mbeki did not allow for was that these dynamics had been utterly changed when the ANC returned home and acquired a mass following organised around regional bases.

Fight back

Up to that point, the numerous people whom Mbeki had discerned as 'enemies' – notably Cyril Ramaphosa, Tokyo Sexwale and Mathews Phosa – had been purged and had disappeared from view. In effect they decided that Mbeki was too powerful to resist and had tried to find a quieter life for themselves beneath the parapet. But Zuma was different. He had already decided in his own mind – and told a few others – that he saw himself as a serious candidate to succeed Mbeki in 2009. Thrown back on his own resources, he was left in no doubt that Mbeki meant to destroy him completely. Every organ of state was mobilised against him, including the police and the bureaucracy of the justice system, with judicious leaks to the press at every juncture. Mbeki was a careful manipulator of the judicial system and he had sent his personal emissary to Durban to ensure that Judge Hilary Squires was chosen to judge Schabir Shaik.[20] Quite why Mbeki wanted Squires is unclear: probably he saw him as the sort of conservative white judge who would not let Shaik off lightly.

Squires judged Shaik with exemplary severity. He could find no evidence of positive wrong-doing. His conclusion that Shaik's extensive bankrolling of Zuma had been done in expectation of future gain was mere mind-reading, however: there had been no future gain. For this 'corruption in the mind' Shaik was sentenced to 15 years, more than any murderer might face. On top of that a text-book 'honey-trap'[21] was organised, which the libidinous Zuma naturally fell for, which then led to a publicly orchestrated rape case against him. Meanwhile the police and the courts closed in on Zuma to try him for corruption. Zuma knew that none of this could have happened unless Mbeki had ordained it.[22]

One has to imagine the scene. As many of us observed during the war between Inkatha and the UDF and then the ANC, when Zulu hostel-dwellers faced a hostile UDF/ANC community outside the hostel gates, incidents would multiply until the hostel-dwellers went into warrior mode. They would do this by 'camping against' their enemy, which essentially meant sitting around in a circle in the evenings, drinking, smoking dagga (marijuana) and talking menacingly about their enemies. This period of 'camping' could go on for many months before the warriors sallied forth to do battle, by now quite saturated with hatred against their foes, whom they would usually summarily despatch. This is what happened at Boipatong in 1992 when Inkatha hostel-dwellers, infuriated by attacks from the surrounding community, burst out after months of camping, slaughtering 45 people and maiming others.

So when Zuma, stripped of the deputy presidency and publicly humiliated, arrived back in KwaZulu-Natal in June 2005 he gathered his many sons, friends and nephews (such as Mandla Gcaba) around him for consultation. The Zuma clan is very extensive and Mandla Gcaba, who also comes from Nkandla, is head of the equally extensive Gcaba clan. Moreover, Gcaba was the boss of the formidable (and often violent) Durban Long Distance Taxi Association. This was not a network to be taken lightly, though it is doubtful if Mbeki realised what he was taking on, for Zuma's world was so different from his own. It was a strange mix of the modern and the highly traditional. Thus Zuma had four wives and some 20 children, but even by the age of 42 Mandla Gcaba had three wives and 12 children and had also absorbed into his family the 22 children of his slain brothers, together with a host of cousins, nephews and nieces. Mandla's father, Simon, had had five wives. Like Zuma, Gcaba liked nothing better than being back in Nkandla, where he grew up herding cattle.[23]

It may be that Mbeki was awaiting a signal of complete surrender from Zuma. If so, he had mistaken his man. Zuma was thrown back on his own and the inevitable view of his support group was that, if confronted by an arrogant Xhosa intellectual like Mbeki, a proper Zulu man fights back. From that moment on, an extensive period of 'camping against' Mbeki effectively began.

Jacob Zuma is an extremely pleasant and genial man, almost universally popular among those who know him. His fine singing voice and joviality meant that he was in great demand to sing at weddings and funerals. He also has a strong and genuine identification with poor, rural Zulu people – that is to say, his own roots. All of which meant that he was able to add a large friendship circle to his already very large extended family.

The search for allies – and funders

Zuma's rock-solid base was his own Zulu heartland, but it was obvious that this was not enough. It became clear that Mbeki – whose intelligence network had, of course, swiftly apprised him of Zuma's determination to fight back – was now set on finishing Zuma off completely by having him sent to jail for corruption, presumably for 15 years like Schabir Shaik. Zuma was already 63, so that would mean jail for the rest of his life. It was an utterly desperate situation, particularly since Mbeki was bound to use the entire machinery of state against Zuma – the intelligence service, the police, the prosecutors, and so on. Moreover, Mbeki was paranoid and relied heavily on spies, phone-taps and 'dirty tricks' of every kind.[24] He had already largely won over the press into somehow believing that Zuma was a major beneficiary of the Arms Deal of the mid-1990s, although Mbeki, together with the defence minister, Joe Modise, had orchestrated the deal while Zuma had been a mere provincial minister at that time, far from the action. Zuma could not even rule out the possibility of assassination and quickly recruited a number of burly bodyguards who searched everyone who came near him (including the present writer).

So Zuma was fighting for his life against an overwhelmingly powerful opponent. Above all, he needed money – not just for his own and his family's survival and for his growing political campaign, but for the expensive lawyers necessary to keep him out of jail. Mandla Gcaba was of primary importance in this. By then he had become a director of Remant Alton, the private bus service to which Durban city council had sold off its own bus service (for just R70 million) in 2003. Remant Alton was, from the first, an obvious vehicle of Durban ANC sleaze. It was chaired by Diliza Mji, the ANC's former provincial treasurer, and run by Daniel Jagadasan, who had been convicted of bribing municipal officials. Remant Alton utterly failed to run a sustainable service and had to be frequently bailed out by the council which then generously purchased the whole company back in 2008 for R405 million.[25] That is to say, Durban municipal corruption produced substantial revenue flows and, inevitably, some of these too would eventuate in donations to the Zuma camp.

But inevitably Zuma also had to turn to Durban's wealthy Indian community, starting with Schabir Shaik's brothers – already thirsting for revenge against Mbeki – but extending outwards from there to anyone willing to help. Among his larger donors were his lawyer, Julie Mahomed, the Durban businessman Vivian Reddy, the Namibian businessman Jürgen Kögl, various members of the Zuma family, and his old friend Nora Fakude-Nkuna. Nelson Mandela also gave him R1 million, despite his obvious implication in the Schabir Shaik case.[26] This suggests a certain lack of concern about corruption on Mandela's part.

Zuma was greatly helped by the special relationship between Zulus and Indians. And any Indian involved in ANC (or Inkatha) politics knows that his entire career depends on Zulu support which he can never risk alienating. (Later, Zuma was to choose a Durban Indian, Pravin Gordhan, to be his first finance minister. Gordhan could never show the same independence as his predecessor, Trevor Manuel, a man of the Cape Flats.) Naturally, there were a number of Indian businessmen willing to place a side-bet on Zuma as, perhaps, the next president. Moreover, Mac Maharaj, the most senior Indian in the ANC and a struggle hero, immediately came out for Zuma. (He treated somewhat startled diners at an official banquet to a diatribe about 'that little shit, Mbeki'.[27]) And Indian support did not just mean money. Maharaj was an extremely wily strategic adviser, as was Schabir Shaik's brother, Mo.

Zuma, for his part, was in no position to pick and choose his friends. Since all the avenues of respectability were closed to him, he had to fall back on taxi bosses and shady financiers: there were no questions asked. Similarly, Zuma happily courted the SACP, the wild men of the ANC Youth League, Cosatu, anyone who would listen – all alienated from Mbeki because of the way in which they had been deliberately marginalised in the key turn towards economic orthodoxy in 1996 under his so-called Growth, Employment and Redistribution Policy (Gear). Mbeki had realised that South Africa was drifting towards an IMF bail-out and knew that he would never be forgiven if that happened. So he took tough pre-emptive action – which was highly successful. The budget was brought back into balance and the debt paid down. But the left was deeply shocked that it could simply be left out of policy decision-making in this way. Thereafter Mbeki and those who supported him were vilified as part of 'the 1996 class project'.

Zuma had gone along with Gear – he had little understanding of economics – but was perfectly happy to benefit from the populist reaction against it. Soon there were Zuma factions within almost every state bureaucracy.

Mbeki's downfall

Mbeki threw the book at Zuma – and there was plenty to throw. Soon Zuma was facing charges on more than 700 counts of fraud, money-laundering, corruption and racketeering. In response he rallied his supporters and raised money for teams of expensive lawyers. Their aim, from the outset, was to use every possible means to defer and delay the case on the assumption that if Zuma could win the intra-party battle against Mbeki it would not be difficult to find a legal means to make all these charges go away. This turned out to be a winning strategy. Zuma was quite frank about this and told me: 'The case against Schabir and me was essentially political, so we needed political lawyers. Schabir didn't understand this. I warned him he had the wrong kind of lawyers but he didn't listen to me.'[28]

Mbeki had made a fatal mistake by believing the standard ANC line that tribalism was just a creation of apartheid and, with liberation, would naturally fall away. The fact is, of course, that ethnic feelings continue in South Africa, just as they do throughout Africa. It could hardly be otherwise. Perceiving his mistake too late, Mbeki made last-minute attempts to rally the Xhosas to his side, but this was never really effective. According to Mark Gevisser, he was also 'worried that Zuma and his backers had no respect for the rule of law, and would be unaccountable to the constitutional dispensation … There was also the worry of a resurgence of ethnic politics and … that Zuma's leftist advisors would undo all the meticulous stitching of South Africa into the global economy … It would be, in effect, a dream shattered, irrevocably, as South Africa turned into yet another post-colonial kleptocracy; another "footprint of despair" in the path of destruction away from the promises of *uhuru*.'[29] Gevisser also reported that Mbeki saw a South Africa governed by Zuma as 'just another neo-colonial basket case.'[30] All of which seems remarkably prescient now, though one has to remember that it was under Mbeki that corruption really took off and that there was no sharp break between the Mbeki and Zuma presiden-cies. Instead, they are part of a steady downward slide. Indeed, the only real question is whether that slide did not begin even earlier. Certainly, by Zuma's second term the country was wrestling not only with the legacy of apartheid but with the accumulated weight of ANC corruption and policy errors over 20 years.

Zulu-speakers are South Africa's largest single ethnic group and they are also the most cohesive. Whatever their political views, Zulus tend to be proud of their king, their history, and their legend as one of Africa's supreme warrior nations. By contrast, the Xhosas are still split among Thembu, Mpondo, Mfengu and so on; they have no unified history or sim-ilar cohesion. The ANC was founded by a Zulu – John Dube – and when it finally became a mass movement in the 1950s its leader was a Zulu chief, Albert Luthuli. Zulus then patiently put up with a succession of Xhosa ANC leaders,[31] but with Zuma's ascension to the deputy presidency there was a feeling that at last the ANC was 'coming home' to where it belonged. So when Mbeki decided to shatter such notions, he was not only taking on Zuma. He was creating a bruised, indignant Zulu consciousness to which Zuma inevitably appealed – with growing success. It did not help that Mbeki comes from the Mfengu group, often referred to by white historians of old as 'the loyal Mfengu' because of their eagerness to collaborate with white rule.

I have elsewhere described in detail the battle which culminated in Zuma's sweeping victory over Mbeki at the ANC's Polokwane conference in 2007,[32] so there is no need to repeat that story here. Suffice it to say that this was an epochal victory for grass-roots democracy. Like so many other African rulers, Mbeki had tried to perpetuate himself in power – and was brought down to earth with a thump. He was forced from office in 2008 and Zuma became president in 2009.

Payback time

Much of the story of the years that followed consisted in the paying-off of the debts incurred in the desperate years of 2005–2007. Zuma himself, of course, became a virtual Zulu monarch with his multiple wives, palatial establishment at Nkandla and many cattle. In effect, South Africa was now ruled by a cunning but semi-literate Zulu chief. Naturally, Zuma and his lawyers fended off all remaining legal charges connected to the Arms Deal and any other embarrassing questions to do with Nkandla: in effect, the assumption was that the conquest of executive power nullified all other notions of legal responsibility. Indeed, as was later revealed, Zuma argued that criminal charges against him should be dropped because corruption was 'a victimless crime' and only a crime at all 'in a Western paradigm'.[33] Sure enough, Schabir Shaik was quickly freed on 'health' grounds, though he was soon to be seen out on the golf course. Mo Shaik became head of the intelligence service. Mac Maharaj, whose plain speaking about Mbeki had resulted in him being pushed back into exile, where he kept body and soul together through a lowly teaching post in America, returned in triumph to become Zuma's spokesman and canny personal adviser. Just as Mbeki had depended on the bullying Essop Pahad as his virtual prime minister, so Maharaj was now Zuma's right-hand man.

Zuma himself became head of the Masibambisane Rural Development Initiative (MRDI), the Jacob Zuma Foundation and the Jacob Zuma RDP Education Trust, to which companies that wanted government favour were wise to contribute. This gave him access to what were in effect large slush funds from which he could disburse at will, the great chief bestowing favours. The MRDI was used to fund high-profile gifts of tractors, seeds and implements to rural people in the run-up the elections – and just to make sure it was nicely topped up, the Ministry of Agriculture gave it R800 million in state funds. MRDI's deputy chair is Sibusiso Mzobe, Zuma's cousin.[34] Other provincial government departments gave the MRDI another R95 million.[35] The minister of agriculture who so helpfully pushed this largesse Zuma's way was Tina Joemat-Pettersson. When she was later moved to the energy portfolio this coincided exactly with Zuma's wish to sign a R1-trillion nuclear deal with Russia. It was popularly assumed that any such deal would be likely to include large kickbacks.

As soon as Zuma won the ANC leadership contest many members of his family began to set up companies at bewildering speed in anticipation of economic gains. These were not long in coming. His second wife (actually the fourth, counting one died and another divorced), Nompumelelo 'Ma' Ntuli, is a one-woman business on her own, with a large portfolio of interests. She is a director of seven companies and also runs the MaNtuli Zuma Foundation. Each of his other wives – Thobeka Madiba-Zuma and Bongekile Ngema-Zuma – also have their own foundations and an array of business interests. Thobeka bought a large house in Durban in 2011 through her family trust, commissioning renovations of R9 million. Bongekile also bought a luxury home in 2011, in Pretoria.

No fewer than five Zuma family members either sit on the board or serve in executive positions in the Isthebe group of companies. Isthebe was founded by the family as a major vehicle for its interests. It is involved in energy, oil, exploration, agriculture, engineering, mining and IT. It uses its BEE credentials and above all the Zuma name to push for contracts. Among the family members involved are Zuma's younger brother, Michael, and his eldest son, Edward.

These are, inevitably, Zuma's two closest henchmen. Michael, who freely admits to using the Zuma name to get business, is involved in 25 companies and is a director of 15 of them. He is listed as a director of the Midway Two group, which was investigated by the police for tender irregularities – including a R1-billion tender for the police themselves. Naturally, Michael claimed there was no case to answer, and as always seemed to happen with cases involving Zuma family members, no one was interested in taking the matter further.

Edward joined no fewer than 34 companies once his father became president and remains a director of 10 of them. Edward has encountered much public odium for his alleged links with the super-lucrative business of cigarette smuggling. Enormous quantities of illegal cigarettes are smuggled into South Africa from Zimbabwe and Malawi and numerous figures in the business are under investigation for fraud, money laundering and tax evasion. One of these is Yusuf Kajee, the CEO of Amalgamated Tobacco Manufacturing (ATM). Edward was on ATM's board till 2011 and remains Kajee's fellow director on the board of Fastjet, the budget airline. Another Fastjet director, Paul de Robillard, has had to face allegations of involvement in fraud and murder, which of course he denies.

Duduzane, another Zuma son, became a director of numerous companies as his father climbed to power. His interests are tightly intermeshed with those of the Gupta brothers, Ajay, Atul and Rajesh (Tony), who have made themselves greatly useful to Zuma, not least by their financial patronage of his children. Duduzane Zuma sits on the board of JIC Mining along with Rajesh Gupta and he also sits on the boards of two other Gupta companies, Sahara Holdings and Shiva Uranium. Duduzane and Rajesh also hold a 25.1 per cent stake in VR Laser Services which had a multi-billion-rand sub-contract to supply armoured vehicles to the army.[36] In addition Duduzane owns 30 per cent of the company that controls the TV station ANN7 and was also involved with Imperial Crown Trading, a company controversially granted a share of the lucrative Sishen mineral deposits, even though these had already been allocated elsewhere. The result was a major scandal: in effect mineral rights were simply stolen through manipulation of state registration, with the minimum objective that ICT would have to be bought off. In 2012 press reports linked Duduzane and the Guptas to an illegal mining venture in Mpumalanga. Idwala Coal, which naturally got large contracts from the state-owned utility, Eskom, was found to have broken environmental laws and to have operated illegally for years. In August 2014 Duduzane's silver Porsche was in an accident in which two people were killed and Duduzane earned the ire of the magistracy by failing to attend the inquest. This drew public criticism that, like the Guptas, he was acting as if he believed that he was above the law.

Zuma's eldest daughter, Duduzile, is also involved in many different companies and was for some time a director of the Guptas' Sahara Holdings. One of her directorships is with Duzi Investment Holdings, presumably named after the Msunduzi River, which flows between Pietermaritzburg and Durban. It holds investments in Zambia's financial sector, Angolan housing projects and infrastructure development in the DRC.

Three other daughters, Gugulethu, Thuthukile and Nokothula, have all been able to indulge their teenage fantasies of appearing in TV soaps as well as having interests in various companies.

A family business

However the Zuma family's biggest (and most controversial) businessman is Zuma's nephew, Khulubuse, whose ultra-corpulent figure is seldom out of the news. He has been involved in over 30 companies in recent years. In many of them he works alongside his uncle's lawyer, Michael Hulley, who is apparently being rewarded for his role in helping Zuma escape the various legal charges against him. Most controversial was the directorship of Khulubuse and Hulley, alongside Mandela's grandson, Zondwa, of Aurora Empowerment Systems, which owned two mines.[37] To growing public scandal, the mines were looted while the workers went unpaid. In the end the Chinese (in the shape of China African Precious Metals) obligingly bought Aurora out. This at least brought down the curtain on an affair which had acutely embarrassed the government, for it demonstrated all too plainly how the ANC-linked elite were profiting while their workers (literally) starved.

In order to get out of Aurora Khulubuse relied heavily on the Taiwanese fixer, Jen-Chih 'Robert' Huang,[38] who, somewhat mysteriously, was convicted and sentenced to 12 years for murder in 1998 but managed never to serve time in jail. Huang was instrumental in arranging Chinese partners for Khulubuse. In June 2014 Huang's assets were frozen over a R541-million tax claim.[39] Court papers alleged that he had operated a whole network of companies as fronts to dodge tax and had been running a multibillion rand racket through Durban harbour. Huang's main company was Mpisi Trading, of which Khulubuse was the chairman for some years. Khulubuse has also been involved with the Lithuanian businessman and gold trader, Boris Bershtein, the head of Royal HTM investments, of which Khulubuse has been a director since 2009.[40] Bershtein's CV boasts three fake PhDs and the *New York Times* has linked him to Russian organised crime figures; he is also alleged to have ferried gold in his private jet from Kyrgyzstan to Switzerland.[41]

Zuma seemed entirely happy to use his official role to support his family's ventures. He met with Nam Sang-Tae, CEO of Daewoo Shipbuilding, to smooth the way for Khulubuse to make a deal between Daewoo and Impinda Group, covering oil, gas and coal transport.[42] His links with

China also helped Khulubuse make a deal with DongFeng Automobile Company, with plans for a South African dealership and an assembly plant.[43] Similarly, Zuma intervened to support a hydro-electric deal from the Mphanda Nkuwa dam in Mozambique, a project for which his son Mxolisi had been a lobbyist.[44] And so on it went.

Mandla Gcaba, who shares directorships in six companies with Khulubuse, naturally thrived too. Having bought back the municipal bus service from Remant Alton in 2008, Durban city council quickly sold it off again in 2009 – without a tender – to Transnat Africa, another company linked to Mandla Gcaba. When this proved unprofitable the bus company was hurriedly taken over once more by the city but operated by Transnat Africa at a fee of R136 million a month.[45] Durban city council also lent itself to favourable deals for S'bu Mpisane and his wife, who won over R200 million worth of housing tenders. The houses built by the Mpisanes often started to crumble within months,[46] so that, for example, of the low-cost houses built for the council in 2010, 60 per cent had to be rectified or rebuilt. But this sort of profiteering was common: of the 27 000 low-cost houses built under the Reconstruction and Development Programme (RDP) that were inspected by the provincial housing department in 2010, 80 per cent had to be demolished or rebuilt.[47]

While Durban under ANC rule was already a corrupt city, there seems little doubt that Zuma's accession to power saw a smart step-up, as the city's budget was used to pay off political debts and reward those who had backed him. R40 million in construction tenders, for example, was handed to John Mchunu, the chairman of the Durban ANC.[48] The mayor of Durban, Obed Mlaba, hijacked a R3-billion waste management project, which he described as 'my pension fund'.[49] This led to a volley of legal claims and counter-claims, but the allegations against Mlaba and the Mlaba Family Trust were ultimately upheld by the Manase Report into corruption in the city, published in 2013 after Durban city council had tried as hard as it could to prevent its publication. Despite this, Zuma rewarded Mlaba with the country's top diplomatic posting to the Court of St James, London.

Pork barrel

Inevitably, Zuma's election to the presidency was taken by the KZN ANC to mean that they were now the top dogs and should be rewarded accordingly. At the same time, it was clear now that the KwaZulu-Natal ANC 'owned' the presidency and was the dominant voice in the ANC. This had diverse results. An immediate one was that KwaZulu-Natal benefited from all manner of pork-barrel expenditure. A R3.4 billion stadium was built in Durban – Moses Mabhida stadium, after the old communist and ANC leader – for the Soccer World Cup in 2010. It was an absurd waste, right next to a large existing stadium, and immediately became a white elephant which nobody could possibly fill, costing Durban ratepayers R100 million a year in maintenance alone. More billions were lavished on the new King Shaka International Airport, which was equally uneconomic: the moment this decision was taken Aeroporti di Roma sold its stake in Acsa (Airports Company South Africa), for it knew there was no way of commercially justifying this huge capital expenditure. At the airport a new John Dube Trade Port was established and was given Special Economic Zone status by the government. Huge new spending plans were unveiled to enable Durban Harbour to double its capacity. There was brave talk of Durban hosting the Commonwealth Games, even the Olympics. All over the province new roads were built, even those which did not lead to Nkandla.

This euphoria was perhaps most notably reflected in the province's historic capital, Pietermaritzburg, an elegant old Victorian city founded in 1838, whose city hall was housed in the largest brick building of Victorian vintage in the Southern Hemisphere. In 2010 the city was placed under administration and the mayor and city manager were stripped of their powers – this following an orgy of corruption and maladministration. The city's cash reserve had fallen from R120 million in 2007 to R1.7 million. The auditor-general had repeatedly cited the city for 'irregular, fruitless and wasteful expenditure' but the city council had virtually refused to exercise proper oversight. The result was that the city was 'in turmoil' and on the point of collapse. There was a deep symbolism in the fact that this proud old city had weathered colonialism, Union and apartheid but that ANC rule had so quickly reduced it to beggary and the loss of its autonomy.

At a far lower level, the effect was felt in repeated assassinations of coun-cillors and key political activists. The point – not lost on even the humblest militant – was that the KwaZulu-Natal ANC now ruled the national ANC and thus the country. This dominance was easily translated into power, money and patronage. Accordingly, even humble town councillorships now had a definite cash value and were well worth fighting over. Inevitably, incipient warlords wanted to capture them and were not prepared to stand by while rival factions stepped in. It was dog eat dog.

Bheki Cele, one of Zuma's strongest supporters, was made the boss of the entire South African Police Service (the SAPS). He awarded himself the rank of general but lived far beyond his official annual salary of R1.3 million. Thus, for example, he bought his then fiancée, Thembeka Ngcobo, a house and a Mercedes[50] – before later breaking off the relationship. Many questions were raised over Cele's tenure as police chief, not least his close association with S'bu Mpisane, the mysteriously rich Durban policeman. When Cele paid *lobola* (bride price) for Ngcobo, his *lobola* delegation was led by S'bu Mpisane, the soccer boss Irvin Khoza, the minister of justice, Jeff Radebe, and Zuma's son, Edward.[51] Moreover, Cele, like Mpisane, had some history in taxi war violence. In his earlier career as provincial min-ister for safety and security in KwaZulu-Natal, Cele had been cited in an interdict obtained by Bongani Mkhize, chairman of the KwaMaphumulo Taxi Association, preventing the police from killing him. Mkhize was at that time involved in a taxi war in which the police seemed to take a strongly partisan interest, shooting seven suspects dead. Mkhize's interdict didn't work: he was soon also shot dead by the police, who claimed he had fired on them first – a view strongly questioned by a ballistics expert hired by the Mkhize family.[52]

One of the reasons why Bheki Cele excited interest was that his Umhlanga home cost many times his annual salary. Secondly, he boasted of getting his suits from Lafayette in Paris. And he often seemed to have large sums of cash about his person. In May 2010 he lost a bag apparently containing R40 000 aboard an SAA flight but he simply waved the theft aside and claimed that no money was involved. Similarly, shortly before his planned wedding there was a theft of between R1 million and R5 million in cash from his home (denied by Cele but asserted by police sources).[53] As head of the SAPS Cele followed Jackie Selebi, Thabo Mbeki's right-hand man who served as head of Interpol before being sentenced to 15 years for corruption (a first for Interpol, one imagines).[54] Selebi was, however, an ANC old-timer so in 2012 Zuma had him released on 'medical parole'. The fact is that a police chief in today's South Africa has easy access to almost unlimited amounts of cash from those anxious to avoid justice and it takes an unusual character to resist such a temptation. Finally, in 2012 Zuma had to suspend Cele from his post after a board of inquiry headed by Judge Jake Moloi found him unfit for office after he had spent R1.7 billion on leases which were 'unlawful, improper and constituted maladministration'.[55]

Cele took his dismissal extremely badly. Quite apart from the fact that he could see Zuma's allies and clients benefiting from corruption wherever he looked, he doubtless also knew the extent of corruption within the police. Inevitably, in such an environment anyone dismissed for corruption feels unfairly discriminated against. In any modern South African city one is likely to be told that the head of the local police drugs squad is being paid off by the drug dealers, the head of the CID is being paid off by major gangsters and so on. Selebi, by consorting with – and getting paid off by – mafia bosses, was merely par for the course. In addition, anything to do with police intelligence is riddled by Zulu tribalism, for Zuma has been careful to keep the intelligence services and the ministries of justice, prisons and police all under Zulu control. Knowing all this, Cele was indignant that he had been singled out for public disgrace – and this was no small matter, for he had retained a popular political base in KwaZulu-Natal. In the end Zuma gave way and appointed Cele as deputy minister of agriculture in May 2014.

A chief, not a president

Thus the pattern which emerges from this dense forest of family corporate behaviour is that the (large) Zuma family – no doubt with the President's backing – have seen his ascent to political leadership as a once-in-a-lifetime opportunity to get rich quick – and to ensure that the Zuma family will remain rich, whatever happens to the President's career. In their hurry to do this they have been willing to secure the services of some extremely dubious business partners. It is all of a piece with Jacob Zuma's own rise to power, his path smoothed by a number of unsavoury characters, but ending in a spectacular recreation of Zulu chieftaincy among his many wives and cattle at Nkandla. In that sense, Zuma is a conservative character, for he has taken South Africa's chief executive role and turned the clock back, returning it to a de facto Zulu chieftaincy. At the same time he has returned power and possessions as far as he can to South Africa's traditional rulers.[56] The great irony is that he has done this at the head of a party which claims to be progressive and leftist, and with the enthusiastic support of the SACP.

In July 2014 one of Zuma's daughters, Thuthukile (25), was appointed as the chief of staff for the minister of telecommunications. This highly paid job had never been advertised and it was understood that she had been the personal choice of the minister, Siyabonga Cwele, a Zulu and a Zuma loyalist.[57] The fact that Thuthukile was by some way the youngest person ever to occupy such a post provoked a brief storm over the nepotism allegedly involved.[58] What enraged critics was that, despite Zuma's ritual denunciations of corruption, it was all so natural, so unapologetic. It is little wonder that ministers in Zuma's cabinet paid no heed to the Executive Members' Ethics Act and quite brazenly continue to hold directorships in private companies. No fewer than 27 ministers did this in Zuma's first administration. The comparable number at the start of his second administration was 18, but that number would doubtless grow as ministers sought to benefit their own companies with an expectation of complete immunity.[59]

Similarly, Zuma attempted to deflect the storm of criticism over the R246-million 'security upgrade' to his Nkandla home by insisting (on the basis of no evidence) that he had paid for it himself. Yet for a man earning R2 million a year, that posed obvious and unanswerable questions about where such money had come from. Moreover, despite the continuing furore over Nkandla, Zuma pressed ahead with government plans to spend R2 billion more on turning his local village of Nxamalala (just 3 kilometres from his homestead) into 'the first town built by black people after democracy'. This new town (immediately dubbed 'Zumaville') would be linked to Kranskop by a new road costing R290 million. Typically, when this project drew parliamentary criticism, Zuma replied: 'Why must people of Nkandla starve? Why should they be isolated? Should they be punished because they are neighbours to Zuma? Developing that area does not trouble me. It makes me very proud.'[60] Yet this solicitude for his neighbours is only partly genuine. Thus part of the spending on Zuma's Nkandla homestead is for a private clinic, because the KwaNxamalala clinic, which the locals use, provides very poor care and often doesn't even have a nurse on duty.[61]

A truer picture could be obtained by observing Christmas in Nkandla, when Zuma handed out food, toiletries and blankets (all emblazoned with his own face) to a hall full of old people, sternly telling them to ignore the furore about the cost of his home. 'You must not listen to people who criticise the government,' he told them. He also received a deputation of local people led by Councillor Sibongiseni Bhengu, who declared that: 'The President is being insulted. He is being compared to ordinary people. We do not have a problem with the amount of money that was spent ... It doesn't matter how much was used.'[62] Thus the Authorised Version. Zuma seems to have assumed, in effect, that all South Africans would be willing to behave like deferential rural Zulus towards their chief. It was a major misjudgement, even though he was able to make the ANC behave like that. Public criticism over Nkandla continued to mount and in August 2014 Zuma virtually fled from a parliamentary question session in which Julius Malema and his Economic Freedom Fighters (EFF) chanted 'Pay back the the money.' Zuma then complained that he was being 'persecuted' over Nkandla, again suggesting that he barely understood the charges against him.[63]

The criminalisation of the state

More serious, however, is the fact that the Zuma era has brought about the sweeping criminalisation of the South African state. It is not just that Zuma himself is still facing 700 unsettled counts of corruption, fraud, money-laundering and racketeering, or that he has been the happy recipient of support from many extremely dubious sources, or even that he has clearly broken the law by spending hundreds of millions of public money on his private residence. He also seems to have no problem with the fact that his son Edward has several associates with serious criminal records and is still fighting a furious rearguard action against the tax authorities over his alleged involvement in the illegal cigarette trade. This trade costs the South African state at least R12 billion a year in lost taxes. Yet Edward set up his Amalgamated Tobacco Manufacturing company (ATM) as soon as his father became president, using Chinese machinery and Chinese technicians. The tax authorities successfully showed that ATM had failed to pay its correct taxes and that its documents wilfully hid the true nature of its business. Thus in 2013 ATM declared that it had manufactured 15 800 boxes of cigarettes while the true figure was 190 000 boxes. Edward implausibly explained these charges as being the product of racism.[64]

The case of Zuma's nephew, Khulubuse, was even worse. As we have seen, Khulubuse's business dealings also left much to be desired. But on at least two occasions Zuma apparently intervened to push business his way. When Khulubuse's Aurora Empowerment Systems was in deep trouble over the mismanagement of mines it had bought, Zuma allegedly intervened to woo the international investment firm, Global Emerging Markets (GEM) and persuade it to inject $2 million into Aurora. GEM's director, Chris Brown, claimed that he had met with Zuma in the living room of his official residence and been persuaded to invest in Aurora. This he did, but it turned out that he had been directed to pay into a dummy account, from which the money was quickly stolen. Brown insisted that even at the time of his meeting with the President 'they had arranged to steal the funds'.[65]

No sooner had Zuma become president than he made a state visit to the Democratic Republic of Congo in September 2009. Mbeki had tended to ignore the DRC and Angola on the grounds that they were such bywords for corruption by their respective rulers that they undermined his vision of an African Renaissance. Zuma had no such reservations – and nor was he interested in an African Renaissance. President Joseph Kabila, then only 38, was grateful not only for this recognition but also desperately needed South Africa's military help against the M23 rebels then threatening the Eastern DRC, which Zuma was happy to provide. Kabila drew attention to the rich oilfields in the Eastern Congo and argued that if South Africa could arrange security around the oil installations, their exploitation could go ahead – and that it was only reasonable that this should be of benefit to 'South Africa, the ruling party and even the Zuma family'.[66]

Six months later Khulubuse Zuma set up two companies in the British Virgin Islands, Caprikat and Foxwhelp, and Kabila took over two oilfields from Tullow Oil and instead allocated them to Khulubuse for the payment of a mere $6 million, although the two fields were valued at about $10 billion. Tullow protested fiercely but in vain that there was no sense in allocating these oilfields to companies with zero experience or expertise. But, of course, Khulubuse had no plan to operate the oilfields – what he wanted was to be able to sell that right for a good price. So Caprikat/Foxwhelp quickly established Oil of DRCongo to operate the fields – a company owned by Fleurette, belonging to the youthful Israeli billionaire Dan Gertler, who is a bosom friend of Kabila's. Khulubuse is also reported to have acquired large mining and construction interests in the DRC.[67]

When Nelson Mandela was president he attracted much criticism for the shameless way in which he used South African policy as a means to enrich the ANC, raising enormous funds from dictators and despots around the Third World. Mandela could see nothing wrong with this any more than he could see anything wrong with calling for 'everyone' to join the ANC in order to create a one-party state. Moreover, it was known that when, for example, Mandela travelled to Gaddafi's Libya, a whole party of dodgy businessmen and arms dealers would travel in train, hoping to benefit. But Zuma's diplomacy in the DRC was aimed not at the enrichment of the ANC but of his own family. This was how the worst African dictators – Mobutu, Obiang Nguema, Arap Moi – had behaved. Such behaviour was new in South African history. The fact that the ANC could applaud and support it told one all that one needed to know of its degradation.

Zuma was known to travel to and from Nkandla with a fleet of helicopters and also to use a luxury Boeing business jet to go abroad. The Opposition spokesman, David Maynier, estimated that over R230 million had been spent on flights in the Boeing alone, but the government refused to divulge any details of costs on the (absurd) grounds that all such information about the President was 'sensitive'.[68] For Zuma, seeing himself as a chief more than a president, felt that his person must be respected, and his followers have repeatedly suggested that South Africa should follow other African states in having a law forbidding all criticism of the president. Zuma, though he himself is ordained as a Christian preacher in an Africanist church, espouses polygamy, and makes no secret of his homophobia or his belief that women are second-class citizens. He also practises all manner of traditional pre-Christian rituals. He has attacked Christianity for undermining traditional African values and threatened voters who do not vote for the ANC that their ancestors will not forgive them. He has also inveighed against 'clever blacks' who think they know better than the old ways.[69]

In his celebrated dystopian novel written in 1947, *When Smuts Goes. A History of South Africa from 1952 to 2010*, Arthur Keppel-Jones foresaw South Africa meeting its ruin at the hands of a primitive Zulu leader, Sixpens. There are many points of comparison between Zuma and Sixpens. Indeed, in many respects, Zuma has fulfilled the predictive vision of rightwing whites who resisted majority rule on the grounds that it would bring authoritarianism, corruption and incompetence sufficient to ruin the country. The surprise is how quickly the ANC in power regressed to this sort of rule and, even more, how it rallied behind Zuma, defending him against any criticism.

But let us not leave the story there. The scene is the Durban beachfront on the eve of the 2014 elections. On 2 May the beach lit up for a huge party thrown by S'bu and Shauwn Mpisane at a cost of some R1 million, all in honour of the ANC. There is Khulubuse Zuma, enormous in a scarlet suit with an SACP hat, improbably suggesting that he supports communist ideals. Champagne and expensive whiskies flow in copious amounts and large numbers of beautiful young women in short skirts and high heels pick their way across the sand. There, dancing in line with the socialites, models and soap opera stars, are Bheki Cele (in shorts) and sundry businessmen. Everywhere the yellow, black and green of the ANC. Shauwn Mpisane in gold-studded jeans. No one is keen to discuss the many and various charges levelled against the Mpisanes over S'bu's role in the shootings on the Embankment, his wondrous resurrection since then, the long list of allegations about the way the Mpisanes have earned their enormous wealth through tenders for the Durban city council, or, indeed, exactly why Bheki

Cele had to be fired as police commissioner. Shauwn Mpisane is adamant that the party is not about 'a certain person' (Zuma) but about the 'legacy that our forefathers left for us'.[70]

But what were those revellers really celebrating? Clearly, a degree of amnesia was an essential quality, a belief that celebrity alone was quite enough to hold the law at bay, that pouring out money in such conspicuous and wasteful expenditure was perfectly acceptable in a country with 40 per cent unemployment, that ANC government was all about a small elite having the time of their lives. What these party-goers were happy about was that their patronage line had come to power. But what they were really celebrating, consciously or not, was the criminalisation of the South African state.

CHAPTER THREE

The ANC Under Zuma

J acob Zuma's conquest of the ANC at Polokwane in 2007 and, even more, his accession to the presidency in 2009 were seen by many of his critics as heralding an era of unparalleled corruption in which the ANC became unrecognisable as the old Mandela ANC. Zuma himself was seen as both the symbol and the cause of this degradation. In fact this was simplistic. As I have argued elsewhere,[1] the ANC was headed in this direction even before it took power in 1994 as the leadership – Mandela included – quickly availed themselves of new sources of income from a variety of 'godfathers', that is to say wealthy figures of the *ancien régime* who moved rapidly to buy the favours of the new elite. Contrary to later suggestions from the left, no systematic deal was brokered between 'white capital' and the new elite. Instead there were multiple individual arrangements and the ANC itself made no constitutional or ideological concessions in return. The only bargain the ANC made was the new constitution it hammered out at the Convention for a Democratic South Africa (Codesa) and the only concession made to capital there lay in the basic recognition of property rights. The ANC remained wholly free to devise its own policies on every subject, the economy included.

The ANC's slide into corruption and warlordism actually derived from the nature of African nationalism itself. Everywhere on the continent where African nationalism had triumphed the result had been the same – a period of rapid appropriation by the new elite which took the seats of political power and set about a headlong process of primary accumulation. Whatever its more populist or socialist promises, it was everywhere clear that the new elite was set on becoming rich or, at the very least, acquiring middle-class status overnight. That is, the real heart of the movement lay not with the masses but this much smaller class of would-be plutocrats.[2] In most African states the appetites of the new elite were constrained by the simple fact that the countries themselves were very poor. In South Africa, however – like Nigeria – the country contained considerable resources and the result was an immense and competitive feeding frenzy.

In South Africa it took several years for the new elite to complete its capture of every aspect of the old white state, to institutionalise a new system of racial preference, this time in favour of Africans, and to push forcefully into the private sector – hence the impression that these early years under Mandela were fundamentally more benign. In fact it is easy to see in retrospect that the Mandela period laid the foundations for all that followed. It was then that strong racial preferences were introduced in the labour market; then that the labour market itself was deliberately distorted to favour a small labour aristocracy; and it was then that corruption began to soar, symbolised by the Arms Deal, which remains the single biggest example of corruption in government to date. Moreover, as we have seen, Mandela was the direct father of the Zuma period, for he it was who insisted on Zuma's elevation to the deputy presidency, just as it was he who was later a prominent funder of Zuma's. This is hardly a surprising conclusion: African nationalism is all of a piece, just as Afrikaner nationalism was.

Zuma takes power

Although Zuma had decisively defeated Mbeki at the ANC's Polokwane conference of 2007, there was nervousness about forcing Mbeki out, so he continued as president. To the annoyance of the Zuma camp, the attempt to prosecute Zuma continued. Since Zuma regarded this as merely a form of political persecution, it was seen as evidence of Mbeki's continuing bad faith. Matters finally came to a head in September 2008 when Judge Chris Nicholson confirmed Zuma's view by declaring that there had been improper political interference with the National Prosecuting Authority (NPA), a view later confirmed by the release of phone tap data from the prosecutors' phones. The Zuma camp leapt into action and the ANC's National Executive Committee (NEC) asked Mbeki to resign. Mbeki knew better than to resist and was replaced by the ANC secretary-general, Kgalema Motlanthe. Motlanthe, a former head of the National Union of Mineworkers, was an SACP member and a vulgar Marxist who had demanded that the nation's children must be 'taught to hate capitalism'. But age had somewhat tempered his fire and he was seen as a reassuring, avuncular figure. Everyone knew, however, that he was merely serving *pro tem* until Zuma could lead the ANC to victory in the election due in May 2009.

Zuma's own particular style was immediately visible. In January 2009 he announced his engagement to what would be his fifth wife. Most ANC politicians would not have chosen to flaunt their polygamy just months before an election. Already, during his wedding to his fourth wife the previous year, Zuma had happily accepted a contribution towards his wedding expenses of R400 000 from David Mabuza, the former head of the teachers' union, Sadtu, who, it was known, was anxious to become premier of Mpumalanga province. The accusations that Mabuza was thus buying his premiership were simply brushed aside by Zuma, but Mabuza indeed became premier – and was doubtless more than able to recoup his costs.[3]

Mbeki's much-offended supporters now launched the Congress of the People (Cope) and it became evident that it had particular appeal in the (Xhosa) Eastern Cape. Mbeki's rule had led many to talk of the 'Xhosa Nostra' – and indeed, his cabinets had become increasingly dominated by Xhosas. The sight of a Xhosa president being dispossessed by a Zulu naturally alarmed many Xhosas and Zuma moved quickly to offer prominent positions on the ANC list to such Xhosa heavyweights as Enoch Godongwana and Phathekile Holomisa, head of the chiefs' association, Contralesa. But the more striking fact was the sweeping purge of Mbekiites. Of the ANC's 315 sitting MPs, 132 were jettisoned. The major beneficiaries were Zuma's allies in the SACP and Cosatu. Among those to feature prominently were Buti Manamela, head of the Young Communist League; Songezo Mjongile, former leader of the ANC Youth League; Thulas Nxesi, Sadtu's general secretary, and General Siphiwe Nyanda, ex-head of the SANDF – reflecting Zuma's strong base in former MK circles. In addition, it was notable that Zuma, a former head of ANC Intelligence, included in his inner circle such figures as Lindiwe Sisulu, a former minister for intelligence, and Billy Masethla, a former director-general of national intelligence. On the campaign trail he handed out food parcels and, like any Tammany[4] boss, could see nothing wrong with it or any need to explain where the money for this had come from.

The 2009 election itself saw Cope win 7.42 per cent of the vote and 30 seats – in the Xhosa heartland of the Eastern Cape it got 13.67 per cent. This represented the relative containment of the Cope threat. The ANC's share of the vote fell from 69.69 per cent to 65.9 per cent, which meant the loss of 15 parliamentary seats, but the party still had a huge majority. In fact the ANC vote fell everywhere except in Zuma's KwaZulu-Natal, where it soared from 1 287 823 (46.98 per cent) in 2004 to 2 192 516 (62.95 per cent), and in Mpumalanga where, thanks to a large Zulu population, the ANC vote stayed flat.[5] Thus while KwaZulu-Natal had seen only the fourth biggest ANC vote in 2004, now it was second only to Gauteng. South African commentators are peculiarly loath to believe in the power of tribalism, but for anyone else it was unmissable.

Zuma's cabinet appointments rewarded his supporters. Pravin Gordhan was at finance, Lindiwe Sisulu at defence, and Siphiwe Nyanda at communications. Both the leader (Blade Nzimande) and deputy leader (Jeremy Cronin) of the SACP got posts – as minister for higher education and deputy minister of transport. All the security cluster of ministries went to Zulus – Jeff Radebe at justice, Nathi Mthethwa at police and Siyabonga Cwele at state security. In addition, there were Zulus at the head of the Constitutional Court (Sandile Ngcobo), the SABC (Ben Ngubane), the SAPS (Bheki Cele), the National Intelligence Agency (Lizo Njenje) and the National Prosecuting Authority (Menzi Simelane), while Zuma's confidant, Mo Shaik, headed the South African Secret Service. But Zuma remained wary of his intelligence chiefs, replacing almost all of them by 2011 and then again in 2014.

Trevor Manuel, previously Mbeki's minister of finance, remained pre-
cariously as head of the National Development Plan, producing a document that was widely acclaimed and largely ignored. A late lobby by
Cosatu saw the creation of a new Department of Economic Development,
headed by Ebrahim Patel, a hardline Cosatu activist – the idea being to
counterbalance the Department of Finance, always suspected of economic
'neo-liberalism' by the left. Another key player in economic policy was the
minister for trade and industry, Rob Davies, a high-ranking communist
whose Marxism-Leninism was of almost mechanical rigidity.

Origins of the Zuma system

Another key appointment was the confirmation of Ace Magashule as premier of the Free State, a post he had already held for 10 years. Magashule
had made the crucial step of becoming a Zuma ally and this carried him
back to power. Under him the Free State had become legendary for corruption of every kind – none of the province's 20 municipalities has ever
received a clean audit.[6] Within months of taking office this time Magashule
was involved in a lawsuit in which Zuma's associate, Vivian Reddy, was
accused of arranging a R3-million bribe for a casino licence.[7] It was pure
Tammany politics: Magashule was allowed to turn the Free State into his
own private kingdom, making him immensely rich – in return for which he
gave Zuma total loyalty. The result was the formation of a political alliance
between KwaZulu-Natal and the neighbouring provinces of Mpumalanga
(where premier David Mabuza ran a similarly corrupt fiefdom[8]) and the
Free State, creating a pro-Zuma bloc which controlled some 40 per cent of
the votes at any ANC conference. In effect Zuma had thus already insured
himself against any possibility of the sort of insurrection that had deposed
Mbeki.

A similar deal was done in Limpopo province, where Cassel Mathale – a
close ally of Julius Malema, head of the ANC Youth League, who had been
a key Zuma supporter against Mbeki – became premier. Both Mathale and
Malema prospered mightily as a result. In the Northern Cape, the ANC
provincial chairman, John Block, who was also the provincial finance

minister, became the pivotal figure in a similar web of corruption revolving, as such things generally did, around tenders and procurement. Block went on trial for fraud, corruption and money-laundering but the ANC refused to suspend him from office and he meanwhile redoubled his vows of loyalty: 'Walking with Zuma is like you are walking with God,' he told his followers.[9]

The same applied exactly to the MK veterans. As an old MK man, Zuma had benefited from their support against Mbeki. After his victory he sought to give the MK Military Veterans Association (MKMVA) an enhanced role within the ANC. However, a number of dissidents, with undoubted cause, accused the leadership of MKMVA of having stolen much of the institution's funds, leaving ordinary MK veterans to live in poverty. A forensic survey by auditors backed this up: 'The top brass of MKMVA turned its investment holdings into their personal piggy bank, using funds to pay for jewellery, spa treatments and school drama lessons, and to withdraw large sums in cash before Christmas ... the report directly fingers former association treasurer Dumisani Khoza, former chairperson Deacon Mathe, current treasurer Johannes "Sparks" Motseki and current chairperson Kebby Maphatsoe. It alleges that they helped themselves to R5.4m ...'.[10]

To add insult to injury, Maphatsoe, the apparent ringleader, had managed to avoid doing any actual fighting when in MK (he had been a cook and then run away) but was now stealing funds intended for those who had fought. Maphatsoe was also a beneficiary in the notorious Gold Fields BEE scheme. Zuma reacted to this potentially awkward situation by giving the MKMVA leadership his whole-hearted support and even making Maphatsoe deputy minister for defence with special responsibility for veterans. The result was that the MKMVA remained utterly corrupt and slavishly loyal to Zuma in all he did. When the Public Protector, Thuli Madonsela, issued a report on Nkandla demanding that Zuma pay back some of the state's money spent on the project, Maphatsoe attacked Madonsela as a CIA agent and demanded that 'Thuli must tell us who her handler is'. He retracted only when Madonsela sued him for libel.[11]

Thus the Zuma system. In effect, provincial premiers and party bosses were given a licence to plunder provided they stayed loyal to the chief at the centre. Since the chief and his family were themselves becoming rich at a great rate, everyone understood the game. Hence the description of Zuma's ANC (offered to me by one who fought in these wars) as 'a federation of warlords'. Each province in turn became a microcosm of the whole with local mayors and councillors plundering their municipalities, knowing that they could probably get away with this provided they remained staunchly loyal to the local party boss and premier. Problems arose when, as often in the Eastern Cape, the chairman of the provincial ANC and the premier were at odds, or when this dichotomy was seen at local level – for example in Nelson Mandela metropole (Port Elizabeth) – or when someone down the food-chain simply went too far and stole so much that major scandals or real political trouble erupted. Such eruptions happened continuously, for example when gross theft resulted in the breakdown of the health system in the Free State or in the failure of the water supply in Grahamstown and other parts of the Eastern Cape.

The Zuma system resembled a medieval state in which the king or mafia don was owed fealty by mighty barons who paid him tribute and gave him political and military support if needed. Within their own baronies, the barons were almost absolute rulers, exacting tribute from those beneath them and exercising powers of patronage over lower-level appointments. Normally speaking, the king would not interfere with their administration though he did exercise powers of taxation over the whole populace. Only if a baron or his underlings exacted so much tribute as to cause a peasants' revolt or create major scandal within the kingdom, would the king be forced to act – though naturally, any sign that a baron was no longer loyal to the king would trigger more severe action.

The heart of the system was KwaZulu-Natal. Although the ANC there was just as prone to factional feuding as anywhere else, when it came to the crunch it would be bound to support the first Zulu president not only out of tribal loyalty but because of the rich rewards of patronage the province received as a result of its central position. With KwaZulu-Natal effectively sewn up, together with Free State and Mpumalanga, Zuma was invulnerable. Many commentators failed to understand this and, the wish being father to the thought, frequently speculated that the ANC might grow weary of the incessant cloud of scandal which hung over Zuma and decide to eject him, as it had ejected Mbeki. In fact this was quite impossible while the whole weight of tribal loyalty and patronage lay behind Zuma. Mbeki, in his time, had viewed with concern the way in which ANC municipal governance had simply become institutionalised looting and, in an effort to stop or at least control this, had sought ever greater presidential powers over the naming of provincial premiers and mayors. This had threatened the whole incipient mafia system of (as it were) delegated looting and Mbeki's proposals had been explosively rejected at Polokwane. Zuma not only made no move to revive such proposals but positively embraced the resulting system. It was, after all, the 'traditional' system, allowing for African 'big men' to dominate government at every level.

The final fruit of the Zuma system was seen in the incessant popular protests in townships and informal settlements. These were endemic almost everywhere, with marches, demonstrations, burning tyres, stoning of cars and municipal buildings, and so on. Such protestors usually aimed at some failure in service delivery and at the corruption of their local mayor and councillors. In fact this was misleading. Lawrie Schlemmer investigated several dozen of such protests and found that they were *invariably* caused by other elements within the local ANC.[12] What was happening was that everywhere local factions would form, conscious of the rich pickings enjoyed by their local mayor and councillors, and would attempt to use their muscle to change the balance within the local ANC so that the pickings could, instead, come the way of their own faction. That is to say, at the very bottom of the patronage system there was a sort of eternal dog-fight over the bones falling from the tables of the better-off.

When Zuma appointed so many leading communists and Cosatu activists to his government – and the ANC's new secretary-general, Gwede Mantashe, was also chairman of the SACP – many wondered if this presaged a major swing to the left. Zuma denied this: ANC policy would stay as it was, he said. He seemed to have no policy ideas of his own: everything would be decided by the ANC. In fact, while these appointments gave major opportunities to the left – and Mantashe became the *de facto* prime minister – what Zuma had done was to distribute jobs to the allies who had helped him against Mbeki. They could be barons now too, could share in the spoils – Mantashe, for all his Marxism-Leninism, was now a prosperous farm-owner (at Elliot in the Eastern Cape), always keen to talk of his herds of cattle and sheep.[13] But Zuma very specifically warned the SACP against any notion of changing the balance of power. Some, he knew, had argued that now the Tripartite Alliance would rule, and not just the ANC. This was, he said, quite wrong. The ANC 'would always play a leading role in the alliance' and 'the role of the SACP in the alliance is to assist the ANC'.[14]

And this was indeed the case. The SACP ministers enjoyed the perks of office and – with the exception of Rob Davies, who showed an energetic and dogmatic protectionism – they made no attempt to change the government's overall direction. There was vague talk of a 'second transition', but that was all. Ideological differences were weak forces compared to the hidebound strength of the Zuma system.

A shambolic party

The ANC remained a continuous site of struggle as the various factions fought for more power and patronage. ANC headquarters at Luthuli House in downtown Johannesburg frequently dictated or vetoed policy initiatives, while in cabinet Siphiwe Nyanda often seemed more powerful than Zuma and was meanwhile helping himself to numerous and lucrative contracts with state entities.[15] Tokyo Sexwale's presidential ambitions, backed by his vast wealth, were always a problem, as was the wild and intemperate rhetoric coming from the Youth League. Deputy President Kgalema Motlanthe reprimanded Malema but, typically, Zuma remained silent. Ministers came out with policy proposals in all directions and Zuma himself made regular big promises of infrastructural spending – but little actually happened. In the midst of the cacophony Zuma sat, never taking any decisive view on any issue, never pushing for implementation. Mainly the President got into the news when he took another wife or had another child out of wedlock. He was openly jeered at by journalists and cartoonists.

The ANC itself was a continuous source of concern, starting with the fact that it didn't pay its bills. In January 2010 the advertising agency Ogilvy's obtained a court judgment against the party for R17.5 million for bills still unpaid from the previous year. The court heard of the party's repeated broken promises, delaying tactics and sheer dishonesty.[16] This was just one of many scandals. The wife of the minister for security, Siyabonga Cwele, was jailed for being a drug trafficker.[17] Worse still, an intraparty committee found evidence of corruption and mismanagement of funds within the ANC. On top of that the ANC chief whip, Mathole Motshekga, was the source of continuous complaint from within the ANC caucus.[18] Yet he was already the ANC's tenth chief whip in 15 years and his predecessors included Tony Yengeni (jailed for fraud) and Mbulelo Goniwe (dismissed for repeated sexual harassment of MPs and staffers). By 2013 Motshekga too had been forced out and replaced by Stone Sizani, not long after which Sizani's wife was charged with involvement in an elaborate fraud to draw salaries from phantom teachers in the Eastern Cape.[19] It was difficult to imagine that Sizani – a former MEC for Education of the Eastern Cape – had been ignorant of his wife's activities.

Tokyo Sexwale, the minister for human settlements (ie housing), submitted his own report about the party which spoke of 'rapidly escalating levels of inter- and intra-alliance political tensions, hostility, mistrust, mutual suspicion, disinformation campaigns, public slander and other ills that have come to characterise our day-to-day political existence'.[20] Sexwale was known to be aiming at the secretary-general, but Mantashe brought out his own report in which he said that the ANC had been transformed from a people-driven to a money-driven organisation in which all and every means including assassination were being used to dispose of rivals within the party. The fundamental activity within the party now, he said, was about 'lobbying and positions'. Often, gate-keepers would prevent others from joining the party if they thought this might strengthen a rival faction. The influence of money and a small group with major resources was pervasive. The manipulation of membership statistics was such that attempts to audit membership were 'a farce'. Cadres were sometimes paid to disrupt meetings. Bribery was widespread. Free travel and cell phones were being used to buy votes. And so on.[21]

Mantashe seems not to have realised that all this was the quite normal, even inevitable result of the ANC becoming essentially a vehicle for personal aggrandisement through the looting of the public exchequer. Zuma, for his part, made occasional formulaic and toothless denunciations of corruption, but that was all. Meanwhile, his various cabinet re-shuffles saw a growing number of Zulus take up position within the Presidency and more and more ministers from KwaZulu-Natal – including Roy Padayachie (communications), Malusi Gigaba and his deputy, Ben Martins (public enterprises), plus Bathabile Dlamini (social development, and thus the controller of the largest source of patronage of all, the social grant system). Most powerful of all was the President's spokesman and closest adviser, Mac Maharaj.

It became clear that the ANC under Zuma was directionless. Zuma seemed to see his job essentially as one of holding the centre ground while balancing and placating all the factions. This caused many to criticise him for lack of leadership – without reflecting much on the fact that this might well be the only way that an ANC leader could now behave. Perhaps the most interesting insight came from a Wikileaks US Embassy cable reporting on a private conversation with the ANC's Gauteng spokesman, Dumisa Ntuli. Ntuli said that the ANC was 'a complete mess', divided not only between Zuma and Mbeki supporters but 'along multiple other lines'. Ntuli said that 'party leaders [read: Gwede Mantashe] are seeking ways to restructure and unify the party so that younger members understand the history and values of the ANC' – but that this was a hopeless task, bound to end in failure. 'The younger cadres have no interest in the history of the ANC. They want access to jobs and personal enrichment ... they will not listen to, or respect, senior officials.' Ntuli also lamented that members were not even focused on the 2011 local elections – they were 'mostly focused on jockeying for positions to be decided upon at the 2012 party congress'. As for the government itself, 'it will not come close to delivering' on its promises.[22] Ntuli naturally denied giving any such interview, but it was a perfectly sound account.

An endless stream of scandals

What was so damaging to Zuma's administration was the combination of drift and corruption. In this respect his Nkandla homestead, so expensively built with taxpayers' money, came to seem symbolic of the whole system.

It was obvious that what Zuma liked most was to be back in Nkandla with his wives and cattle and it was easy to assume that he had become president simply in order to amass wealth for his family and to protect himself from prosecution. This was not really fair: Zuma was undoubtedly keen to improve the lot of poor rural Africans. When he visited Nkandla there were always large numbers of poor supplicants waiting to see him and he would spend long evenings listening to them, often to the despair of his staff who were increasingly worried about the effect of his heavy workload on his health. Similarly, it was too easily forgotten that Thabo Mbeki had shamefully manipulated the prosecution and legal system in order to try to destroy Zuma and that the case against Zuma was thus fatally flawed.[23]

Zuma got little public credit in large part because of the steady flow of scandals, many of them related to the ubiquitous Guptas. It naturally annoyed public opinion that the three brothers, who had only arrived in South Africa from Uttar Pradesh in 1993, should enjoy such wealth and such influence over the government. Not only had they made themselves enormously useful to Zuma personally; they had also founded the pro-ANC *New Age* newspaper, which they ran at a huge loss, and the ANN7 TV news station, a pro-ANC and similarly loss-making operation. The Guptas had interests in computers (Sahara Computers, a copycat of the larger Indian Sahara), air transport, energy and mining. Their Johannesburg estate, Sahara, was palatial and they also acquired the large mansion in Constantia (Cape Town) which had belonged to Sir Mark Thatcher. Their style was arrogant and blatant: over and over again they acted as if they were above the law.

So powerful had the Guptas become through their patronage of the Zuma family that it was widely known that they had advance knowledge of which ministers were to be demoted or promoted in any reshuffle – and ministers who annoyed the Guptas had little chance of preferment. Moreover, the Guptas clearly had advance notice of government decisions and were able to use this for commercial gain – for example when the state-owned Transnet decided to spend R50 billion on new locomotives. In the midst of the tender process Rajesh Gupta and Duduzane Zuma bought into VR Laser Services, which, sure enough, got part of the tender.[24]

Or again, in the Free State, Zuma's client, Ace Magashule, the premier, announced a R570-million scheme for the province to set up a dairy farm at the 4 400-hectare Krynaauwslust holding. Its 370 cows would, he averred, produce 100 000 litres of milk a day – these were clearly ambitious cows, for this would beat normal milk yields ten-fold. The enterprise would be run by Duduzane Zuma, Tshepo Magashule (Ace's son) and Mabengela Pty Ltd (a Gupta vehicle). But the black elite, though keen to own farms, often sees them as essentially for weekend excursions. Looking after cows seven days a week is not on the agenda. By mid-2014 the cows at Krynaauwslust were so neglected that 65 of them had died of starvation and this large public investment was in ruins.[25]

But, in the public eye, worst of all was the Gupta wedding at Sun City in 2013 when an Airbus A330 with 200 guests aboard was allowed to land at the Air Force base at Waterkloof – strictly off-limits to civilian aircraft – and police escorts provided for the guests all the way to Sun City. Moreover, all the black staff there had been dispensed with so that the Gupta guests could be served by whites and not by 'smelly blacks'.[26] This produced a huge and prolonged public furore which should have convinced Zuma that his association with the Guptas was causing him more political damage than could be justified by any amount of family commercial advantage. But it went on. And the public drew the obvious conclusions.[27]

The changing political landscape

The May 2011 local elections provided a major jolt. The ANC had been severely discomfited when the opposition Democratic Alliance (DA) had come to power in Cape Town in the 2006 local elections and there had been much talk of the ANC re-taking and even 'liberating' the city. However in the 2009 elections the DA had progressed further, winning the whole province of the Western Cape as well. This was too much and the ANC launched 'Operation Reclaim' to try to reverse this result by making the Western Cape 'ungovernable' by every possible means – labour agitation, damaging municipal property, hurling human waste at public buildings and so on. It was a bizarre strategy, for it meant that the ANC was trying to revive its struggle mode of the 1980s when the strategy of 'ungovernability' had been extensively used against the apartheid regime. But now this tactic was being used against authorities which had been democratically elected on a universal suffrage franchise.

The 2011 elections showed that this strategy had failed completely. Voters wanted efficient local government and did not appreciate ANC attempts to damage it. Not only did the DA win Cape Town by a heavily increased majority; it also won another 11 Western Cape municipalities and was the biggest party in four more. The ANC was all but ejected from the Western Cape – it was left with the control of just one of the province's 24 municipalities, Beaufort West.

Overall the ANC vote fell from 65.7 per cent in 2006 to 62 per cent in 2011 while the DA rose from 16.3 per cent to 23.9 per cent. The ANC was only saved from a more serious embarrassment by a great surge in its vote in KwaZulu-Natal. This was the result of careful preparation as Zuma sought to make the province his impregnable stronghold. First, almost all the chiefs and also the Zulu king had been wooed away from Chief Buthelezi's Inkatha Freedom Party, using the normal forms of inducement and patronage. Second, the ANC nationally had declared a target of 1 million members by 2012 (the party's centenary) and Zuma had made sure that the membership drive was particularly strong in KwaZulu-Natal – for, of course, the more members a province had, the more delegates it would have at the party's national conference. The early results of this had already been seen in September 2010 at the ANC National General Council (held, of course, in Durban), at which it was announced that party membership in KwaZulu-Natal had soared ahead of all other provinces, reaching 192 618 out of a total of 749 112.[28] This meant that the province would now command over a quarter of the votes at the conference. Third, the ANC had helped exploit a split in the IFP which saw that party's chairperson, Zanele kaMagwaza-Msibi, resign to form the National Freedom Party, taking large numbers of IFP supporters with her. In the municipal elections the NFP took 322 000 votes and won no fewer than 210 council seats in the province's 62 municipalities. This helped reduce the IFP to 341 seats while the ANC soared ahead with 906 seats.[29] It was noticeable that in many municipalities the NFP chose the ANC as its coalition partner, producing furious IFP accusations that the entire party split had been masterminded by the ANC and that kaMagwaza-Msibi was now no more than an ANC client.[30] This furore was hardly dispelled when, in 2014, she was appointed as deputy minister for science and technology in Zuma's cabinet.

These local elections should have been a sharp wake-up call. Not only was the DA expanding vigorously throughout the Western Cape, it was beginning to make serious inroads in the Eastern Cape and the Northern Cape. The ANC had lost ground in all the major cities and was now in retreat. Its advances in KwaZulu-Natal increased the risks of Zulu tribal domination and the likely ethnic response to that. Above all, voters were in open revolt against ANC looting of the municipalities. All of which suggested the need for a sharp change. But, just as in the financial realm, where there was an equal need for a sharp change to avoid the looming 'fiscal cliff', there was no real change. In the Western Cape the now dis-credited 'Operation Reclaim' continued, as if such harassment could bully voters into switching back to the ANC. The only obvious shift – evident in the North Western town of Tlokwe and the Western Cape's Oudtshoorn – was an increased ANC willingness to cheat. This could hardly be a work-able long-term strategy. But drift ruled. There was no long-term strategy any more.

Approaching Mangaung

The year 2012 had long been a key focus for the ANC, not only because it was the party's centenary but because all factional politicking within the ANC was always targeted towards the next party conference – in this case in Mangaung (Bloemfontein). The centenary in January was celebrated with the usual tasteless displays of conspicuous consumption by the ANC elite – Porsches, Mercedes, Range Rovers, French champagne, expen-sive whiskeys, dolly birds, flash clothes, the whole scene surrounded by 'tenderpreneurs' hustling for business.

The more serious issue was that Zuma's underwhelming performance and the growing Zulu predominance had produced sufficient discontent for a challenge to his leadership. Zuma's rustic and unlettered style, his polygamy, his constant claims that God was on the ANC's side and that the ancestors required an ANC vote, all grated on the sensibilities of the new black middle class – which meant that Gauteng, where that class was most highly concentrated, was the centre of the disaffection from Zuma. Lurking behind this was the stereotype of the 'stupid Zulu', prevalent in both black and white circles.[31] The anti-Zuma cause had also been taken up by Julius Malema and the ANC Youth League, in good measure because Malema wanted a larger place in the sun. Malema saw himself as the man who had toppled Mbeki, and the relative ease with which that had been achieved had nourished unrealistic notions that Zuma could similarly be tossed aside. A situation of elite enrichment amidst growing unemployment and inequality inevitably generated considerable popular discontent and Malema, a talented radical populist who campaigned for the full implementation of the Freedom Charter, including a sweeping nationalisation of all banks, mines and major companies, became its spokesman – by definition an oppositional role.

It was clear that Gauteng, which was used to setting the national agenda and resented the slippage of power to Durban and KwaZulu-Natal, would demand a challenge to Zuma's leadership. Given the Northern Sotho preponderance in Gauteng it was not surprising to see that Mathews Phosa, the ANC treasurer-general, backed this group, as did other Northern Sothos such as Tokyo Sexwale, Malema and Motlanthe. Sexwale was ever-ready to run for president but opposition crystallised around Motlanthe. The situation was greatly complicated by fierce factional battles almost everywhere.

Zuma's first move was to launch an official probe into the affairs of the Limpopo ANC,[32] which had just re-elected Cassel Mathale (a Malema henchman) as chairman and given Malema a seat on the provincial executive. The probe was an obvious threat to Malema's base and the source of his patronage – and it sent a clear message to others. Next, he summoned four provincial ANC chairmen – Zweli Mkhize (KwaZulu-Natal), Phumulo Masualle (Eastern Cape), Ace Magashule (Free State) and David Mabuza (Mpumalanga). Mkhize had been Zuma's key henchman in KwaZulu-Natal, Mabuza and Magashule were both regional godfathers, and Masualle, the chairman of the Eastern Cape ANC, had played a crucial role in swinging much of that province behind Zuma and against Mbeki.

The Eastern Cape had been the largest province in terms of ANC membership in Mbeki's time but it had never provided Mbeki with a solid regional base, even though he came from there. In part this was just because he was never a grass-roots politician, but it was also because the divisions between the Xhosa tribes were still sharp, as were those between inhabitants of the old Ciskei and Transkei bantustans and the part of the province which had never been a bantustan at all. In addition, Mbeki's more centrist economic policies sat awkwardly with the province's radical traditions, with both the SACP and Cosatu playing important roles there. Phumulo Masualle, a former post office engineer from the poverty-stricken little Transkei town of Mount Frere, was a leading communist and also the boss of the OR Tambo region which centres on Mthatha and includes most of the old Transkei bantustan. For this region, still dominated by traditional chiefs, to be headed by a communist was, of course, a fantastic denial of its sociology – but such freakish situations often occur in ANC-ruled South Africa. At Polokwane, the OR Tambo region was the largest in delegate terms not only in the Eastern Cape but in the country as a whole. And it had cast these votes for Zuma. The irony was considerable: Mbeki's whole career had been built on his close relationship with Tambo and he succeeded to the ANC leadership as Tambo's heir. In the end Mbeki won the Eastern Cape vote at Polokwane by only 51 per cent to 49 per cent. His lack of a solid regional base was fatal.

Mabuza, Magashule and Mkhize were all premiers of their provinces (and Masualle was to become premier in his in 2014). They were also all chairmen of their ANC provincial executives. As such, they were all also ex-officio members of the party's NEC. However, most power resided within the NEC's inner cabinet, the National Working Committee, and membership of that was restricted to the directly elected members of the NEC. Jacob Zuma had famously been allowed to be an exception to this rule in the 1990s when he had been both an ANC provincial chairman and an elected NEC member. As mentioned, Mandela had allowed this partly in order to block Harry Gwala and partly because, in an era of sharp competition with Inkatha, it was regarded as essential to have a prominent Zulu in the top echelons of the ANC.

Now, however, the situation was quite different. The overthrow of Mbeki at Polokwane had in good part also been the victory of the party's great regional barons and mayors who did not want to be subject to Mbeki's ultra-centralised rule. So the reason for this multiple – and unconstitutional – office-holding by Mabuza, Magashule, Mkhize and Masualle was simply that the four men were all great regional barons who naturally accumulated all the offices they could in order to consolidate their power. Zuma had allowed something similar for the premier of North West province, Thandi Modise, who was also ANC deputy secretary-general, although the rules quite clearly stated that the deputy SG must hold no other office. Modise, however, threw her lot in with the anti-Zuma faction, which immediately opened the door to her rival, the North West ANC chairman, Supra Mahumapelo, to pledge support for Zuma in the hope of being able to displace Modise from her premiership. (The stratagem worked: Mahumapelo became premier after the 2014 election.)

This practice of adding one political office to another had been common in nineteenth- and twentieth-century France (where it was known as the *cumul des mandats)*, where it had similarly reflected the regional dominance of local notables. Zuma had embraced this practice in South Africa simply to 'go with the flow' though, as we have seen, this also allowed him to bolster his own position. He now summoned the four party bosses because the Motlanthe camp was disputing their position in order to weaken the Zuma camp. Indeed, Motlanthe had launched a warning shot as early as 2010 when Nomvula Mokonyane, the premier of Gauteng, had decided to run for chairperson of the Gauteng ANC, even though she was already an NEC member. Mokonyane was another regional boss, whose elevation to the premiership in 2009 had been supported by Zuma in order to displace Paul Mashatile, a noted critic of Zuma. She had immediately started to accumulate power and office like any other regional baron. Motlanthe, by his public objection, had stopped her[33] – but this was only a prelude to an attempt to rein in all the other regional barons as well.

Gwede Mantashe, as ANC secretary-general, had to take Motlanthe's objections seriously,[34] but Zuma put his foot down with considerable force on this issue, for such objections were a threat to his entire system. Not only did the four men all keep their positions but, as we have seen, Masualle was later allowed to succeed to the premiership of the Eastern Cape as well. Mokonyane was promoted to the national cabinet and Thandi Modise was later forced to swap her premiership for the relatively powerless job of speaker of the upper house, the National Council of Provinces. Mantashe had to accept this. He was often a powerful and virtually independent force, but he was also the SACP's chairman and the SACP's policy was one of unconditional support for Zuma.

It might seem that once Zuma had confirmed these provincial bosses in power, the game was essentially over, though in fact all of them faced factional battles within their own provinces. This was particularly true in the Eastern Cape: OR Tambo region was still safe for Zuma, but the other four regions were all up for grabs. There were many divisions too in KwaZulu-Natal, and both the Sexwale and Motlanthe factions went looking for allies there, for there was now a general realisation that Zuma could not be beaten provided his home province remained united behind him. Bheki Cele, the sacked police commissioner, was still in rebellious mood and was naturally wooed by both opposing factions, but there were also persistent reports that relations between Zuma and KwaZulu-Natal's premier, Zweli Mkhize, had frosted over – to the point where Zuma no longer bothered to tell the premier when he was coming to the province.[35]

KwaZulu-Natal: the engine room

These reports were indignantly denied by Mkhize, though there does seem to have been some deterioration in their relationship. Be that as it may, Mkhize had played a fundamental role in originally rallying KwaZulu-Natal behind Zuma and he was certainly not going to let the country's first Zulu president be defeated.

But Mkhize was already thinking beyond that. An educated man – a medical doctor by profession – Mkhize was himself a potential president. In 2009 he could have had any cabinet post of his choice but opted instead to be premier of his home province (and chairman of its ANC), knowing full well that a regional base had become a *sine qua non* for any South African leadership pretender. He had, naturally, thrived in office – his wife and daughters soon had their own businesses – and he was accused of receiving R20 million from the corrupt Uruguayan businessman, Gaston

Savoi,[36] in the Intaka scandal. He was also accused of having spent over R1 million of state money on private airplanes. In the end he apologised and paid back the money – though more eyebrows were raised by the revelation that he had sums of that size to give away, money he could never have accumulated from his salary.[37]

With Jacob Zuma presumably about to enter his final term as president, Mkhize knew that the succession would be bound to go to someone already in the ANC's executive 'top six', so he had decided to go for the post of treasurer-general (he had earlier been the ANC's provincial treasurer). It was easy enough to arrange that KwaZulu-Natal should nominate him for this post and to ensure that Free State and Mpumalanga quickly followed. The Northern Cape, Eastern Cape and the North West soon jumped on the bandwagon, making his election a formality. The fact that Mkhize so easily beat his opponent for the post, Paul Mashatile of Gauteng, was another striking display of KwaZulu-Natal's dominance. But naturally, since KwaZulu-Natal was now the centre of power, there was also no shortage of ambitious men keen to kick Mkhize upstairs and take his place in the province. This posed a delicate question for Mkhize, who naturally wished to keep his provincial base as well.[38]

But KwaZulu-Natal was not at Zweli Mkhize's personal disposal. As the engine-room of the Zuma faction and the ANC, it was naturally full of powerful Zulu politicians. Most powerful of all had been John Mchunu, the chairman of the ANC's Durban region until his death in 2010. Mchunu, a former Inkatha warlord, was a consummate political organiser and a hard man. He had played a crucial role in Zuma's triumph against Mbeki and then became boss of the province, ruling largely through his domination of Durban. Together with Bheki Cele he controlled the city's patronage in jobs and tenders and used it to dominate the whole province, naturally becoming rich himself in the process. Mike Sutcliffe might be Durban's city manager and Obed Mlaba its mayor, but Mchunu and Cele had the final word on everything, including how long Sutcliffe and Mlaba could stay in their jobs. Mchunu and Cele, both senior figures in the SACP, ruled the city like New York 'godfathers'.[39]

In fact the balance of power within the KwaZulu-Natal ANC was complex. Mchunu's unexpected and early death saw his post go to Dr

Sibongiseni Dhlomo, who immediately became a key player in the province. He was soon at work diverting tenders in an ANC direction. (When a municipal official failed to allocate a waste-management tender to an ANC-backed consortium, he was sacked by Dhlomo who angrily accused him of 'lacking respect for the ANC'.[40]) Zweli Mkhize had originally come from Nkandla, another reason for his early closeness to Zuma, but his political base lay in Pietermaritzburg. He was thus always at a disadvantage compared to the big power-players of Durban, who had far more patronage to dispense. Another key figure was Nathi Mthethwa, Zuma's minister of police and one of his closest confidants. The ANC provincial secretary, Sihle Zikalala, had been Malema's colleague in the ANC Youth League but had been shrewd enough to throw his lot in with Zuma, a move which had carried him to power. Senzo Mchunu, the former ANC provincial secretary and since then a leading minister in the provincial government, was another young man whose espousal of the Zuma cause had benefited his career. There was also another powerful Mchunu (none of them were related), Willies Mchunu, a senior provincial minister and chairman of the provincial SACP as well as deputy chairman of the provincial ANC.

Such, then, was the alignment of forces within the ANC as the great showdown of Mangaung neared. Certainly the ANC as a 'federation of warlords' differed markedly from the united and euphoric party of the early Mandela era, but there was no doubt that the party's progression towards its new state was due to the 'natural' evolution of forces within African society. Had Mandela or Mbeki stayed in power long enough, the party would have evolved in the same direction, whatever attempts they might have made to hinder it. The real difference about Zuma was that he treated that evolution as natural and embraced it. The resultant party was not a pretty sight. But, of course, the ANC ruled with two partners, the SACP and Cosatu. Unfortunately, neither of them had been able to resist the forces of decline either.

The SACP, the tail on the dog

Theoretically, the SACP had never been stronger than in the Zuma period. In his 2009 government the Party counted four ministers and four deputy ministers, and the ANC secretary-general was also the SACP chairman. The Party had also had its own membership drive, carrying it up from 50 000 members in 2008 to 152 000 by 2013.[41] Moreover, a large proportion of Cosatu and individual trade union leaders were SACP members. In fact the Party was in a peculiar and in many ways weak position. Its great days of struggle were behind it, as were its iconic leaders, Chris Hani and Joe Slovo. Indeed, the generation of white Jewish intellectuals who dominated the Party in the 1940s–60s had almost completely died out. They had been an extremely able, determined and dedicated group, so the fact that they had not been replaced has meant that the Party's intellectual leadership was far weaker than before. Blade Nzimande, the SACP leader since 1998, was a man of very modest talents with no struggle record to his name. Although the party professed an old-fashioned brand of Marxism-Leninism, most of its actual policy positions were highly voluntarist and often black national- ist, so it had drifted free of its own supposed intellectual moorings.

Nzimande, himself a Zulu, had strongly supported Zuma against Mbeki and was rewarded in 2009 with a cabinet position. This meant he would draw two salaries – as leader and minister – and he immediately celebrated by awarding himself a R1.1-million ministerial BMW. This drew consid- erable criticism from the Cosatu leader, Zwelinzima Vavi, who felt that Nzimande was becoming a Gucci communist and that he would now neglect the Party while enjoying life as a highly paid and privileged minis- ter. Certainly, Nzimande seemed to feel that the SACP's inclusion in gov- ernment signalled the success of his strategy and he was utterly fulsome in his praise for and loyalty to Zuma.[42]

At the same time, the Party was bankrupt. By February 2012 it could no longer pay the rent for its offices or the salaries of its officials and had to run to Cosatu for help. The Party already had office space at Cosatu House in Johannesburg but now it had not only to move there lock, stock and barrel but also to beg Cosatu to pay the R140 000 relocation expenses involved.[43] Soon the Party was accommodated in Cosatu offices in every regional centre as well. Moreover, the unions had committed themselves to helping the SACP as 'their' party. What this meant was that the rent they were supposed to receive was simply deducted from their grants to the SACP – that is, the Party lived rent-free on Cosatu's charity.[44]

Meanwhile, in its drive for members the SACP had pursued the easy path, which was to follow up behind Zuma's phenomenally successful ANC membership drive in KwaZulu-Natal and get many of the same people – often unlettered peasants – to sign up for SACP as well as ANC membership. No wonder Kgalema Motlanthe was to complain that SACP members lacked the political education of old.[45] By June 2012 the results were clear. A full 25 per cent of the Party's members were now from KwaZulu-Natal, giving it a distinct ethnic Zulu tinge.[46] Moreover, the Party's congress was held – not, as one might imagine, in Johannesburg or even Durban, where the proletariat was, but at Empangeni in Zululand. The fact that Nzimande now referred to KwaZulu-Natal as Moses Mabhida province (after a previous Zulu leader of the Party) reinforced the general impression that Nzimande and the Party had simply been folded into a larger Zulu enterprise and was committed to all-out support for Zuma as a Zulu leader.

This impression was only strengthened when in November 2012 Nzimande advocated a law to punish anyone who impugned President Zuma's dignity. Such 'insult laws', as they are known, are a feature only of the most backward Third World states and fit naturally into a chiefly conception of leadership. Similarly, the SACP was the shrillest of all in its defence of Zuma over Nkandla – which it termed 'rural development' – and it had no word of criticism for Zuma when he opened the doors for traditional leaders like the Zulu king to make enormous land claims. Everything suggested that the Party was now completely comfortable with chiefly traditionalism.

In fact this was a mask. The key to understanding the Party lay elsewhere, in two rather unexpected directions. First was the fact that when Nzimande became a cabinet minister he took up residence in the five-star Mount Nelson Hotel in Cape Town and was thenceforth not much seen in Party circles.[47] In 2012 two Party secretaries were appointed to fill his role. This was an exact reversal of 1998 when Nzimande first became SACP leader. He then immediately resigned as chairman of the parliamentary education committee and even as an MP altogether in order to give his full attention to his job. Clearly, government office had led Nzimande to make a dramatic downward revaluation of the importance of his Party role. The second place to look was the car park at the University of Zululand in

Empangeni when the Party congress took place there. Whereas most delegates arrived in buses or crowded taxis, the leaders' cars were in the car park – Range Rovers, large Mercedes and BMWs, SUVs, Jaguars, Lexuses, even a few Cadillacs. In the main hall Nzimande spoke of the Party as the vanguard of the workers and the poor. The car park told a different and much more truthful story.

That is to say, the SACP had become the vehicle which allowed the Party leadership to become part of the predatory elite which rules and despoils South Africa. Naturally, the ministers lived highest on the hog, but behind them came a small army of SACP MPs, mayors and councillors all just as anxious as any other ANC activist to make sure their public position worked to their private benefit. This was now the main *raison d'être* of the Party. Zuma had allowed it a larger number of seats at the banquet table and its gratitude to him was boundless. Of course the Party might not really believe that Nkandla represented rural development or that the Zulu king ought to be allowed to own most of KwaZulu-Natal: it is extremely difficult to believe such things. But under Nzimande it would sing whatever song Zuma would like to hear.

The crisis of Cosatu

The increasingly obvious corruption within the government, including the grotesque expenditure on Nkandla and the controversial relationship with the Guptas, posed a major problem for Cosatu. Its general secretary, Zwelinzima Vavi, was an instinctive egalitarian and had criticised the ANC's 'predatory elite' in increasingly direct terms. Vavi was a popular figure and carried significant weight with ordinary Cosatu members. Inevitably the Zuma faction began to view him as a problem. There was an ethnic edge: Vavi was Xhosa, and the Cosatu president, Sdumo Dlamini, a Swazi, was strongly pro-Zuma. Swaziland and Zululand are contiguous, both have monarchies and there is much inter-marriage between the two groups (Dlamini is a common Zulu name as well as a Swazi name). Moreover, Blade Nzimande, another Zulu, was at daggers drawn with Vavi.

Dlamini strongly opposed Vavi and tried to rein in his criticism of the government. In the end Vavi was found to have appointed a young woman with whom he had then had an affair. As a result he was suspended as general secretary. Vavi did not deny the affair but his supporters, knowing full well that sexual misdemeanours were ten a penny within Cosatu, were sure that this matter was simply being used as ammunition. They therefore demanded a special Cosatu congress to discuss the matter. Dlamini and his faction, despite an adverse court ruling that Vavi had been unjustly treated, continued to hold out against a special congress, fearing that it might provide an opportunity for grass roots support for Vavi to manifest itself. Yet grass roots feeling in favour of Vavi did continually show itself, with Dlamini booed at a number of Cosatu gatherings.[48]

This stalemate became explosive when Numsa, the second biggest – and then the biggest – Cosatu union, took Vavi's side. In part this may have been ideological – Numsa had always taken a radical communist line. But it was also true that Numsa's leader, Irvin Jim, aspired to the Cosatu leadership and that his aspirations were blocked in part because he was a coloured. Jim furiously tried to demonstrate that he was more radical than anyone. The result was a stand-off, with Numsa increasingly an outcast within Cosatu and openly stating that it would not call for an ANC vote in the 2014 elections. This split threatened to endanger the entire trade union movement, so in April 2014 the ANC deputy president, Cyril Ramaphosa, and deputy secretary-general, Jessie Duarte, were called in to mediate the struggle. In effect this handed control of the federation over to two ANC outsiders, leading to suggestions that Cosatu had now merely become the ANC's labour desk.[49]

The fact that Ramaphosa was now a multi-millionaire with business interests that had prompted him to call in the police against striking platinum miners (see chapter four), merely emphasised the dire straits in which Cosatu now found itself. In the early 1980s the Federation of South African Trade Unions (Fosatu) had strongly resisted the idea of any alliance with the ANC on the grounds that once any political affiliation was allowed, workers' interests would inevitably be subordinated to party interests. Despite that, Fosatu, swept away by revolutionary enthusiasm, had become the Congress of South African Trade Unions in 1985 – and now the dire predictions of the old 'workerists' had come true. Cosatu's executive spent a whole day in deciding on such a prostration to political control. Ramaphosa immediately declared a truce in the struggle between Vavi and Dlamini, but it seemed clear that all this meant was that everything would be postponed till the elections were over and the ANC's interests were secure.[50]

This soap opera obscured a deeper truth, which was that Cosatu, as part of the ruling alliance, had become part of the Establishment. Although virtually all its leaders were SACP members they tended to see their union jobs merely as stepping stones to elite status. Many achieved this by becoming MPs and ministers, others by benefiting from BEE deals, yet others through the management of union pension funds (not a few corruptly) – and even those who remained in the trade union movement generally benefited from middle-class lifestyles and salaries (paid by the employers, to whom they inevitably became closer).

This process of embourgeoisement had no keener observer than Vavi, who realised that many of his strictures about the ANC applied with almost equal force to Cosatu. Looking back, he felt that something fundamental had changed after 1994 when Cosatu was able to use its political leverage to create full-time shop stewards, men and women who theoretically represented shopfloor workers but who were themselves excused all work, were given their own offices and could devote themselves entirely to union affairs. This tended to make them more political and they spent their time passing motions and taking political positions – a situation mirrored at national level where all the major Cosatu unions issued a continuous flow of press releases on every aspect of public life. Moreover, employers quickly realised the benefits of cutting the shop stewards in on procurements that affected workers, such as catering. 'The shop stewards are now unofficial tender boards,' as Vavi put it. 'That's why the tender providers take them out and pummel them with gifts. You get overseas trips, you get cars, you get a *per diem*. You get invited for dinner right, left and centre, so you never spend a cent of that *per diem*. Some are even invited to go overseas to watch cricket and rugby.'[51] Vavi thought that it was this embourgeoisement of the National Union of Mineworkers that had opened the door for the breakaway Association of Mineworkers and Construction Union (AMCU). Moreover, other breakaway unions had been launched in other

spheres and even if these were contained, the problem of embourgeoisement remained. The biggest game in South Africa's soccer calendar is the
Soweto derby between Orlando Pirates and Kaiser Chiefs – and Vavi had
no illusions about what one would see there: 'Go to the stadium … and you
will see the boxes are full of Cosatu shop stewards.'[52] He had no answer to
this other than a premonition that Cosatu risked finding itself outflanked
by the next uprising of the poor.

In fact these trends had already produced a growing crisis of relevance
for the unions. Between 2003 and 2014 total union membership fell from
3.9 million to 3 million – and it was common knowledge that even then
those figures were grossly inflated. This shrinkage led to a large loss of
income, made a career in politics even more attractive to union officials
and encouraged both breakaway unions and greater militancy, as union
leaders strove desperately to keep their members by promises of higher
wages. The overall unionisation rate of the workforce was down to 29 per
cent by 2014, and if one excluded civil servants the rate fell to just 12 per
cent.[53]

Vavi's predecessor, Jay Naidoo, had trodden exactly the elite path that
Vavi described – cabinet minister, successful businessman, career at the SA
Development Bank – but he was also a man who wished to be taken seriously for his social conscience. Yet it was he who had led the unions into
alliance with the ANC and SACP, a step never mandated by the rank and
file and one which guaranteed the complete politicisation of the unions.
He now declared himself horrified by what had occurred and claimed that
in all his negotiations with the SACP and the ANC 'there was an explicit
commitment to the political independence of Cosatu'.[54] Yet the whole history of African trade unionism was one of subordination to a hegemonic
party destroying union independence. The writing was on the wall.

Naidoo argued that it was 'suicidal' for Cosatu to expel Numsa on political grounds because it ignored the whole basis of trade unionism, that
workers joined a union to defend their rights in the workplace, not because
of politics – 'that the Cosatu central committee is pondering the expulsion
of hundreds of thousands of workers strikes me as lunacy'.[55] In retrospect,
Naidoo felt that joining the Tripartite Alliance had been a terrible mistake
for Cosatu. 'Sucked into co-governing a political and economic system that

is failing to deliver the promise of a better life we made to our people in 1994, Cosatu teeters and threatens to fall. Cosatu's masters used to be its members. Now it takes orders from other quarters.' 'Thousands of workers,' he pointed out, 'are deserting the Cosatu unions. They have lost trust in their branch leaders. I have been in many places where I have been personally told, "Comrade, we do not see union organisers. We don't know what is happening in our union. Our leaders are too involved in politics and we do not get the services and education that we did in the past."'[56]

Worse still, Naidoo said, because of ever-increasing unemployment the number of dependants that each union member had to support had increased markedly. This had driven many workers to seek loans from 'marauding micro-loan sharks, often connected to political leadership [who] lurk around factories or mines in order to plunge workers into a spiralling debt trap'.[57] Meanwhile, the government had squandered the most precious thing of all – time. Given the advancing digital revolution, nothing was more important than that the nation's children should be properly educated to face that future – but instead, educational standards had collapsed. (Even Naidoo was not bold enough to point the finger at Sadtu.) 'These are the children of workers and we have failed them ... we are our own worst enemy.'[58]

Naidoo's lament reveals perhaps the greatest weakness of the South African left, its simple lack of comparative historical knowledge. Anyone with a reasonable knowledge of how African trade unions had been co-opted, corrupted and suppressed by dominant parties, and anyone with any acquaintance with international labour history, would have predicted pretty much what has come to pass.

Many South Africans felt deeply disappointed at the way the promise of 1994 had been thrown away and tended to blame Zuma personally for all that had gone wrong. This was naïve. What had gone wrong was systemic, not personal. There is a linear development from 1994 to today. When Nelson Mandela was freed and universal suffrage was conceded a set of social processes was set in motion which only now, after more than 20 years of liberation, is nearing maturity.

But what has come to pass? Both the SACP and Cosatu have been reduced to mere satellites of the ANC, while the ANC itself is racked ever more by corruption, dominated by 'big man' figures and increasingly in sway to tribal factors. It is a highly unstable mix and it cannot guarantee the competent and stable management of the country through the difficult period ahead. Everything is up for grabs. Zuma is not a dictator: indeed he endures a daily diet of insult and ridicule suffered by no other African leader. He does what is necessary to keep the hugely unstable coalition under him fed and happy. It is difficult to believe that any other ANC leader could be very different.

That this is not at all how the ANC envisaged things would evolve is merely a testament to how poorly it understood the processes which would be unleashed by its own conquest of power. Its primitive Marxism had not even prepared it for the way in which the acquisitive instincts of its own leaders would take over as soon as they returned home, let alone what came next. The ANC made the assumption that it could operate as a governing and ideologically pure vanguard elite over and above the normality of South African capitalist society, but this failed at the first hurdle. Thereafter, things progressively fell apart, torn between warring egos and clans while the country stagnated. This was, however, unlikely to be where matters ended. The game had not yet all been played.

CHAPTER FOUR

Mangaung and After

As the ANC approached the Mangaung conference there was a lot of talk about 'a second transition', the nationalisation of industry and 'sweeping socio-economic transformation', these being the sort of things that excite ANC audiences. In reality, as we have seen, a modern ANC conference is far more about jobs, patronage, tenders and the ability to loot. Many of the barefoot revolutionaries of Polokwane had become rich in the intervening five years. Should they lose their positions most would, lacking education or skills, be without visible means of support. Naturally enough, such folk were willing to fight very hard in order to keep what they had, dispossess others or gain more.

Even the ANC had begun to worry about what such processes were doing to the party. After the 2011 municipal elections it had set up a commission under the home affairs minister, Nkosazana Dlamini-Zuma, to examine allegations of irregularities in the party's list process. The commission had reported that ANC membership was now pursued by those with no interest in politics, merely a get-rich-quick attitude. There was large-scale manipulation of membership lists, with instances of 'bulk membership' – that is, creating a large number of ghost members by contributing their membership fees and then voting in their names, and 'gatekeeping' by turning down bona fide members who might change the political balance in an undesired direction. The commission also found many candidates who knew nothing of the ANC or who had only joined the party after having been nominated for office. When faced with branches which obstinately voted the 'wrong' way, some party leaders were creating parallel branches, often using the names of dead members. The commission had no real answers to any of this.[1]

The re-emergence of ethnicity

If one stood back from the endless detail of factional politicking, the larger picture was about the growing role of ethnicity in the ANC. When Mandela left the scene in 1999 there was little trace of this (other than outbursts of anti-white and anti-Indian feeling) and he had taken care to leave the party carefully balanced between the two largest black groups, with a Xhosa president and a Zulu deputy president. Mbeki quickly upset that by firing Zuma and thereafter his cabinet became and more heavily Xhosa-dominated. Zuma defeated Mbeki thanks in large part to a solid Zulu bloc behind him and by the 2009 election it was already clear that this increasing Zulu predominance was matched by the erosion of support among other groups. By 2012 this process had gone a stage further. As we have seen, Zuma commanded a KwaZulu-Natal-centred bloc of three provinces. But beyond that the erosion had continued apace. Of the two provinces in which Xhosas were the predominant group behind the ANC – the Western and Eastern Cape – it became clear that there was now an anti-Zuma majority. It was also clear that the multi-ethnic province of Gauteng was anti-Zuma.

Beyond that the pattern of opposition to Zuma was clear. The two men opting to run against him, Sexwale and Motlanthe, were both Northern Sothos. Zuma's tormentor, Julius Malema, and his ally, the Limpopo provincial premier, Cassel Mathale, were also both Northern Sothos, as was Mathews Phosa, who had defected from the top six to attack Zuma. And these dissidents were backed by the North West's Tswana premier.

In other African countries this growing ethnicisation of politics would have drawn obvious comment but in South Africa all mention of tribalism had been de-legitimated both by the ANC's century-long struggle to repress tribal divisions and, even more, by the apartheid government's attempt to base its bantustan policy on African tribal differences. The result, perversely, was that those groups which resented the growing Zulu predominance would not appeal to an anti-Zulu tribal sense but would instead accuse KwaZulu-Natal of tribalism. Zweli Mkhize angrily denounced such talk as an attempt to muzzle his province – but the fact was, of course, that clean contrary to ANC rules, the KwaZulu-Natal regions had been openly lobbying for Zuma's re-election, and somehow Luthuli House had failed to reprimand them for this.[2]

Hanging over everything was the province's remarkable ANC membership drive. In 2005 KwaZulu-Natal had counted 75 035 ANC members; by 2007, 102 742; by 2008, 112 525; by January 2012, 244 000; by May 2012, 252 637, and finally, at Mangaung, 331 820.[3] Everyone knew that this gave the province a dominant voice in the ANC. Hence Zuma, at the province's ANC conference, told delegates that their responsibility was to lead the party: 'Your behaviour should be devoid of any sense of arrogance because of your strength.'[4]

This was all very well, but the stakes were too high for that, as became clear at the ANC national policy conference in late July 2012. It began with the KwaZulu-Natal delegates singing songs in favour of Zuma and Limpopo singing songs against him, from which it soon escalated into fist-fights between delegates, one delegate being prevented from speaking by others manhandling her away from the microphone, and another delegate being assaulted with a bottle. The entire platform party, including Zuma, was powerless and retreated at speed. Journalists were kept corralled away from the action because the organisers had anticipated trouble.[5] On the crucial votes it was soon apparent that Free State, Mpumalanga and KwaZulu-Natal formed a solid bloc accounting for over 40 per cent of all delegates. (Mpumalanga, which has a significant Zulu population, had also seen a boom in ANC membership, rising from 55 000 in 2007 to over 130 000 by 2012.) Since other provinces were all more divided, the result was, inevitably, a victory for the Zuma forces on every key matter. The Zulu delegates poured scorn on Malema: 'How can a Pedi boy stand against a

81

Zulu man?' They also made it clear that anyone who wanted to overthrow the country's first Zulu president would have to reckon with his massed impis.

The power of events

The stakes would, however, be a lot higher at Mangaung. They were made all the higher by two key events. First there was the problem of Julius Malema, whose frequent outbursts had attracted a large audience as well as two convictions for hate speech. Zuma was long urged to discipline him but was reluctant to do so. Soon, however, Malema was seen as a direct challenger to the President's authority and in November 2011 he was suspended from the ANC for five years. Malema's wild behaviour continued and in February 2012 he was sentenced to expulsion. This verdict had, however, to be confirmed by a full disciplinary commission and for this task Zuma picked Cyril Ramaphosa, who had played only a backbench role for the previous 17 years. It was a dirty job and it soon became clear that Ramaphosa had agreed to do it only as part of a larger bargain, which was that he should succeed Motlanthe as Zuma's deputy president.

Tremendous efforts were made by the Zuma camp to get both Sexwale and Motlanthe to withdraw their candidacies. That they refused to do so was seen as a major sign of disrespect. After all, no one had opposed Mandela or Mbeki's nominations for president: why should the first Zulu president be treated differently? But nothing envenomed Zuma sentiment against Motlanthe (and Mathews Phosa) so much as their refusal to disavow Malema. For even Zuma's opponents who felt no ethnic solidarity with Malema found him a useful attack-dog. Malema's expulsion altered the political landscape, for he refused to melt into obscurity in the way that those expelled from the ANC usually had. Instead he campaigned ever more fiercely, accusing Zuma of trying to kill him[6] – and finally launching his own party, the Economic Freedom Fighters (EFF).

The second event was the massacre of 34 striking mine-workers at the Lonmin platinum mine at Marikana on 16 August 2012. The strike originated in the bitter split in the National Union of Mineworkers, with the rival union, AMCU, pulling away more and more members. Since NUM was the biggest union, the backbone of Cosatu, the SACP and the ANC, this was an extremely threatening development for the government. There had been persistent violence between the two sides in the weeks before, leaving 10 dead. When the police finally gunned down the 34 AMCU members there was a strong suspicion that, in effect, they had been brought in to suppress a threat to the ANC – a suspicion which grew when it was discovered that most of the 34 had been shot in the back, many of them hunted down and on the run. Certainly, everyone knew that it was inconceivable that NUM members could have been shot in that way.

Marikana was a watershed. The obvious analogy of the Sharpeville massacre brought immediate comparisons between the ANC and the apartheid governments, both apparently equally distant from and uncaring of the lives of poorer Africans. The pigs had taken over *Animal Farm* and were behaving just as the humans had. The government was so alarmed by this comparison that it tried, unavailingly, to prevent the media from labelling the event as 'a massacre'; instead it had to be 'the Marikana tragedy'. Malema naturally took up the cause of the AMCU miners until he was escorted away by angry policemen. The minister of defence insisted that the police had acted correctly because Malema was 'a counter-revolutionary'. Malema's assertion that his sources within the government had told him a plan had been hatched 'to get rid of me'[7] could not be lightly dismissed, given that in that year alone there had already been 12 political assassinations in the ANC.

As the different regions met to choose their conference delegates it became clear that Zuma had lost much of his support in the Eastern Cape. A potent sign of this was the abandonment of the regional ANC conference of the OR Tambo region amidst allegations of vote-rigging. The pro-Zuma forces were accused of deliberately collapsing the conference after they had lost the contest for regional chairman by a vote of 296–295.[8] It emerged that over 100 delegates had been fraudulently registered while 134 claimed they had been wrongly denied registration by gatekeepers.[9] This was a microcosm of what was happening on a far wider scale – but it was ominous for Zuma that he seemed likely to lose a region which had been pivotal to his victory in 2007. Residual resentment over Mbeki's axing now reacted much more powerfully with popular anger over Marikana – many of those killed had been Pondos from the Eastern Cape.

As Mangaung neared, things got rougher. Infighting became so fierce that even in the Ward 1 branch of KwaXimba (KwaZulu-Natal) – the country's biggest branch, with a safe pro-Zuma majority – the branch meeting had to be abandoned in chaos after large numbers of members arrived armed with dangerous weapons.[10] Also in KwaZulu-Natal, Bheki Cele was suddenly dropped even from the voters' roll in his ward. There were denials that this meant anything, though it seemed clear that Cele was being punished for his dissidence. Soon he and Zuma buried the hatchet and Cele magically re-appeared in a prominent role.

In the Northern Cape a police raid saw the arrest of more than half the province's ANC leadership in an enquiry into alleged kickbacks.[11] The point was not lost on the Northern Cape's resident baron, John Block, who engineered a pro-Zuma majority in the province. In Gauteng a gang of nine men and a woman, members of the MKVMA, stormed an ANC meeting and threatened to shoot anti-Zuma delegates. There were persistent reports that the MKVMA was now Zuma's private army. In Mpumalanga, Joe Ndimande, leader of an anti-Zuma faction, was forced into hiding after his house was petrol-bombed. In Limpopo, Aluruli Nelwamondo, an anti-Zuma activist, narrowly avoided assassination when four armed men stormed his house. In Thaba Nchu in the Free State an ANC ward councillor had to run for his life when MKVMA members started shooting at an ANC branch meeting. In Port Shepstone in KwaZulu-Natal, Sifiso Khumalo, an ANC Youth League leader, had to plead guilty to murdering two local ANC leaders. Almost everywhere there were fist-fights, stabbings, fights with broken bottles and, often, shootings.[12]

The violence extended to the ANC branches in the Western Cape, though there the party had been reduced to a bankrupt wreck, having lost first Cape Town and then almost every other town in the province. The remnants of the party, run by the provincial chairman, Marius Fransman, and the Cosatu activist, Tony Ehrenreich, had vaingloriously hired the Cape Town International Convention Centre for an ANC conference, which left them with a bill for R1.8 million. Moreover, the provincial ANC treasurer admitted that funds raised for the party by its leaders were never actually reaching the party.[13] All told, the party owed R3 million and bailiffs moved in to seize furniture and cut off phones. Thereafter the party lived on charity. Neither its predominant Xhosa membership nor its residual coloured membership was in any mood to support Zuma, but Fransman, a junior minister in the Zuma government, desperately – though ineffectually – tried to prevent the party from plumping for the anti-Zuma side. He repeatedly managed to prevent the ANC's Western Cape general council from meeting[14] and, ludicrously, sought favour with his bosses by advocating a 10-year term for all the party's executive Top Six, thus avoiding the need for recurrent elections.[15]

The showdown

The conference met in the usual welter of contradictions – the leadership in enormous and expensive vehicles, the delegates in buses and taxis. The accommodation for leaders and delegates might also have been on different planets. Most of the delegates were jammed into the student residences at the University of the Free State – the university had to threaten to kick them all out and close down the conference if the ANC didn't stump up the rental.[16] The extreme affluence of the party elite contrasted with the fact that the party, having overspent on the conference, failed to pay its staff's salaries that Christmas, while the ANC's security staff and cleaners had, by then, gone unpaid for five months.[17]

Already the provincial nominations for ANC president were rolling in. Limpopo, Western Cape and North West were all locked in disputes which prevented their provincial conferences going ahead. The situation in the Free State was even more serious, for the Constitutional Court had ruled that its provincial conference had been 'unlawful and invalid'. The Zuma forces were not to be deflected: Free State was too important to the Zuma coalition, so Mantashe ruled that the Court's ruling would not prevent the Free State delegates thus illegally elected from participating fully in the conference. He also struck the chiefly tone favoured by the Zuma camp: 'The president is coming to the conference. He is not contesting. He is the incumbent. He is being contested.'[18] Tokyo Sexwale got the point. Early on he had risen to offer an amendment but was shouted down with such force that he quickly abandoned his presidential bid and backed Zuma instead.[19] This was to do him no good: soon afterwards he was sacked from the cabinet.

To no one's surprise the Free State delegates cast a vote of 324-0 for Zuma against Motlanthe. Then came KwaZulu-Natal with 858-0 and Mpumalanga with 427-17. Since there were only 4 076 accredited delegates and by no means all were certain to vote, these three provinces alone had thus given Zuma 80 per cent of the votes he needed for re-election. After that it was a formality because the powers of incumbency and patronage guaranteed Zuma useful numbers of votes even where he was in the minority. He had expected to lose the Eastern Cape but in the end this crumbled his way by 392–211. (Many in the Eastern Cape were surprised by this result and blamed it on Motlanthe's virtual refusal to campaign.) Motlanthe won by 238–173 in Gauteng, by 268-7 in Limpopo and by 99–90 in the Western Cape. Thanks to John Block's efforts in the Northern Cape, Zuma won there by 169–25, and a similar effort by Supra Mahumapelo in North West carried Zuma to victory there by 162–14. Overall Zuma had won by 2 983 to 991. Thus Zuma had carried KwaZulu-Natal, Free State and Mpumalanga by a combined vote of 1609 to 17 – but despite even the enormous advantages bestowed by incumbency, he had carried the other six provinces by the far tighter margin of 993 to 855. Naturally, the party bosses who delivered the 'right' result by such huge margins had to resort to every means of persuasion to whip delegates into line – threats, job offers, cash payments and so on.

Motlanthe had come under enormous pressure to withdraw; repeated deputations beat a path to his door. Meanwhile Zuma had prevented him from making any foreign trips and had also given him responsibility for any unpleasant matters arising, like the unrest in the mining sector or the new road tolls in Johannesburg. Motlanthe had remained detached and philosophical and had failed to campaign with even minimal energy. He felt simply that the ANC must have a choice. This attitude was completely unacceptable to the Zuma camp. A senior cabinet minister told the *Mail & Guardian* that senior party leaders 'are shocked and they are asking themselves: where does he get the guts to challenge JZ? They see it more as an attempt to tear the ANC apart. The shock has become anger now.'[20] An ANC leader from KwaZulu-Natal said that Motlanthe 'under-estimated the power of KwaZulu-Natal ... Nobody can win the conference of the ANC without the support of KwaZulu-Natal.'[21] The Motlanthe camp attacked this as 'feudal'. Motlanthe had a perfect right to stand, they said: 'It can't be right that some positions are ring-fenced and are no-go areas because there is a tribal leader on the throne.'[22]

Zuma's crushing victory saw tremendous scenes of Zulu triumphalism and the singing of songs depicting Motlanthe, Sexwale, Fikile Mbalula (who had foolishly challenged for Mantashe's job), Thandi Modise, Mathews Phosa and Paul Mashatile as 'enemies', not just opponents but people who had dared to defy the Chief and who should now be firmly punished. There were also numerous Zulu praise songs about Zuma. On the other side there was dejection and much talk about this really being a victory for the Guptas. Motlanthe spoke very carefully about how as ANC leaders 'we always strive to ensure that the expression of the will of members is not interfered with, because we are well aware that if processes are fraudulent, they also contaminate the end product'.[23]

This was a strong hint that the Motlanthe camp was extremely suspicious about many elements of Zuma's victory. There were big questions as to whether the Free State delegation should have been allowed inside the hall at all, let alone allowed to vote. Then again, there was the thunderous vote from KwaZulu-Natal which had all but settled the conference on its own: the province had a whole quarter of the vote and the thought of denying Zuma victory and thus affronting that solid mass of angry Zulus was pretty much untenable. But everyone knew there were lots of divisions and splits in KwaZulu-Natal, so how did it end up with a 858-0 vote? That meant that every single branch in the province had nominated Zuma, which seemed most improbable. Most ANC members were passive non-attenders and it was extremely difficult to get them to come to branch meetings. And for a branch nomination meeting to be valid it had to achieve an attendance of 50 per cent+1 of its members. It seemed virtually impossible that every branch in KwaZulu-Natal had really achieved that.

And of course, there had been so much violence during the nomination process. The vote in Limpopo was held up as warring factions had to be broken up by police using teargas and guns. In North West – the Wild West, as it was now called – armed gunmen attacked the ANC provincial secretary, Kabelo Mataboge (who was known to be anti-Zuma), on the steps of his house. Were they Zuma's private army, the MKVMA? Or forces in the control of the North West party boss, Supra Mahumapelo, a strong pro-Zuma partisan who was known to hate Mataboge? No one knew, but it seemed like a warning and no doubt helped the North West to go for Zuma.

All of this and more was in the minds of Zuma's opponents and their bitterness was considerable. They knew they had been beaten not just by numbers but by the might of a ruthless political machine. But there was no time for grieving as the Zuma machine swept on. First, Ramaphosa was voted in as deputy president by a huge majority and then there was a night of the long knives in the NEC elections, with the pro-Zuma wave sweeping all before it. All those who had opposed Zuma were swept away. Delegates voted mainly on the basis of lists which were circulated by faction managers and in effect the list put up by KwaZulu-Natal was voted through *en bloc*, just as the policy programme advocated by KwaZulu-Natal was. The ANC had never seen such domination by one region and one ethnic group before. Not surprisingly, it was decided to hold the conference after-party in Durban, which also hosted the finale of the year-long ANC centenary celebrations. Symbolically, the ANC centenary flame was brought back to the province of its first president, John Dube. The party held rallies and banquets, had its first new NEC meeting, and issued its annual 8 January (Foundation Day) statement – all in Durban.

Understanding Mangaung

Mangaung was greeted with some bemusement by commentators – especially white commentators such as Allister Sparks who had, from the outset, suggested that it would be almost suicidal for the ANC to re-elect Zuma for a second term because he was clearly unpopular with the electorate at large. The polls were indeed terrible – a *Sunday Times* poll of urban voters in March 2013[24] found that Zuma's approval rating had fallen to 41 per cent (with 51 per cent disapproving), a terrible result for someone whose party was running at a roughly 63 per cent level. By year end a similar poll found that even among ANC voters 51 per cent believed that Zuma should resign over the Nkandla corruption saga. When 'don't knows' were excluded this figure rose to 59 per cent.[25]

Among the wider electorate, the picture was far worse. Inevitably, the pundits all preferred Motlanthe. They were anything but happy when Zuma romped home. Yet the result was, as Marxists say, over-determined. Zuma had come to power at the head of a coalition of the SACP, Cosatu, Zulus and the ANC Youth League. The Youth League was gone, but the rest was still intact, and to the mix had been added a number of powerful regional barons. Not only ethnicity but the whole weight of in-possession power and patronage had been on Zuma's side, creating a quite invincible Tammany machine. So while the disposition of the electorate might point in one direction, the balance of forces within the ANC pointed in quite another.

Zuma's problem was that the type of support from often inarticulate backwoodsmen that had brought him to power simply didn't translate well into the world of government, Parliament or newspaper editors. A good example was Phindisile 'Ma Mkhize' Xaba, who had risen to fame as Zuma's most passionate supporter during his rape trial, when she could be seen daily dancing outside the Johannesburg High Court, wielding a wooden replica AK-47. When Zuma came to power she was rewarded, becoming a well-paid MP. But in all her time in Parliament, she said not a single word. She was hardly an asset with the media. When asked why she supported Zuma she replied: 'Because he comes from my province, KwaZulu-Natal. It has nothing to do with you. Please leave me alone.'[26]

No sooner had Ramaphosa been elected deputy president than the same pundits began to speculate on his becoming president, something which both business and white opinion thought would be far preferable, and might provide a far cleaner and more decisive leadership. It is worth spelling out the reasons why this outcome is problematic. Ramaphosa is a Venda – a small and somewhat low status group – and he has no regional or organisational base within the ANC. It is, of course, possible that he could succeed if, for example, Zuma died in office or had to retire suddenly on health grounds. There is a presumption in the ANC that a deputy president is the presumptive heir and if the question of succession had to be settled quickly, it could go Ramaphosa's way. But if the election of a successor is conducted in the normal style, it would be very difficult for Ramaphosa to succeed.

Moreover, anyone who studies the way the ANC has developed should realise that any successor would face a series of well-dug-in regional barons of great wealth and power – indeed, they would determine the succession in the first place. It would also be difficult for any successor to be very different from Zuma. He/she would have to tolerate a great deal of corruption and misbehaviour and would spend much time just balancing the factions. Of course, in theory one could have a Henry VIII who shakes the system to its roots, dissolves the monasteries and accumulates unbridled power. Africa has seen many such leaders. An ANC leader like that might scythe down the great barons and the factions, but he would also do the same to the Opposition, Parliament and the press. And it almost certainly would be a 'he', despite a certain amount of speculation about Nkosazana Dlamini-Zuma. The ANC is a fundamentally male chauvinist institution. It will be a long time before it chooses to be led by anyone who is female, gay or non-African. But the resistances to autocratic rule are very great: no one should forget that in the last 25 years South Africa has had six different presidents.

It will also be some time before the ANC picks a non-Nguni. The Eastern coastal lands of South Africa get the most rain so there is more verdant grassland there and thus more cattle and thus more people. The people who live down that Eastern littoral – the Swazis, Zulus and Xhosas – are the Nguni. Their languages are closely related, they live in close proximity to one another, they are more numerous and more densely settled than other African tribes in South Africa. These are the people who resisted the whites most fiercely, the people who have retained their kings and their national consciousness. Almost axiomatically, they are the people who exercise power.

This is evident in ANC history. The party was founded in 1912 and its first president was John Dube, a Zulu. Thereafter he was followed for the next 40 years by a Northern Sotho, a Southern Sotho, a Xhosa, a Zulu, a Southern Sotho (the same man again), a Xhosa and a Tswana. Eight leaders in 40 years. But in those years the ANC counted for very little: it was a minor fringe movement with little support. By the 1950s, however, the great wave of post-war national awakening which swept the continent also reached South Africa and the ANC began to grow as a mass, national movement. As soon as this happened two things occurred. First the Ngunis took over, and second, they became 'big men' who stayed far longer in office. The first was Albert Luthuli, president from 1952 to 1967 – a Zulu. Then Oliver Tambo, a Xhosa, 1967–91. Then Nelson Mandela, a Xhosa, 1991–97. Then Thabo Mbeki, a Xhosa, 1997–2007, and since then Zuma, a Zulu. So by 2014 the ANC presidency had been a closed Nguni preserve for 62 years, a period in which there had been just five presidents.

Thus the political sociology of South Africa suggests strongly that the next president will be an Nguni man, and very likely a Zulu. Anyone who wants to bet upon a Venda man (Ramaphosa) or Zulu woman (Dlamini-Zuma) is wagering against a lot of history. Zuma's presidency signalled that the Zulus had re-conquered the ANC presidency, just as Mwai Kibaki's victory in the Kenyan election of 2002 signalled the re-conquest of the presidency by Kikuyus. It was no accident at all that he was followed by Uhuru Kenyatta, another Kikuyu. In opposition Kibaki had railed against the wealth and corruption of the Kenyatta and Moi families. All his presidency actually meant was that at the end of 10 years they had been joined in wealth by the Kibaki family, just as Zuma's presidency will establish the Zuma family as wealthy oligarchs in South Africa. Such precedents must be borne in mind. This is how African politics work. Anyone who wants to see South Africa avoid this trajectory has to hope for regime change.

On to 2014

The first thought of ANC activists was of how Mangaung would affect the balance within the party. It was now a clear possibility that the ANC parliamentary caucus would be purged of its anti-Zuma elements once nominations for the 2014 election began. There was also a question over Ace Magashule's future in the Free State: the Constitutional Court had, in effect, found him guilty of rigging his own ANC provincial conference.

More or less inevitably, Magashule returned to power.

In KwaZulu-Natal Zweli Mkhize, despite his election to the Top Six, was in no hurry at all to quit his posts as ANC chairman or premier. South African politicians are very reluctant to relinquish their base. In the end he handed over to Senzo Mchunu as chairman in February 2013 but insisted that he would continue as premier until the end of his term in mid-2014.[27] This produced an immediate revolt in the ANC's provincial executive committee, which 'overwhelmingly' voted to remove Mkhize.[28] The overthrow of this, the greatest of the regional barons, was an event of such importance that the whole Top Six of the national ANC came down to Durban to discuss the matter, but in the end the premier had to go. There were simply too many eager competitors for his position, too many place-seekers jostling behind him, too many mouths to feed. Mkhize resigned in late August. Already KwaZulu-Natal had begun to beat the drum for Nkosazana Dlamini-Zuma to succeed her ex-husband as president in 2019. Some commentators even took this seriously, apparently not noticing that the lady would already be well over 70 at that date. In fact this was merely a way of registering that KwaZulu-Natal did not regard a Ramaphosa succession as inevitable and would prefer a Zulu in that post.

The year after Mangaung was, as might be expected, one of settling accounts. This was generally perceived as a matter of Zuma rewarding those who had supported him and punishing those who hadn't. This was, indeed, often the case, but it was also true that many a party boss or notable had hitched himself or herself to the Zuma bandwagon and now demanded that their underlings be rewarded or their enemies punished, a fact which gave a thoroughness and inevitability to the unfolding process.

Limpopo, Julius Malema's province, had spearheaded the anti-Zuma campaign, so retribution was greatest here. Malema and his executive had all been expelled from the ANC Youth League and multiple charges for fraud, corruption and money-laundering had been laid against Malema. In addition he was pursued for large amounts of back tax and soon lost his house and farm. In Limpopo the ANC intervened to unseat Cassel Mathale as party chairman, dissolve the whole ANC provincial executive beneath him and also place the province under administration, thus deposing Mathale as premier and all his ministers as well. Naturally, the confiscation of such large amounts of power and patronage immediately produced an eager queue of applicants keen to acquire them and swear loyalty to Zuma. In addition, the Limpopo branch of the ANC Youth League – which Malema had taken great care to retain as a base after he had moved on to head the national ANCYL – was dissolved. But this was not enough. Mathale and Malema had built their power on the Mopani, Peter Mokaba and Sekhukhune ANC regions, so all three regional executives were also dissolved. Even the mayors within those regions were not safe as Luthuli House moved to extirpate the Limpopo 'problem' once and for all. The purge went right down to grass roots. The province's 69 local branches were examined and 52 of them were found to have 'parallel structures' (dummy membership lists allowing for the manipulation of branch votes). All these members were now to be verified and even if they were genuine, they would still need to serve a probation period before they could again participate in party activities.[29]

The Eastern Cape, historically the great bastion of the ANC, had been in a state of chaos and corruption ever since 1994, but it was too important to ignore. The ANC appeared to be collapsing there: in three years the province's ANC membership had fallen from 225 597 to 187 585 to 160 000. Of the province's 45 municipalities, 44 were ANC controlled and in 2011–12 not one of them had achieved a clean audit: looting was the norm.[30] Most critical of all was Nelson Mandela metropole (Port Elizabeth) which, almost unbelievably, had come within a whisker of falling to the Opposition in the 2011 local elections. The ex-Robben Islander, Nceba Faku, had been the great regional boss here, ruling the city as mayor for two terms, during which time he became a serial tenderpreneur and was dogged by scandals, many of them involving an Indian family, the Geevas, who supported him just as the Guptas supported Zuma. Faku even built himself a special throne on a raised dais in the council chamber to signal his kingly status. President Mbeki had ultimately forced Faku to step down in favour of Zanoxolo Wayile, a well-meaning Cosatu activist. But Faku remained ANC chairman of the region and retained his grip on patronage so that he was able to retain control of appointments and frustrate Wayile.[31]

The result had been a bitter stand-off between the two camps. The city hovered on the edge of bankruptcy, run into the ground by looting. When the Opposition nearly took the city in 2011, Faku blamed the media and threatened to burn down the *Eastern Province Herald*.[32] Luthuli House now moved in and it was announced that both Faku and Wayile were resigning, the latter becoming an MP. The Eastern Cape ANC secretary, Oscar Mabuyane, in a statement which no one believed, announced that Faku had resigned of his own accord 'in the good interests of himself, his family and the ANC' and that this was 'not political'.[33] As if this were not comical enough, the ANC then turned to an 81-year-old backbencher and ex-Robben Islander, Ben Fihla, to replace both men. It was typical of ANC thinking that it was assumed that the problems of one of the country's largest cities could be solved by imposing an octogenarian with no municipal experience – simply because he was a struggle veteran.

The situation in North West province was equally chaotic. Supra Mahumapelo, the ANC chairman who had backed Zuma, was now the province's major political boss, leaving Thandi Modise, who had opposed Zuma, clinging on to the premiership by her fingernails. Mahumapelo had been locked in combat with the ANC provincial secretary, Kabelo Mataboge (who had so narrowly escaped assassination in the run-up to Mangaung), and his deputy chairman, China Dodovu. Mataboge, incensed by the rigging of the local party conference, had taken the party to court in a (hopeless) bid to prevent it. This was now proclaimed to have been a major offence and he was suspended from the ANC for three years. China Dodovu was also arrested, charged (and finally acquitted) after he was charged with involvement in the murder of an ANC councillor, David 'Aubuti' Chika, in 2012.[34] Other anti-Zuma elements were similarly charged with involvement in the murder. Mahumapelo, now also the speaker of the provincial legislature, had his finger in every pie, from the smallest municipality to even deciding matters in the premier's office. He loomed over the province to such a degree that he was known as 'the Black Jesus'.[35]

In the Northern Cape the great reality was that while premiers came and went, the provincial ANC chairman, John Block, remained the provincial minister of finance, a position from which he utterly dominated the province. Block was, however, continually attended by major scandals and had been charged on various counts of fraud, corruption and money-laundering involving R49 million. Already a R3-million guest-house belonging to Block had been seized by the Asset Forfeiture Unit.[36] Block's court appearances were, however, the occasion for large demonstrations of popular sympathy and support, as if he were a feudal lord supported by his tenants and serfs. For great regional barons like Block controlled much patronage and were never short of clients or would-be clients. This presented Luthuli House with a conundrum: on the one hand they would like to be rid of Block's embarrassments, on the other they feared that any such move might assist the DA's steady progress in the province. Mantashe, when queried about the impact of Block's trial on the party, could only reply, 'He is not in prison.'[37]

Gauteng was a difficult case because it was the richest province with the biggest black middle class and it had, at Mangaung, been strongly anti-Zuma. The fear was that in the 2014 General Election the ANC might even tip under 50 per cent in the province. This rather constrained Luthuli House from disciplining the local ANC leadership, but there was a furious response when it was learned that the provincial ANC were so disenchanted with Zuma that they had invited Thabo Mbeki to help with their campaign in 2014. Mantashe declared this to be 'just unfortunate' and said the Gauteng ANC had 'run ahead of themselves.'[38]

Finally, the Free State had to exist without an ANC provincial executive for six months while multiple charges of rigging the party through suspensions and expulsions were heard against the premier.[39] It naturally took a bit of time for affairs to be settled in Magashule's favour. In the end the 40-plus people whom he had suspended or dismissed were told that they should beg his forgiveness before they could have their jobs back. Most refused.[40] But given how central Magashule was to the Zuma bloc, there could be only one outcome.

Similar accusations were made against the Mpumalanga premier, David Mabuza, but, for the same reasons, these too were waved away. This had a price: by September 2014 Mantashe had to deal with the headache of over 20 ANC branches in Mpumalanga alleging that their attempt to nominate anti-Mabuza candidates had led to fraud and assault. In one case the bodyguards of one of Mabuza's provincial ministers had fired shots during a branch meeting.[41] All of this was highly irregular but again it was disregarded: Mabuza was too important to the Zuma system.

Log-rolling the party

Zuma presided over this unruly and factious party, making constant small adjustments in order to maintain balance and control, rather like a log-roller on a Canadian river. Thus between May 2009 and July 2013 Zuma re-shuffled his cabinet five times so that there was an almost constant game of musical chairs in the governance of the country – which clearly came a long way second to the imperatives of the ever-shifting party balance. In that period only five ministers out of 36 went unchanged.[42] Between 2009 and September 2014 Zuma made 47 ministerial changes, 54 changes of deputy ministers and 177 changes of the director-generals who head the ministries.[43] Zuma was aided by a constant flow of intelligence from the state security agencies about his opponents, friends and clients. Even in exile the first duty of the ANC intelligence agency was to spy on the ANC itself and this has continued throughout the period of liberation. And of course, in exile Zuma was head of ANC intelligence, which greatly facilitated the politicisation of the service.

If the presidency seemed largely paralysed by the demands of party, Parliament was no better. Not only did the ANC accord it little respect but the DA leader, Helen Zille, followed suit and chose not to sit in it but to immerse herself instead in the Western Cape. Even so, the ANC was not happy with the pinpricks of criticism it got from Parliament, looking to its chief whip and the (usually heavily partisan) speaker for protection. Typically, the ANC chief whip was a tough 'big man' and there had been trouble with several: Tony Yengeni had gone to jail and Mbulelo Goniwe had been sacked for sexually harassing ANC women MPs. Now Mathole Motshekga was sacked as chief whip because 'he allowed Opposition parties to force Parliamentary debates to be held that have caused embarrassment to the ANC and Zuma'.[44] That is, for doing his job properly.

Mandela dies

All this time Nelson Mandela was slowly dying. His family and carers admitted that they deliberately kept from him news of ANC developments since they knew it would upset him to see what his beloved party had become. Mandela constituted the ANC's only remaining claim to the 'moral high ground' of which it had asserted sole ownership when it returned from exile in 1990. As such he remained a precious political possession, especially since his popularity both domestically and internationally remained at stellar levels. For a long time the old man was in and out of hospital and finally, his Houghton home was fitted out as a well-equipped medical facility and he stayed there. The news about his condition was very carefully controlled by the ANC but it gradually became clear that Mandela was no longer conscious and that he was being kept alive by various machines controlling his breathing, heart rate and so on. He remained in this condition for several months. At one stage, the younger members of the Mandela family reported that the patriarch was effectively a vegetable, beyond all human interaction. The ANC thunderously denied this perfectly true report for, of course, Mandela's impending death was of huge and sacral importance to the movement and everything now had to be placed at the level of Valhalla and the Gods.

The ANC tends to think in heavily symbolic terms, placing huge emphasis on funerals, anniversaries, bringing back home the mortal remains of long-dead exiles, and the like. The funeral, the memorial service and the period of mourning for Mandela would be of exceptional importance and the ANC was determined to wring from it all it could. But there was a crowded calendar of events, dominated by the elections in April/May 2014, the campaign before that, the ANC's anniversary on 12 January, and so on. The question was, when was Mandela going to die? The longer he was kept on life support, of course, the greater the risk that the old man might decide this by himself. This could turn out to be very inconvenient, so it was better to take the matter in hand. The party would decide when he would die.

As one looked at the calendar, the solution was obvious. Mandela couldn't be allowed to die too near to Christmas or over the long Christmas-New Year break which is the peak of the summer holiday in South Africa, when everyone is otherwise engaged. But the ideal date for the funeral would be 16 December. This was once the day when the whites celebrated victory over Dingaan's Zulus and for that very reason that date had been chosen to launch MK military action in 1961. And now it was the

Day of Reconciliation. Moreover, it annoyed the ANC that the Opposition laid claim to Mandela's heritage, so the party was always keen to emphasise that Mandela had been a revolutionary, a guerrilla, and not just the motherhood-and-apple-pie figure the Opposition liked to remember. Holding the funeral on 16 December would thus be perfect – sufficiently before Christmas and allowing enough time to organise the large international event that it was bound to be. This in turn dictated that Mandela had to die about 10 days before that. And he duly did, on 5 December. One or two family members rather gave the game away by bravely trumpeting that 'Madiba took his last few breaths on his own', thus revealing that he had died seconds after his respirator had been turned off. (In fact the report that he had taken his last breath on his own seems to have been an ANC notion and is variously attributed to family members, Winnie Mandela and Mandla Mandela.[45] Winnie spoke of her 'shock' when she entered his room and saw that 'They'd switched off the dialysis machine. I watched those figures going down, down so slowly. He drew his last breath and just rested.'[46])

The memorial and funeral services that followed were not what everyone had expected. In the presence of British prime ministers and American presidents hideously inappropriate speeches were made attacking their countries. Desmond Tutu, always keen to insert himself at the front of any event, had clearly hoped to be allowed to give the funeral oration but was afforded no special status, offending him so much that he threatened for a while not to attend the funeral. The dreary fact was that it was not a high and holy state funeral, it was an ANC party event from start to finish, enlivened only by the crowd's booing of Zuma at the memorial service. To cap things, the SACP proudly announced that Mandela had been a member of the SACP Central Committee at the time of Rivonia. Which meant that the old man had lied at his trial and ever since. But nobody minded that now or blamed him for it.

The 2014 election

Mandela's name was often invoked as the ANC marched to battle in its fifth election since liberation. This time was different in several ways. First, Malema's EFF provided the ANC with a tough populist challenge on its left, something it had feared for 20 years. The whole idea of the Tripartite Alliance was that Cosatu and the SACP would ensure that there were no enemies on the left. Malema's robust challenge exposed the decrepitude of both organisations and it was, in particular, a sign that the SACP's days were all but over. It had been decisively displaced on the left and no amount of fulminating against the EFF as 'fascist' could deal with that fact. The party's failure to put up its own candidates and build its own distinctive following on the left now rebounded upon it.

Second, although it was expected that Cope would fall back and that many of its voters would return to their old ANC loyalties, it was equally clear that the ANC overall was in retreat. For the first time many of its MPs and activists were gripped by the fear of failure. Psychologically this was more difficult still: the ANC had seen itself as always gaining, always progressing, a dynamic movement always moving ahead. It came as an unpleasant realisation that its high tide was past, that any radical dreams not realised by now were likely to remain just dreams. The defection of an SACP old-stager like Ronnie Kasrils – now calling for a spoiled ballot – was a sign of the times. Inside ANC headquarters all ANC candidates were carefully screened by 'Project Veritas', headed by Thabo Kubu, a senior figure in the notorious ANC security department of old, Mbokodo, which had been responsible for killing and torturing ANC dissidents in the Angolan camps. Other ex-Mbokodo men worked under Kubu, the aim being to ensure that all ANC MPs were totally loyal to Zuma.[47]

As in the 2011 local elections, the contest soon resolved itself into a matter of whether the rising tide of Zulu support for Zuma could compensate for losses suffered almost everywhere else. The registered electorate had risen by 9.52 per cent since 2009 to 25 388 082, but in KwaZulu-Natal registration was up by 14.34 per cent – far more than anywhere else – and in neighbouring Mpumalanga, Zuma's loyal ally, the figure was up by 9.67 per cent.[48] However, South Africa's voter turnout had been on a declining path ever since 1994 as voter apathy and anti-political feeling rose. Turnout now fell again to 73.48 per cent, though that still meant that 734 805 more people voted in 2014 than in 2009.[49] Almost half (361 445) that increase came from just one province – KwaZulu-Natal – while in three provinces the number of votes cast fell in absolute terms.

Despite those extra 734 805 voters, the ANC vote fell by 214 000 votes, from 65.9 per cent to 62.15 per cent. Things would have been very much worse if the party hadn't registered a net gain of 274 579 votes in KwaZulu-Natal. The ANC's losses were particularly steep in Gauteng (-292 265) and Limpopo (-116 654), in both cases due in good part to the incursion of the EFF, which took over 10 per cent of the vote in both provinces. Overall the EFF took 6.35 per cent of the vote (1 169 259 votes) – an impressive showing for a party which had existed for only 10 months. One result was that for the first time, the ANC vote owed more to KwaZulu-Natal than to any other province.

The ANC's Gauteng result was near-traumatic for the party. It had lost a whole 10.39 per cent of its 2009 vote and now, with its vote down to just 54.92 per cent, the party was in real jeopardy. Everyone knew that the DA did better and the ANC worse at municipal elections, thanks to lower turnout, and that could well drag the ANC down below the 50 per cent line in both Johannesburg and Pretoria in 2016. Whether the ANC could really survive the symbolic disaster of losing either of these two cities was a moot point. What was obvious – it had been implicit in the Gauteng ANC's appeal to Mbeki to campaign for them – was that the ANC was losing the urban black middle class. Zuma had summed up all that was wrong when he had torn angrily into 'clever blacks ... people who write in papers are educated. They think they are telling the truth. It is not ... It is propaganda that is very dangerous.' Or again, he savaged 'black people who become too clever ... they become the most eloquent in criticizing themselves about their own traditions.'[50] The whole tradition of the ANC was that it was led by the African intelligentsia, by John Dube, AC Jordan, Professor ZK Matthews – and the upwardly aspirant black middle class of Gauteng wanted nothing more than that their children should be well educated, become 'clever blacks'. They were utterly repelled by Zuma.

Such are the oddities of South African political discourse that it is difficult to say some things aloud. I attended one post-electoral colloquium in which there was repeated reference to 'the KwaZulu-Natal factor' as if some unspecified East Coast regionalism were at work. When I suggested that we were obviously looking at a full-blown process of tribal mobilisation – the highest ANC membership, the highest level of registrations, the highest turnout, the largest rise in the ANC vote at a time when that vote was falling steeply elsewhere, and even the fact that Zulus now constituted the largest fraction of the ANC vote – I was castigated for having dared to mention the dread word 'tribe'. It was suggested, instead, that one was looking at a 'patronage vote' – as if this were somehow a separable phenomenon. For of course Zuma's Zulu hegemony has seen considerable patronage showered on his home province: that is exactly what one would expect and certainly this helps to reinforce the ethnic cohesion behind Zuma. In the classic phrase, it is 'their turn to eat'. It is difficult to believe that this tribal mobilisation will be without consequences. ANC conferences now turn completely around the pivotal KwaZulu-Natal vote. Even non-Zulu pretenders to leadership such as Sexwale and Ramaphosa were quick to visit KwaZulu-Natal and seek favour there, for it is now universally assumed that no one can rise to the top against that province's veto. On the one hand, one must expect the KwaZulu-Natal ANC to attempt to maintain its central position, perhaps anointing another of its own to follow Zuma; on the other hand, it would be surprising if other ethnic groups did not react against Zulu dominance.

The government which eventuated from 2014 was just like its predecessor. It drifted. Zuma's State of the Nation addresses were drab, lifeless affairs. Cabinet ministers began to make proposals of all kinds which were purely their own idea, which had not been adopted as party policy, had not even been through cabinet. One minute the government would announce a plan to buy 6–8 nuclear power stations from Russia at a cost of $50–100 billion. The next day the previous day's announcement would be denied. The day after that the agreement reached with Russia would be declared a state secret. Quite how a matter of such obvious public interest as the nation's future power supply could possibly be made a state secret was unexplained. It was simply a pitiful performance and it was quite plain that the initial statement had been made without any consideration for the fact of international sanctions on Russia over Ukraine. It was universally assumed that any such agreement would be laced with giant kickbacks. And this was no small matter: it could break the government's back, bankrupt the country, cause its bonds to be downgraded to junk status. In the midst of this, the central bank governor, Gill Marcus, resigned, her frequent warnings of the trouble to come having been wholly ignored.

Perhaps what summed up matters best, however, was a far smaller matter. It emerged that the many millions of rands that the government had disbursed to pay for T-shirts, transport, food and other services for mourners at the Mandela funeral at Qunu in the Eastern Cape had simply vanished.[51] Further investigation revealed a great chain of politicians and local businessmen peculating and filling one another's pockets, headed by the ANC mayor of Buffalo City (East London). The mayor, Zukiswa Ncitha (a leading communist), was arrested, charged and bailed. Not only her bank account was frozen; so were the accounts of her deputy, Temba Tinta, the speaker, Luleka Simon-Ndzele and the Buffalo City ANC secretary, Phumlani Mkolo.[52] The national ANC repeatedly appealed for these officials to resign but, quite brazenly, none of them did. Yet for the ANC Mandela's funeral had been an utterly sacred occasion. Hardly a day went by without evidence that this or that ANC official was looting the health, education or infrastructure budget, but if money for Mandela's funeral could be looted, then nothing at all was off limits. Clearly, things had changed. In the days of Mandela or even Mbeki, such local officials would never have dared defy the central ANC. But now everywhere a predatory elite had sunk its teeth deep into the body politic and was loath to let go. And, given the example of Nkandla, why should it, after all? So things were different now. And nothing was sacred.

CHAPTER FIVE

The New Class Structure

One of the great ironies of contemporary South Africa is that while Marxism is the philosophy shared by all three elements of the ruling alliance – the ANC, Cosatu and the SACP, as well as by many intellectuals – one thing that none of the above wishes to discuss is the class structure of the new South Africa. This is a significant instance of bad faith in the Sartrean sense. In their own eyes the ruling alliance are working towards a National Democratic Revolution (NDR), a long-discredited Soviet formula, disowned even by its progenitors[1] – a sort of African socialist nirvana in which not only will poverty, inequality and unemployment be abolished but 'the antagonistic contradictions between the oppressed majority and their oppressors, as well as the resolution of the national grievance arising from the colonial rule' will be resolved.[2] It will, indeed, be a sort of heaven, apparently.

It is a clearly racist vision. In its original formulation the SACP aimed at the abolition of all racial and class differences and the creation of 'a common society'. But once the Party adopted the slogan of 'colonialism of a special type', the whites (and perhaps other minorities) were cast as foreign oppressors, settlers to be got rid of – and the vision of a common society was lost. In a sense, this hardly matters, for essentially this is a vision of 'socialism in one country'. If that failed even in Stalin's Russia, the idea that such a thing could succeed on the tip of Africa, in the post-Soviet world of the twenty-first century, is simply laughable. That anyone can believe in anything so crazy is a testament to the terrible ingrown passions which the long struggle in South Africa has left behind. The struggle itself has been over for a quarter of a century now, but the passions are still not spent.

In effect the goal of the NDR means that the ANC-Cosatu-SACP Alliance must remain in power more or less permanently – in 2014 party discussions were under way as to how the Alliance might remain in power for the next 100 years. 'We will continue to run this government forever and ever,' President Zuma declared.[3] The notion was that the ANC would steadily build party hegemony and a socialist order, although in an initial phase a 'patriotic bourgeoisie' of black capitalists could play a useful role. Although the ANC indignantly insists that it alone is majoritarian and thus democratic, in practice it is difficult to reconcile such pretensions with real democracy. What happens, after all, if it is voted out of power? In ANC terms this would necessarily be defined as a victory for reaction and counter-revolution and many within the party would think that this should be resisted with violence. Short of that, of course, the ANC could be expected to use whatever electoral sharp practice was required to prevent such an outcome. In January 2014 allegations of ANC vote-rigging were made in connection with six municipal by-elections in Tlokwe (Potchefstroom) after thousands of voters had been bused in from outside, food parcels distributed liberally to voters in the electoral run-up and so on.[4] If the ANC was willing to play fast and loose with the rules of democracy merely to retain power in a small town in the North West, one can easily imagine how it would behave to prevent its loss of power in, say, Johannesburg or Pretoria, let alone nationally.

While South Africa waits for the NDR to bring about the promised paradise, 20 years have gone by since the ANC came to power in 1994. Thus far the biggest change achieved is unemployment among the highest in the world and the virtual halving in size of the manufacturing sector – that is, exactly the opposite of what was promised.[5] In that time the ANC has provided the country with four presidents, starting with a man nearly 76 years old when he took office, who quite publicly made it clear that he wanted to give it up as soon as possible. He was followed by a man disabled by his paranoia and grandiosity, who was responsible for inflicting well over 300 000 unnecessary Aids deaths on his own people. Thirdly and briefly, there was an old communist and trade union militant who might just have passed muster as a backbench Labour MP in Britain. And finally there was an only just literate Zulu tribesman whose vision did not rise above the feudal. Apart from the generally downward tendency, the most striking thing about this group is that they were all already part of the ANC elite in 1994. If one asked who the coming man was in 2014, it was Cyril Ramaphosa, already a major figure in the 1980s. There is no renewal. It is quite a stretch to imagine that a movement with such leadership will lead the country to the promised land.

Meanwhile, many of the old inequalities of the apartheid order have been retained and on top of that a small and politically connected black elite has attempted to imitate or exceed the lifestyles of the old white elite. Yet this new elite is entirely unproductive: it generates no new wealth. Accordingly, its appetites can only be met by redistribution away from others. This has added a whole new (and very extreme) layer of inequality and explains why post-apartheid South Africa has become the world's most unequal society. This is not some form of aberration from the liberation struggle. A glance around Africa shows that this *is* liberation.

The new stratification

In order to understand the new order the first thing one must do is disregard the 'analysis' provided by the ruling Tripartite Alliance. The Alliance frequently inveighs against 'white capital' (a term which Marx would regard as a racist abomination); it also refers to Cosatu's membership as 'the working class', when in fact it is predominantly white collar and middle income. Similarly, ANC and SACP supporters show no interest in the changing economic substructure, which is the key for any Marxist analysis. In effect there is a complete refusal to do any proper analysis.

It is sometimes claimed that everything is as it was for the white bourgeoisie. This is not true. At the top end, of course, there are a few individual billionaires who have done prodigiously well, but for the white middle class, with salaries between R250 000 and R1 million a year, taxation is now far higher than in the UK or Australia. In addition, such folk are pay-ing for private schools, private health and private security because they do not trust the public providers of such services, and they are now also paying some of the highest electricity costs in the world. In effect, the gov-ernment has made it entirely rational for such people to emigrate. By the same token, however, this small minority is paying the vast bulk of taxes and cannot really be taxed any higher. Many comparative studies show that to increase taxes in such a situation is merely to increase tax evasion. It is doubtful if the government has much considered the risk it is running by creating such incentives to emigration for the group that provides its principal tax base.

The old social structure remains, but in modified form. At the very top there is a super-rich class of businessmen and upper professionals which is multiracial but still predominantly white. Beneath that is an old white mid-dle class which is now considerably squeezed and which in income terms is being steadily overtaken by Asian South Africans, just as the whites have been demographically overtaken by coloureds. There is still a class of white commercial farmers, but it has shrunk by more than half in the past 20 years and is still depleting fast. There is a small number of black farmers, nothing like enough to fill the gap left by their white colleagues. The white working class has essentially ceased to exist and there is a considerable white under-class, evident in the number of white beggars and the dozens of white squatter camps around Pretoria. The really dynamic class, and the one which, because of its political connections, largely dictates terms to the rest, is the new black bourgeoisie.

The key insight remains that of René Dumont who, over 50 years ago, wrote of how the new states of Francophone Africa were governed by a 'bureaucratic bourgeoisie',[6] pointing out that everywhere those who manned the public service – *les fonctionnaires d'état* – were using their position to enrich themselves by all and every means. This included nepo-tism, corruption, moonlighting, the manipulation of political links with the ruling party or junta, pay for phantom workers or pensioners, procure-ment fraud and so on, with the proximate aim of equalling the privileges of the departed white *colons* and administrators. Indeed, for some time one of the chief demands of (black) civil service unions in French West Africa was for paid annual leave *in France*. Naturally, the political elite was largely recruited from this class and was highly responsive to it, for running even a broken-backed state depended upon it.

In fact, Dumont was pointing to a phenomenon which applies to the whole of Africa and which appears quite indifferently of whether a state is deemed conservative or radical. Thus the bureaucratic bourgeoisie is by far the greatest beneficiary of ANC rule in South Africa but the same is true in Swaziland, the state with the highest ratio of civil servants to population in the whole of Africa. In states which have been independent for longer, such as Kenya, this bourgeoisie has often acquired significant landed and commercial interests – and already in South Africa a large number of ANC politicians are also farm-owners and businessmen. A large majority of the ANC National Executive has business interests.

This bureaucratic bourgeoisie is everywhere engaged in a frantic effort of primary accumulation and tends to fasten on rent-seeking opportunities in any direction – and, indeed, on a great deal of straightforward theft. Feeding the ravenous appetites of this class is a precondition for the retention of political power. In some states leaders keep themselves in power essentially by ransacking the national economy in order to be able to keep paying off factions amongst this bourgeoisie – this was seen in Banda's Malawi and Mugabe's Zimbabwe, for example (the distinctions of right and left again being immaterial). Similarly, King Mswati III of Swaziland is currently using up the modest reserves of the Central Bank of Swaziland to pay the exorbitant civil service wage bill plus the royal family's equally astronomical budget. The R2.4 billion loan which Swaziland has negotiated from South Africa will undoubtedly be used for the same purposes.[7]

South Africa's bureaucratic bourgeoisie has several distinguishing features. First, it is heavily unionised. Only two groups in South Africa enjoy unionisation rates of over 70 per cent – miners and public servants. Hence, public sector and white collar workers have come to be predominant within Cosatu, a feature further accentuated by the ongoing collapse of NUM, previously the largest union. Although Cosatu enjoys the support of less than one worker in six, its membership of the Tripartite Alliance and the key supportive role it plays *vis-à-vis* the ANC elite mean that it enjoys a highly privileged position.

Second, and peculiarly given its class position, the bureaucratic bourgeoisie which now drives Cosatu still speaks the language of Marxism-Leninism. This has two practical consequences. Public service workers who are at the least a labour aristocracy and often a straightforward middle class, still depict themselves as downtrodden victims and thus have a strong culture of entitlement. Second, Cosatu unions representing genuinely working-class constituencies have been able very successfully to ride along on the impetus provided by public service workers to gain large inflation-plus wage settlements themselves. The result has been a wage inflation affecting most of the labour force – a staggering defiance of market forces when one considers that there is 40 per cent unemployment and also that labour productivity has not increased. Indeed, by some measures it has actually decreased. This is certainly true of the civil service, where a far larger corps of civil servants fail, by a large margin, to do the work their predecessors did.

Only occasionally does one glimpse the real forces in the labour market – for example in September 2012 when 15 500 people applied for just 90 police jobs in Pietermaritzburg and were set fitness tests in which seven died and 230 collapsed.[8] Similarly, when miners' strikes caused dismissals at Glencore's chrome mines in Limpopo in June 2013, there were 40 000 applicants for the resulting 1 000 jobs.[9] Logically, such prodigious job hunger would imply a downward pressure on wages. Yet this has not happened. For the most part Cosatu is able to use its political connections and the labour laws to preserve a highly protected space for a small labour aristocracy.

The final respect in which the South African bureaucratic bourgeoisie is different is simply that it has come to power in a far richer and more developed economy than any of its African peers, with the result that opportunities for theft and rent-seeking are far greater than elsewhere. The result has been not only a virtual orgy of corruption and looting but also an attempt to reorganise the whole national economy so as to maximise rent-seeking opportunities for the new black elite. Sometimes the argument is made that the old National Party regime was corrupt and so is the ANC, so there has merely been continuity. This is untrue. Of course, there was corruption under apartheid but whatever their other faults and crimes, no apartheid president or premier spent hundreds of millions of rands on his private dwelling. Moreover, the National Party elite were often serious Calvinists. Strijdom, when prime minister, used to refund the state every month for stamps used on his private correspondence. Such a penny-pinching refusal of privilege would be simply laughable to the ANC elite.

An almost endless variety of mechanisms have been instituted in order to enrich the black elite – affirmative action, black economic empowerment (BEE), the funding of black businesses with soft loans, the deliberate creation of wide areas of ministerial discretion over the granting of licences, mining rights, and so on. The hardly accidental result is that ministers or their nominees have to be bought off, and all manner of state intervention in the economy is used to create similar rent-seeking opportunities. Thus in the recent BEE deal concluded at Gold Fields, the company was told which named individuals had to benefit and when the chairperson of the ANC, Baleka Mbete, was dissatisfied with her share she threatened to torpedo the entire deal. She ended up with R28.6 million.[10] The deal is under investigation by the US Securities and Exchange Commission. Mbete was also on hand to cheer Tony Yengeni when he went to jail for fraud, and she herself was earlier found to have acquired a fake driving licence.[11] That despite all this she could become both ANC chairperson and Speaker of Parliament tells its own story of the ANC elite's legal impunity. An Ernst and Young survey in June 2014 found that South Africa was seen as the third-worst country out of 59 when it came to corruption – only Kenya and Nigeria were worse. At the same time, 78 per cent of all South African executives (compared to 67 per cent two years before) thought corruption and bribery were 'widespread in the country'.[12]

The ruling culture of theft

On top of that there is a great deal of straightforward theft. In effect this can be committed with impunity for it is assumed that anything which serves to enrich the new bourgeoisie is good. This is the only way to understand the fact that the ANC government refuses to punish public service corruption. Thus, for example, a report by Edward Nathan Sonnenberg, based on parliamentary committee reports and research by the Public Service Commission, evaluated public service 'corruption, theft, fraud, extortion and forgery' in 2011–2012 as costing the taxpayers at least R1 billion a year. 'Financial misconduct continues,' the report said, 'because there is no real consequence for offenders.'[13]

There are endless and egregious examples of how theft-tolerant the new elite is. A recent case of note is that of Dina Pule, minister for communications, who used her position to enrich herself and her boyfriend, while continuously lying to Parliament that he was her boyfriend. In the end her corruption was so public and overwhelming – R25 million simply 'disappeared' from a communications indaba which Pule had chaired in Cape Town in July 2012 – that she lost her post and her case was referred to Parliament's Ethics Committee, chaired by the veteran communist, Ben Turok. The Committee found her guilty on all counts and she was publicly disgraced. Throughout the Committee hearings, however, Turok received death threats and it emerged that a hit-man had been hired to kill him and other parliamentary officials concerned with the affair. When, however, Pule apologised to Parliament, she was embraced by ANC MPs who angrily attacked Turok for being 'culturally insensitive' and took particular umbrage that his report had been made public and that he had recommended that the case be referred to the law enforcement authorities.[14] But within weeks Pule had missed the deadline for reporting her financial interests to Parliament. Turok was livid: 'Is she going to comply honestly?' he asked pointedly, saying he wasn't bothered about the delay as such.[15]

The Public Protector, Thuli Madonsela, later issued a report which said that Pule had still not owned up fully. She had, for example, pressured the staff of her own department into making a donation of R10 million to the company organising the indaba, from whose account Pule had then personally siphoned off R6 million. When Pule's thieving was exposed by the (Johannesburg) *Sunday Times*, she had fiercely attacked the paper and denied its stories. The Public Protector said that Pule should apologise to the paper 'for persistently lying and for unethical conduct'. Pule ignored this and did not repay any of the money she had stolen. The Opposition DA demanded her expulsion from Parliament but this did not occur. Instead there was talk within the ANC that she might be given an ambassadorial appointment in order to remove her without embarrassment.[16]

Equally striking was the case of Enoch Godongwana, who holds an economics degree from London University. As finance MEC for the Eastern Cape he was implicated in corrupt activities by an inquiry led by Judge Rajarithinam Pillay.[17] Nearly R200 million had been siphoned off from public funds by the then sports minister, Makhenkesi Stofile, and Godongwana had been one of the beneficiaries. He and his wife then emerged as the major shareholders of Canyon Springs, which acquired an investment of R100 million from the SA Clothing and Textile Workers Union pension fund. This money then simply disappeared.[18] The fraud was so embarrassingly public that President Zuma had to ask Godongwana to step down from government, but he immediately re-emerged as the head of the ANC's Economic Transformation Committee. At the ANC's Mangaung conference he gave an interview to Bloomberg in which he said that the ANC should ignore warnings from the credit ratings agencies and push ahead with much higher taxation and aggressive redistributive measures in the mining industry.[19] What was striking in this case is that even a fraud which dashed the pension hopes of Sactwu workers – part of the Tripartite Alliance – could be forgiven if the beneficiary was a member of the ANC elite.

A similar case arose with the R97 billion that President Muammar Gaddafi placed for investment in South Africa. The money quickly disappeared and when, after the fall and death of Gaddafi, Libya and the UN wanted to get it back the head of ANC security, Tito Maleka, was dismissed essentially because he had co-operated with inquiries.[20] News of his dismissal was suppressed by Luthuli House because of the potential embarrassment to those who had benefited. As may be imagined, a sum of such size was likely to be garnered only by those at the very top of the tree.

One could go and on. As Mamphela Ramphele put it, 'We don't have leaders, instead we have thieves. The corruption starts at national level with a President who builds himself a palace and doesn't declare his wealth to the people.'[21]

Another form of elite thieving is the simple failure to pay debts. President

Zuma himself has a patchy record when it comes to repaying bank loans. Typically these were paid off for him by benefactors like the Shaiks or Guptas. In addition some R240 million of state money has been spent on an ostensible security update at his royal kraal at Nkandla where, with his many cattle and multiple wives (each of whom costs the taxpayer R36 000 a month), he lives in a passable imitation of the Zulu king. Over R400 million has also been spent on building a tarred road to the compound. Zuma's son, Edward, spent R2.7 million on his wedding in 2011 and simply refused to settle this bill. Court papers were filed alleging that Edward was hiding his assets so that these could not be attached,[22] and he finally paid up the outstanding R450 000 to his wedding organisers, though only after facing a sequestration application in court.[23] By 2014 the ANC still owed media owners and communications agencies over R10 million dating from the 2011 local elections.[24] Winnie Mandela has similarly refused to pay her debts. When the sheriff moved in to repossess her assets on 21 May 2013, she blockaded herself into her house. Locksmiths called to effect entry were all too frightened of Mrs Mandela to come and when entry was eventually effected there were no bidders for any of the assets because of what *Business Day* termed 'the fear'.[25] Or again, the ANC simply failed to pay the R11 million bill for its centenary celebrations until legal action forced a settlement.[26] One could go on *ad infinitum*.

Ramphele is thus hardly exaggerating: it is rule by thieves. The criminalisation of the state, an acknowledged reality elsewhere on the continent, is now a going concern in South Africa. Naturally, the government's spokesmen try hard to deny this flow of damning facts, leading Njabulo Ndebele to write that: 'Stealing has carved a special place for itself in South Africa. It joined lying as co-mediator between the powerful and the powerless. Stealing and lying become a principle of social and political interaction when lying is used ... to justify stealing as a form of social and political activism. This kind of lying glorified stealing and accorded it something close to heroic legitimacy.'[27] This should be set against the report by the UCT African Food Security Unit Network of January 2013, showing that over 12 million South Africans went to bed hungry each night.[28] As Mondli Makhanya points out, the SACP's clamant defence of the spending on Nkandla was 'a defence of theft from the poor'.[29]

The astonishing public sector

Naturally, the ANC has vastly expanded the public sector in order to be able to offer highly paid jobs to its cadres. The figures are breathtaking. Take, for example, the top level of the elite. In 1973 there were 18 ministers, 6 deputy ministers and 18 directors-general. By May 2014 there were 35 ministers, 38 deputy ministers, 159 directors-general – and an additional 2 501 chief directors and 7 782 directors, posts for which there was no exact equivalent in 1973.[30] Moreover, all of these posts are now far more highly paid, not just in nominal but in real terms. A similar and startling infla- tion has taken place at provincial and municipal levels where the elected members and officials and their staff enjoy salaries undreamt of by their predecessors – and there are now nine provinces in place of four. In addi- tion, between 2008 and 2011 national and local governments spent R102 billion on consultants, many of whom were hired to do civil servants' jobs for them.[31]

What has to be understood is that the new black middle class – and the 'wannabes' – exert enormous pressure on any public sector organisation not only for higher salaries but to provide extra places for their friends, family members and so on. Government as a whole feels this huge, insistent and immanent pressure, which is what explains the continuous expansion of public sector employment. This process ends up with large numbers of supernumerary and superfluous people doing very little but drawing their salaries – and it also leads to the appointment of large numbers of under- qualified people. Falsified CVs and plagiarism are both rampant. At the SABC, the Chief Operating Officer, Mr Hlaudi Motsoeneng, was found to have lied about passing matric and also put up his own salary three times in a year, so that he was earning more than President Zuma.[32] The chair- person of the SABC board, Ellen Tshabalala, also lied about a degree she had not got.[33] Both these errant figures were close to Zuma, as was Dudu Myeni, the similarly unqualified chairperson of SAA. Several newspapers referred to the two women as Zuma's 'girlfriends' without provoking any denial from the presidency.

The same factors push organisations out of shape, because – since the real pressure is to provide salaried white-collar employment for ANC cadres – any area of highly skilled expertise within an organisation (for example, the forensic department of the police) will tend to be starved of resources and personnel because such skills are held mainly by whites and thus offer little prospect for the growth of the black bureaucratic bourgeoisie. One can see these processes at work in any municipality where the ANC holds power. Thus, for example, in DA-controlled Cape Town, in 2014 the city employed 348 engineers and 54 financial managers. Engineers are mostly white, highly qualified and hard to fake. Financial management is, however, a far looser category and almost anyone who has basic clerical skills might qualify. Thus in ANC-controlled Johannesburg the city employed 211 engineers – 40 per cent fewer than Cape Town; but the city also employed 713 financial managers – more than 13 times as many as Cape Town.[34]

Throughout the state and the parastatals one finds a similar pattern, with a ludicrous number of generals in the police and the army, for example. An internal police staffing report leaked to the press in September 2013 showed that 14 000 officers had been placed in posts which were either non-existent or already occupied. In Limpopo province, for example, there were supposed to be (an already excessive) 300 posts for lieutenants and majors. Yet there were 999 such officers in the province.[35]

Moreover, the state has continued to hire more and more public servants, though this can only be justified as 'creating jobs' for it is impossible to argue that more are needed. Thus in the first quarter of 2013 an additional 44 000 public servants were recruited, bringing the total to 3.07 million or 22.6 per cent of the total labour force.[36] In all, 250 000 extra personnel have been added to the government payroll since 2005.[37] At the same time, the number of private sector jobs has been shrinking, so in effect a declining but productive private sector is being more heavily taxed in order to swell an unproductive public sector.[38] This is the economics of the madhouse.

When the economic downturn took place in 2009, for the ruling Tripartite Alliance the key question was, of course, that of the pampered public sector workforce. By this stage their salaries constituted nearly 40 per cent of all government spending. For no less than 20 years their pay had consistently outstripped inflation.[39] Business Unity SA, representing South Africa's major companies, cited research showing that by 2010 public service salary levels were almost 45 per cent above comparable private sector salaries.[40] This was only possible without a spill-over into private sector salaries, because in effect the workforce is racially segregated, with public sector jobs reserved for the rising bureaucratic (black) bourgeoisie. But the problem was that many of them had gone on spending sprees and were deeply in debt. As Trevor Manuel pointed out, 'If we disaggregate … we will see that the middle classes are in way above 100 per cent – all of next year's earnings are already spent.'[41] Naturally, the public sector unions exerted huge pressure, with the result that in 2009–2012 their pay increased by 54 per cent, an annual compound rate of 15.5 per cent.[42]

The finance minister who presided over this malign development, Pravin Gordhan, probably had little choice. Like all Durban Indians with political ambitions, he owed his career entirely to Zulu votes and was thus effectively part of Zuma's Zulu bloc. Having pleaded ineffectually for a moderation in public sector wages, he was reduced, in his medium-term financial statement, to futile attacks on the rating agencies and assertions that South Africa was 'not in terminal crisis'.

Yet the facts were apparent. The national debt was increasing fast and with it, interest payments on the debt – which would reach R115 billion a year by 2015/16, by which time another trillion rand would have been added to the national debt. Even Gordhan had to admit that the latest public sector pay settlement – inflation plus 1 per cent for the next three years – was 'larger than expected'.[43] In fact the settlement was even worse than it looked, for in addition it had been agreed to institute a housing allowance of R900 a month for every public servant, to give a bonus of 10 per cent of total salary to anyone gaining an extra qualification while in post and to grant six weeks' paid leave a year to all public servants with 10 years in post. The public service salary bill thus doubled in just five years.[44] The overall results were little short of fantastic. In 2000–2012 there had been inflation of 105 per cent but public service salaries had increased by 400 per cent.[45] This was an exact replication on a national scale of the story of innumerable ANC-run municipalities where salaries devoured almost 100 per cent of the budget, leaving nothing to spend on municipal infrastructure. In fact just 4.3 per cent of the 2011/12 budget was dedicated to spending on national assets.[46]

The civil service was, at every level, a basket case – but so were the parastatals. Almost all of them were making losses and in 2006–2010 there were huge bail-outs for the Land Bank, SAA, the SABC and Eskom. Yet even in 2009 the directors of Transnet and the Industrial Development Corporation had average salaries of R3.7 million per annum and directors of Eskom averaged R5.8 million each.[47] In fact Transnet would be bankrupt had it not welshed on its pension fund commitments, allowing pensions to fall so far behind inflation that many pensioners were left with nothing once their medical aid costs were paid. Enraged Transnet pensioners have launched suit for R80 billion against their former employer.[48] This is only part of a larger problem, namely the quite cavalier misuse of public sector pension funds for entirely political purposes without any apparent regard for getting a decent return for pensioners.

The public sector salariat is increasingly unanswerable to government. This is visible not only in the way it seems able to bully its political patrons into paying ever-higher salaries and creating ever more public sector jobs, quite irrespective of what the state can afford. But, to take just two examples, it is clear that both the police and the teachers (in the shape of the teachers' union, Sadtu) have largely escaped from state control. Ministers of education have generally quailed before the might of Sadtu, which is helpfully reinforced by the ease with which the union's leaders themselves become government ministers. Sometimes Sadtu officials buy and sell headmasterships and other school posts. When the minister of education appointed a panel to investigate this malpractice, it was immediately flooded with approaches by whistleblowers. The minister was greatly concerned to protect their anonymity, saying they might easily be assassinated for speaking out. This was no exaggeration: in April 2014 two school principals on the KwaZulu-Natal south coast, together with an ANC councillor and the Ugu district director of the provincial education department, were all charged with having murdered a primary school principal and regional Sadtu chairman who had blown the whistle on corruption.[49] It became clear that the practice of selling posts or promotions had been going on since the mid-1990s but that the prices charged had risen three-fold.

Sadtu's response to these revelations was to threaten to declare war on anyone who attempted 'to fight' them. The union also demanded that all posts in the education ministry be given to Sadtu members since they alone 'understand transformation'. In addition, the union called for a halt to all disciplinary actions against teachers and also demanded that school governing bodies be prevented from 'encroaching in schools'.[50] Sadtu also refused all school inspections or other measures aimed at monitoring teacher quality or behaviour. Teacher absenteeism, neglect and abuse of their pupils is rampant. Without doubt the poor quality of teaching in government schools is one reason why South Africa came next-to-bottom (out of 149 countries) in maths in a recent survey by the World Economic Forum.[51] And yet Sadtu protects and perpetuates that poor quality. It is perfectly obvious that South Africa can make no real progress towards producing a better educated workforce unless Sadtu is tamed – but it is a matter of belling the cat and government ministers are frankly scared of the union's power.

But the trouble goes back further. South Africa's universities are now flooded with often ineducable black students produced by these poor government schools. Some of these students, to their very great credit, rise to the challenge and get good degrees. But a far larger number scrape through only thanks to merciful marking – itself the result of strong government pressure to increase pass rates. It is precisely the beneficiaries of such 'affirmative marking' – they are often barely literate – who form the next generation of teachers. To grasp the nettle one would need to begin by taking a far more robust attitude towards meritocracy in university entrance and marking. This too would meet huge social resistance and most universities, knowing this, would be horrified at the thought of raising their standards.

The police too are largely a law unto themselves. This was, of course, most obvious at Marikana where they massacred 34 striking miners on 16 August 2012. The final responsibility for the shootings is unclear – the government's role is unproven – but it also seems that some of the strikers were hunted down and executed by police in cold blood while others were deliberately crushed by police vehicles.[52] Several hundred more strikers were then held in police cells where, according to their lawyers, they were beaten and tortured by the police. The minister of police, Nathi Mthethwa, made no attempt to dispute the allegations and merely suggested that the strikers be handed over to army custody because he could not control the police.

Corruption within the police is legendary – no motorist is without his story of having been stopped by a police officer wanting a bribe. Files and dockets disappear, nullifying cases, depending on who pays what. Both Mthethwa and the National Police Commissioner, Riah Phiyega, seem thoroughly alarmed at the idea that they should be expected to tame what has now become a wild animal. Thus Dr Liza Grobler, who conducted an enquiry into police corruption, found that of the 892 policemen who faced criminal charges for corruption in 2012 (a drop in a far wider ocean), only 22 were suspended. 'There is no leadership on the issue of police corruption besides the odd sound bite,' she reported, and spoke of 'a stony silence and a clear lack of political will' on the part of the minister and commissioner.[53] Both Phiyega's two predecessors had to be removed for corruption (though one was spared jail on health grounds and the other then promoted to deputy minister) so there is no doubt that corruption is rife at the very top of the force.

What is still worse is that both the minister and the commissioner routinely break their oaths of office by deliberately starving the Opposition-ruled Western Cape, where 85 per cent of police stations are understaffed and over 1 000 police posts are vacant – two-thirds of the national total. When the Western Cape premier, Helen Zille, sought to appoint the Khayelitsha commission of enquiry into policing in the province, the minister tried desperately to prevent her, doubtless aware of just how damning its report would be. In the virtual absence of a police force in Khayelitsha, vigilantism is rampant and necklacings a regular event. Research in 2008 found that among African youths aged 10–19, almost half had witnessed a stabbing and almost a third had seen someone shot. A study of young offenders on the Cape Flats showed that 86 per cent had witnessed a stabbing and 77 per cent a murder before going on to commit such crimes themselves.[54] In this way the minister and commissioner, by their deliberate policy of neglect, are incubating crime – and are concerned only to suppress the evidence.

Under such circumstances, the police clearly feel able to act with impunity. Worse, they have been corrupted by violence in just the same way that the trade unions have. During the struggle the unions were encouraged by the ANC to use violent means – they were part of a 'people's war', after all – and found that this often yielded quicker and more certain results than a mere withdrawal of labour. Similarly, under apartheid the police often tortured political prisoners and gradually allowed the practice to spread to criminal suspects: it was so much quicker and easier than the whole uncertain rigmarole of a detective investigation, and you could be sure to end up with a confession and thus a conviction. As Professor Peter Jordi of the Wits Law Clinic puts it, 'Torture was carried out at local police stations before and it continues today. The police torture people all the time – in their homes, in police cells, in the veld, in cars – torture is standard police investigation practice. These policemen are serial criminals.' Given that the police can literally get away with murder, it is hardly surprising that they routinely get away with corruption and with shoddy work practices – leading, for example, to a huge R680-million bill for police sick pay[55] in 2013 as policemen took off time more or less when they felt like it.

The criminalisation of the state, it should be realised, necessarily proceeds via the criminalisation of the police. The ministry of public works has been reduced to a shambles by persistent corruption, causing the auditor-general to refuse to sign the books when well over R3 billion went missing in 2013 alone.[56] One of the earliest and biggest frauds perpetrated was by the chief of police. A report by the Centre for the Study of Violence and Reconciliation in April 2014 suggested that assaults on prisoners, murders and torture by policemen were still on the rise. One officer actually testified that 'If I'm a plumber, you'll see the grease and dirt on my hands. So, if I'm a policeman you must expect that I will have blood on my hands.'[57] When the police recovered R100 million stolen in a heist at OR Tambo Airport in Johannesburg in 2006, the police themselves robbed the safe in which the money was held and ultimately the minister had to pay the consigners R40 million in compensation.[58] The deputy commissioner for prisons, Lucky Thekiso, is himself a convicted murderer who served time in jail for his crime.

Prosecutions for such criminal behaviour are, however, virtually non-existent for the same reason: the minister and commissioner long ago lost control and don't wish to fight to regain it. Trials only occur (sometimes) when the police actually kill people in their custody – but even then, of the 217 deaths in police custody in 2011/2012 investigated by the Independent Police Investigative Directorate, only one resulted in a conviction. For IPID too is a broken reed, not greatly concerned to do its statutory job.[59]

A pattern one finds over and over again is that actors seek political patronage which they then use to give themselves impunity from legal pursuit. One example would be Major-General Phumzo Gela, a policeman who made himself useful to the Gupta family (and thus Zuma) by authorising the irregular use of police vehicles and personnel to escort guests to the Gupta wedding at Sun City in May 2013. Gela was simultaneously facing allegations of various misdemeanours within the police but replied that he would not respond to them since he was 'too senior to be subjected to such processes'. By January 2014 he had got away with this brazen defiance of the law for 22 months.[60]

The point about such cases is that they show the collapse of both the rule of law and the justice system, and also how absurd it would be to expect the Zuma government to take any serious action against corruption.

Thus both the teachers and the police are runaways, progressively escaping from government control. Which in turn means that state education and law and order largely escape from government control. But in one way or another this is happening to more and more elements of the state – municipal bosses set themselves up as local big men, looting their fiefdoms and defying the law. The ANC in Luthuli House tells ministers – and even the President – what to do. At the same time the state is more and more criminalised at every level. This has happened not just because of misgovernance; more through the lack of any governance at all. But through it all run the acquisitive appetite and behaviour of the new public sector bourgeoisie. This is what is literally ripping the South African state apart.

Supporting the new ruling class

For the present the anxieties generated by the situation above are dwarfed by the political need to cosset the new black (and mainly public sector) bourgeoisie. Precisely because so many public servants have run up unpayable debts, the government has twice ordained a credit amnesty, against the warnings of all the banks. The first such amnesty in 2006 was a disaster. Frank Lenisa, of the Credit Bureau Association, has revealed that the beneficiaries of the 2006 amnesty were more than twice as likely as others to end up with bad debts again – indeed, a study of 600 000 beneficiaries of the 2006 amnesty showed that no less than 74 per cent immediately plunged into bad debt again.[61] This is, after all, definitionally, a moral hazard. But the problem exists on an enormous scale – by 2014 South Africa had 20.6 million credit-active consumers (far more people than those who vote in elections), almost half of whom have impaired credit records. Moreover, the phenomenon of unsecured loans has increasingly become a white-collar rather than blue-collar one.[62]

Despite this, the pressure on government exerted by the African bourgeoisie – the only Africans likely to have credit cards – is such that the government again opted to enforce this provenly disastrous policy. The current plan is to remove the names of the 1.6 million people blacklisted by credit bureaux, 'many of whom are public servants',[63] although the banks are emphatic that this will reduce credit, increase the cost of credit and lead to even greater credit defaults in the future. Similarly, because so many public servants are subject to garnishee orders, the government has sought to 'reform' the garnishee order system. And the great sensitivity over e-tolling (electronic charging for highway usage) in Gauteng stems from the fact that so many public service workers have become car owners and are also stretched to the limit financially.

Micro-lenders, who lend at exorbitant rates, attest that the most frequent applicants for loans – often just to pay for groceries or transport – are policemen, teachers, soldiers and other public servants. 'When we say they can't have a loan, some men cry in front of us. They want anything we can give them, from R50 to R50 000,' said the manager of one micro-loan company.[64] The Public Service Commission expressed alarm that of the 1.2 million central government employees at that point (2008) no fewer than 216 857 (18.1 per cent) had garnishee orders paid off their salaries – and most of these were middle-income workers, though a few were senior managers. As the Commission commented, 'Any doubt about the ability of public servants to manage their own resources creates uncertainty about the level of trust, honesty and integrity with which they would manage departmental budgets and assets.'[65] This is a rather delicate way of saying that the situation encourages runaway corruption.

It is worth pointing out that this is not a situation born of poverty but rather the opposite: in effect many of the post-1994 recruits to the public service are enjoying the first middle-class jobs of their life. The political change in the country encouraged an atmosphere of almost frantic self-enrichment and, often, an anxiety that one might be missing out when so many others were feeding heavily at the trough. (When the author reproached one ANC minister for his evident corruption, he replied: 'But absolutely everyone else is doing it! Why should I miss out?') The sight of politicians becoming rich men almost overnight made many feel that the sky was the limit. If Cyril Ramaphosa could go, in a few years, from zero net worth to assets of over $600 million, anything was possible. So while the ANC might talk of socialism, the message received by most of its activists was Guizot's famous *enrichissez-vous!*

Very few of the new recruits had any experience of budgeting or managing a middle-class lifestyle: many rushed out and bought expensive cars and other consumer goods on credit, while simultaneously taking out large mortgages, and only discovered too late that they were way over-committed.

This situation was greatly compounded by the very high rate of family breakdown among Africans: only a quarter of African children grow up in a household with two parents. Indeed, the situation in South Africa is similar to that which Daniel Moynihan described in his famous Moynihan Report. And just as black Americans were furious at being told the home truth that their community's fundamental weakness was the collapse of the black family, so this is not an easily acceptable truth in South Africa either.

Yet the truth is indeed that the collapse of family structures within the African community is probably the single most powerful force in holding that community back. Frequently that collapse has been put down to apartheid, but the fact is that apartheid has been over for a quarter of a century and yet in that period the plight of the African family has got considerably worse. What one can say with some certainty is that this is another factor which complicates the frantic pursuit of the good life by the new elite. Family breakdown means the need to pay alimony and child maintenance, plus the need to manage on one salary, not two. Typically, in this over-stressed situation, the first thing to go was the payment of child maintenance – time and again, male ANC MPs, despite their handsome parliamentary salaries, were found guilty of not paying child maintenance to former spouses – Mandla Mandela was a prominent example.[66] But the problem was nation-wide.

The frantic pursuit of further resources leads to strategies such as serial job-hopping, setting up family businesses and then ensuring that government tenders go to them, sometimes other forms of corruption, sometimes self-righteous strike action, and so on. It was quite normal in the Johannesburg of 1994–2008 to hire new recruits who, in their first month at work, would ask their employers for large loans: all too frequently, when these were refused, peculation would follow. In effect, when they had asked for a loan this had to be understood not as a request for credit but as a statement: 'I absolutely have to have a lot of money.' In a sense the situation revealed by Schabir Shaik's trial – that Jacob Zuma was living hand-to-mouth on perpetual loans and hand-outs – was symptomatic of a quite common phenomenon.

'A lot of public servants came in during and after last year's strike,' said one micro-lender. 'But now, as the cost of everything keeps increasing, they can't afford to pay, so they live on their loans. Even directors who earn R35 000 a month come in here asking for anything we can give them because they have less than R1 000 in their pockets after they have paid their bond and for their car ... The shortage of finances is most stressful among government people.'[67]

As may be seen, this generates heavy pressures on government. Indeed, the IMF, the credit rating agencies and many private investors have all questioned whether the government really has the political will to stand up against the unrelenting pressures of the bureaucratic bourgeoisie – all the harder because the government itself is part of that class.

A case in point came when the Independent Commission for the Remuneration of Public Office-Bearers reported in December 2013. It recommended 7 per cent increases for the lowest paid, 5 per cent for those earning R500 000 to R800 000 a year and 4 per cent for those earning

R800 000 to R1 million, with no increase at all for those earning over R1 million a year. Zuma simply swept this aside and gave 5 per cent to everyone (backdated to April), including the highest paid.[68] It was a text-book example of what the rating agencies had feared and warned against. In fact, Zuma was in such a hurry to do this that he acted illegally. By law he was obligated to leave 30 days' grace to let the provinces decide on whether they wished to accord their civil servants the same increase. Instead he just went ahead and implemented the increase nation-wide, though the DA-ruled Western Cape decided to reverse the increases for its own civil servants.[69]

Moreover, this followed unexpected 'clerical adjustments' announced two months earlier. It emerged that, quite separately from the annual wage negotiations, the Department of Public Service and Administration had quietly reached a separate agreement with clerical unions involving R5.2 billion of extra payments over three years, which alone meant that the government would break its promise to keep the public sector wage bill in line with inflation.[70]

Public sector wages, interest payments and welfare payments now account for 60 per cent of the budget and all three tend only to push upwards. This means that discretionary spending in general and infrastructural investment in particular are always being squeezed. That is, the government is barely in control of the situation. This is true even at a trivial level. No sooner had Pravin Gordhan announced a ban on future unnecessary or luxurious spending by ministers than (in 2014) the purchase of a new R1.3-million BMW 750i for the premier of North West province, Thandi Modise, was nodded through.[71] Modise, an SACP member and formerly a senior commissar in MK, can point to the fact that the SACP leader, Blade Nzimande, has exactly the same car (among others). Nzimande is seen frequently in 5-star hotels and expensive restaurants, has chauffeurs, bodyguards and the rest of the 'big man' outfit. These are yesterday's egalitarians. As the journalist Sandile Memela puts it, 'When it comes to Nzimande et al., it has to be said that nobody should expect a chicken to lay a duck egg.'[72]

In October 2014, as the government lowered the expected rate of growth to 1.4 per cent and warned that belt-tightening must begin, the unions representing 1.3 million public servants put down a demand for an across-the-board 15 per cent increase, despite the fact that inflation was running at under 6 per cent.[73] Given the huge gains made by the public sector unions in the previous few years it was difficult to justify even an inflation-linked increase. The stage was set for a major battle. If the government gave in, its credit rating would undoubtedly fall, with dire consequences. If it did not give in it would face a crippling strike. There could be no good outcome. Nor could one imagine the new class ever voluntarily restraining its demands.

CHAPTER SIX

Culture Wars

When the ANC was in exile it talked of 'the seizure of state power' and assumed that it would use that power to exercise a complete hegemony over South African society. Instead, the transition was negotiated and the ANC found itself having to rule a pluralist society with a multi-party system and a free press. At first this did not present much of a problem because the party's huge majority and its charismatic leader, Mandela, both intimidated and charmed most South Africans. Many whites were, belatedly, stricken with guilt over apartheid and shared in the general euphoria of the 'new South Africa'. This permitted a rampant and ANC-defined political correctness which gave lasting legitimacy to ANC rhetoric with its stress on 'transformation', an 'African renaissance', affirmative action, black economic empowerment, and so on. All the powerful groups in the white, Indian and coloured communities scrambled to stay onside with their new masters. The press, the churches and the universities all followed suit. Only a few NGOs stood outside this consensus and they were soon denounced both from ANC platforms and by a bill threatening governmental control of all NGOs.

The struggle for a free press

It was very difficult in those early years to preserve any space at all for liberal ideas or any notions critical of the ruling party. The press worshipped Mandela and criticism of him was literally unheard of. Even after Mbeki succeeded, the atmosphere remained much the same, the only criticism coming over his Aids denialism and his support for Mugabe. In those years the country owed a great debt to the old *Rand Daily Mail* editor, Raymond Louw, who played a cardinal role in the SA National Editors' Forum (Sanef). Time and again Mbeki and his hatchet-man, Essop Pahad, would pull all the editors together and suggest that they and government work out an agreed position so that the government could be spared press criticism. The objective was to create the culture of a *de facto*, if not a *de jure*, one-party state. It could have happened: many of the white editors were pusillanimous and many of the younger black editors were novices and all too easily seduced by talk of the necessity of nation-building. Louw was the stand-out man who simply would not agree. In the first place, he pointed out, there could be no such thing as an agreed press position, for the press was pluralist and competitive; and secondly, a press–government consensus broke every rule of a free press. In the end he prevailed and as the black editors gained experience they rallied to his side.

Despite that, the press remained intimidated until Mbeki sacked Zuma. It then gradually realised that in this free-for-all it too was free and began to speak up with a wholly new nerve and vigour. The result was that, very reluctantly, Mbeki had to learn to live with a free press in his declining years. But Zuma was the first president of the new South Africa who had to deal with a vigorous and critical press from the first day of his presidency. It was a striking cultural disjuncture. The South African Broadcasting Corporation (SABC) TV and radio were sycophantically pro-ANC (as, of course, was the Gupta TV channel) but the result was merely a huge loss of audience for the SABC and the increasing popularity of the independent e-TV station. In the rest of the media, Zuma and the ANC were much criticised, even lampooned.

The ANC, of course, insisted that the press was white-controlled. This was not obviously true: most newspaper editors were black. But there was a truth of sorts in the accusation, for whites still accounted for the single biggest bloc of the better educated and thus remained culturally dominant. Western 'white' culture still predominated in the top private schools and the whole of the tertiary education sector; it was pumped out of all the cable TV channels, the cinemas, theatres and most of the independent radio stations as well as in most of the press. Even the biggest 'black' newspapers – the *Sowetan*, the *Sun* and *City Press* – were printed in English. A black commentator like Aubrey Matshiqi would routinely claim that while blacks might be a numerical majority, they remained a cultural minority.

This situation was obviously unacceptable to the ANC, for it deprived it of the Gramscian cultural hegemony for which it longed, so it engaged in a long-running cultural struggle. In this the ANC was handicapped by the fact that it had no real intelligentsia. In the 1950s and 1960s the movement had boasted a number of outstanding intellectuals such as Jack Simons, Lionel Forman, Ruth First, Lionel Bernstein and Michael Harmel – but these were almost invariably white, Jewish communists and they were a one-generation phenomenon. Intellectually, they were without progeny. Although a handful of later ANC leaders considered themselves to be intellectuals their qualifications for such a designation were sparse to non-existent. Few ever wrote books or were formally well educated. Thus the movement lacked the first requirement for cultural hegemony, an organic intelligentsia.

The weakness of the traditional intelligentsia

On the other hand, the traditional intelligentsia (to retain Gramscian terminology) remained cowed and intimidated. This was particularly visible in the two institutions which had provided intellectual leadership for the anti-apartheid struggle, the churches and the universities. After 1990 the churches fell into a deep somnolence from which they could not be awakened. It was as if the anti-apartheid struggle had exhausted them and they simply had no energy or appetite for a new struggle against corruption, inequality and illiberality. The ANC insisted, of course, that the churches belonged at their side and the churches seemed unable to muster the courage to declare their independence.

A similar lack of courage afflicted the universities. They were, in any case, in decline. Wits (the University of the Witwatersrand) had lost its old primacy. The University of KwaZulu-Natal was in tatters. The University of South Africa, long celebrated as one of the world's greatest distance-learning institutions, was a shadow of its former self. Partly this was because the universities were part of the public sector and nervously aware that the ANC government had far less regard for either academic freedom or university autonomy than even the old Nat government. By 2014 four universities were under administration. In addition Walter Sisulu University in the Eastern Cape had to be shut down in 2013 because strike action by its faculty, already the best paid in the country although among the least distinguished, had brought the university to the brink of bankruptcy: a perfect and painful example of public service clamancy.[1]

In general the universities were subservient. At the height of the controversy over the Aids denialism which had made Mbeki an international leper, UCT gave him a special African Leadership Award. Once Jacob Zuma came to power the vice chancellor of the University of KwaZulu-Natal, Professor William Makgoba, though he had been a fervent admirer of Mbeki, quickly declared that Zuma was the perfect man to be president and that Mbeki was a 'classic dictator of our times', comparing him to Mobutu, Idi Amin, Mugabe and other African monsters.[2] Thus even at a time when educated opinion, both in South Africa and internationally, had become highly critical of the ANC, South African universities sounded no critical note. There was none of the bravery and independence of mind that the universities showed under apartheid.

All the universities practised affirmative action, both in their admissions and their faculty appointments. The results were damaging: a high failure and drop-out rate, as students who often should never have been admitted, departed; and a situation in which most worthwhile research and publication was carried out by an ageing core of mainly white males. As this latter group exited the system standards were bound to nose-dive. The entire strategy was based on a historically obvious mistake: one simply cannot create an instant new intelligentsia by affirmative action.[3] In the main the universities knew this but, with few exceptions, were so craven that they voluntarily submitted to this self-destructive policy which was bound to lower standards for the coming generations of black students. It was a classic *trahison des clercs*. Inevitably, South Africa continued to suffer a damaging brain drain.

What was true of the universities applied with equal force to what one might term 'public intellectual life' where a stifling and ANC-centred version of political correctness ruled. The SABC was tightly state controlled and deferred to the ANC to the extent that, on specious grounds, it actually refused to take political commercials from the Opposition parties during the 2014 election. In addition, SABC staffers were warned that their phones were being monitored to prevent any political dissidence.[4]

After the election the ANC appealed to the Human Rights Commission against what it termed 'a racist onslaught' against it. This referred to a cartoon depicting government ministers as clowns (the offending news agency and its cartoonists apologised and the matter was referred to the company's internal ombudsman); a photograph tweeted by a DA MP, Mike Waters (who apologised and withdrew the picture); and the Public Protector, Thuli Madonsela, for something she allegedly said to students at Wits (but which she denied).[5] This was all completely ridiculous. The cartoon would have drawn little comment if published in other countries and did not depict Africans with negroid features; a photograph cannot be racist; and there was no proof that Madonsela had said what was alleged.

Yet the ANC ruled such public spaces with a ferocity which kept others compliant. The result was that many private organisations or individuals were careful to put ANC figures on their board of directors, their panel of judges or whatever. The results were often comic. Thus, for example, South Africa's leading book prize, the Alan Paton award, was quite frequently won by communists or jejune beginners; the one certainty was that someone like Alan Paton – an older white male with liberal views – could never have won. Similarly, JM Coetzee's *Disgrace* won the Man Booker Prize and other awards around the world, and helped Coetzee win the Nobel Prize for Literature. In South Africa the novel was bitterly attacked by the ANC and nobody was brave enough to give it any sort of prize.

Behind the curtain of this new 'progressivism' high culture was dying. To go to a theatre, opera, ballet or orchestral recital was to see the same sea of grey-headed whites. It would be surprising if any of these art forms still existed in 20 years' time. Eighty per cent of South Africa's schools were regarded, even by the government, as 'dysfunctional', which meant that education hardly happened in them. Under the ANC South Africa was retreating at speed to a less-cultured, less-educated, less-skilled society. Unwittingly, and while preaching the doctrines of progress and liberation, the ANC was leading South Africa further and further backward.

The quietism and deference to power of the universities and those who policed public intellectual spaces sat in strange contrast to these facts, as if almost no one was willing to look truth in the face. Yet at a private level, the ANC's failure was obvious. Many businessmen, professionals and academics who publicly deferred to the ANC were scathing about it off the record. Meanwhile, the press, echoing this private consensus rather than the apparent public one, carried endless corruption stories and Zuma was mocked on a regular basis in much of the media.

The growing influence of China

The ANC had lost its old lodestone, the Soviet bloc. Increasingly, however, it transferred its affections to China. ANC leaders from every level of society made frequent pilgrimages to China and Zuma's repeated mantra was that 'South Africa must learn from China, not just economically but politically'. These were widely – but unwisely – assumed to be just empty words. There was, after all, scant chance that ANC-ruled South Africa would imitate China's economic dynamism. But the two ruling parties were based on the same Soviet model and they maintained a close though confidential relationship. Over time it became clear that there was, indeed, quite a strong Chinese influence within the ANC.

The first thing to change was political tactics. The ANC had always attacked its opponents head-on and attempted to anathematise them as reactionaries, racists, CIA agents and the like. The Chinese pointed out that it was often more effective to do the opposite; to get one's own activists to join opposition parties and then foment trouble inside them. The Inkatha Freedom Party was an early target for such tactics, and the breakaway from it of the National Freedom Party in 2011 – widely credited to just such tactics – did the IFP far more damage than any amount of frontal attack. The appointment of the NFP leader, Zanele Magwaza-Msibi, to a ministerial post in Zuma's government, plus the NFP's decision to form coalitions with the ANC in local government (including in Magwaza-Msibi's own constituency, Zululand), was seen as evidence for this thesis. Similarly, Julius Malema, after he had founded the Economic Freedom Fighters, said that he was well aware of how the ANC had used similar infiltration tactics against Cope and warned the EFF to be on guard against the same tactics. Malema claimed, indeed, that he had been part of 'an underground core' of the ANC which planned and executed the destruction of Cope and other black-led parties. 'I know how the ruling party operates. I know what tactics they use. I know the type of resources they use.'[6]

Chinese influence was also apparent when it came to the knotty problem of the press. Zuma had pushed through a new law to try to restrain the press but the resistance was fierce and not much was achieved. The Guptas' new paper, *New Age*, was also little help, for very few people read it and even fewer took it seriously. However, in August 2013 there was a major coup when Independent News and Media, the newspaper chain which Tony O'Reilly had run into the ground en route to his own bankruptcy, was bought by Sekunjalo. Sekunjalo was a conglomerate company run by Iqbal Survé, a somewhat overwrought but pro-ANC Indian. At a stroke this put all the main daily morning and evening newspapers in all of South Africa's major cities into the ANC camp.

This was an eyebrow-raising deal in many respects. Sekunjalo had put up 55 per cent of the money but another 25 per cent came from the Public Investment Corporation (PIC, the state-run civil service pension fund) and another 20 per cent from two state-owned Chinese companies. There was immediate speculation that this was an essentially political deal, cooked up by the ANC and the Chinese, to turn the South African press into something more like its Chinese counterpart. Survé took such speculation by the *Mail & Guardian* very badly and publicly accused it of being CIA-controlled,[7] something of a give-away in view of the propensity of ANC politicians to accuse their opponents of being CIA- or MI5-controlled.

Secondly, Survé had paid R2 billion for the deal, far too much in the eyes of most media professionals, for many of the papers in the Independent stable were already losing both subscribers and money. The newspapers were now to be re-aligned in a more pro-ANC direction (and Survé immediately began to hire and fire journalists in order to achieve such a realignment), but it seemed certain that this would alienate many of the remaining readers. The risk was that the papers would soon be run into the ground, which in turn raised questions as to whether this was a suitable investment for a civil service pension fund or indeed for the two Chinese companies involved, the China-Africa Development Fund and the China International TV Corporation. In fact the situation was even worse than it appeared because the PIC had actually lent Survé most of his stake, so really the pension fund had put up 70 per cent. The SA Clothing and Textile Workers Union (Sactwu) had also put up R150 million through its investment arm, yet neither it nor the PIC had any directors on the new board and Survé, who had no serious journalistic experience, enjoyed sole control and attempted to micro-manage the clearly foundering group.[8]

Already the ANC had launched an attempt to steal *Ilanga lase Natal* (Natal Sun), the Zulu newspaper which is South Africa's oldest and biggest African language paper, owned by Chief Buthelezi's Inkatha movement. *Ilanga*'s long-time editor, Arthur Konigkramer, had turned down several ANC offers to buy the paper when, in its programme for its 2012 centenary celebrations, the ANC announced that one of its projects for the year would be 'to reclaim *Ilanga*'. This, it turned out, was to be achieved by the now normal tactic of infiltrating the organisation with moles. From the beginning of 2012 Cosatu made a drive to enrol all of *Ilanga*'s journalists, a prelude to a prolonged industrial war of attrition. At first the journalists demanded a 20 per cent increase – which they got. The union members then demanded wage parity between whites and blacks, a nonsensical claim for all *Ilanga*'s employees are black. 'I soon discovered that my office was bugged,' says Konigkramer, 'and that anything I said there was immediately known to the ANC.' Konigkramer had little doubt that his paper was the target in another example of Chinese-inspired infiltration tactics.[9]

At this point Paul Mashatile, the national minister of arts and culture, visited Durban and in his speech referred to *Ilanga* as being 'in the wrong hands', something that needed to be remedied. He then hurriedly corrected himself and said 'I shouldn't have said that', for the ANC strategy was supposed to be secret. Meanwhile trouble at the newspaper worsened and union activists began to commit acts of sabotage – on one occasion breaking into the paper's offices and wiping an entire Sunday edition off the computers. Meanwhile, other Cosatu unions organised campaigns to boycott *Ilanga* and its circulation fell. At each critical juncture the Dube Trust or some other ANC intermediary would make a bid to buy the paper in what was, transparently, a pincer movement aimed at bringing the paper to its knees and thus forcing a sale – at a bargain price.

Konigkramer sacked the union members caught on camera committing sabotage and when union members went on sympathy strike, he laid them off too. At an ANC meeting in Durban city hall plans were announced to try to break *Ilanga* by withdrawing all government advertising from the paper. It didn't happen: anyone who wanted to recruit Africans to public sector jobs in KwaZulu-Natal simply had to advertise with *Ilanga*. Moreover, the ANC seemed nervous of the possibility of its 'reclaim *Ilanga*' strategy entering the public realm. The obvious comparison was with the ANC's 'Operation Reclaim' in the Western Cape. There again, a semi-subterranean political campaign was waged to overthrow an uncomfortable political fact whose formal status (the IFP ownership of *Ilanga*, the DA's democratic victory in the Western Cape) could hardly be questioned. There too the ANC tried to act by stealth, delegating the direct action campaign against the Western Cape government to the Ses'Khona People's Rights Movement which it set afoot.

At just the same time that the ANC was trying to steal *Ilanga,* trouble of a similar kind was brewing at the black paper, *City Press*, whose independent and critical spirit had greatly annoyed the ANC. A group of black journalists suddenly laid charges of racism, defamation and sowing division against the editor, Ferial Haffajee. Her sin, it turned out, was to have been too critical of President Zuma over his Nkandla house. The subtext, quite clearly, was that an Indian woman had no right to be editing a paper for Africans. If Haffajee could be forced out *City Press* might be steered towards a more ANC-friendly position. However, the journalists had misjudged the redoubtable Ferial Haffajee, who immediately counter-charged them with racism and gave them a week to decide if they still wanted to work for the paper.[10]

Finally in December 2014 Blackstar, a private equity group, made a take-over bid for the Times Media Group which publishes *Business Day*, the *Times*, the *Sunday Times* and the *Financial Mail*. Blackstar had just merged with Kagiso-Tiso, part of the Kagiso Trust. This was widely suspected of being another tactic to smother virtually all that remained of a critical press, for Kagiso is ANC-aligned and chaired by the Revd Frank Chikane, director-general of the Presidency in 1999–2010 under Mbeki, Motlanthe and Zuma. Should this supposition prove correct, the *Mail & Guardian* would be the sole remaining press critic of government. Already Iqbal Survé has accused Trevor Ncube, owner of the *Mail & Guardian*, of being 'controlled by the CIA', doubtless a reflection of ANC thinking on the matter.[11]

Ever since it came to power the ANC has wanted to set up its own political school and in 2014 it appeared that this might happen at last – thanks to China. The party acquired land between Parys and Potchefstroom which it said would house a political school for cadres, a project expected to cost R800 million. A large party of Chinese officials, including the Chinese ambassador, went into conclave with an ANC team led by Gwede Mantashe, at the end of which it was said that the project would 'proceed with the support of our friends'.[12]

The ANC: party of the bantustans

A new aspect of land reform under Zuma has been an increasing bias towards traditional chiefs. The government tried to push through a Traditional Courts Bill which effectively sought to create a separate legal system in rural areas, reinforcing chiefly power, including the power to dispense land and reducing the status of women to virtual serfs. This was, however, defeated by an unlikely coalition of provincial representatives and the feminist lobby. Nonetheless, this hardly served to halt the ANC's rapprochement with the culture of chiefly traditionalism.

Zuma told the National House of Traditional Leaders that he was taking steps to ensure that they would be able to participate in the Land Management Commission, the Land Rights Management Board and the

Rural Development Agency 'so as to ensure that you are able to influence decisions'.[13] This led to a number of traditional leaders making sweeping land claims – a group of chiefs in the Tshwane area laid claim to the whole of Pretoria, while the Zulu king claimed most of KwaZulu-Natal. Indeed, his claims went all the way back to 1838 and would have the effect of removing land rights from everyone else in the province of KwaZulu-Natal. Already the King behaved as if this was already so, building his eighth palace on land claimed for the last 15 years by landless communities.[14] Zuma also promised chiefs that the government would in future pay for them and their families to be members of the government medical aid scheme, guaranteeing them private health care.[15] The ANC also determined to revive the Communal Land Rights Act (stalled by constitutional challenges) which conferred more power on chiefs and, contrary to previous ANC thinking, would entrench the boundaries of the old bantustans.[16]

As the ANC found its urban base under increasing threat from the DA and the EFF, it leaned ever more heavily on traditional leaders. Zuma's entire behaviour over Nkandla was, of course, that of a rural chief; he even dismissed criticism as prejudice against rural dwellers. Blade Nzimande, who treated the whole row as an opportunity to show almost slavish loyalty to Zuma, led a pro-Zuma demonstration in Nkandla in which Zuma's construction of, effectively, his own royal kraal was held up as an example of 'rural development'.[17] But South Africa has several thousand chiefs and headmen plus 17 kings, queens or paramount chiefs, who collectively give access to some 18 million South Africans. (Only the two richest provinces, Gauteng and the Western Cape, have no chiefs.) It was striking, for example, that as the ANC girded itself for conflict with the EFF in Limpopo (Julius Malema's home province), the ANC elective conference held in Polokwane in February 2014 featured a number of leading chiefs. Most notable was Chief Seshego Sekororo, the Limpopo chairman of Contralesa – recognised as 'Comrade Chief Sekororo' by the chair – and Chief Kennedy Tshivhase, who was elected to the ANC provincial executive.[18]

The ANC's increasing dependence on the rural vote mirrored the way in which Zanu-PF in Zimbabwe (and probably other African nationalist parties elsewhere) lost urban votes early on but clung to rural support. Rural voters were almost all poor and more dependent on patronage and hand-outs. And as the ANC began to lose ground it increasingly used the state Social Security Agency to make mass hand-outs of food parcels, blankets and other items at ANC rallies, ignoring furious Opposition objections at this misuse of state resources for party political gain. All such handouts were in rural areas.[19] Rural voters were easily threatened that failure to support the ANC would result in the loss of this largesse or their welfare or pension payments. They were also more subject to chiefly authority and influence, less exposed to the media – and, in the last analysis, any ruling party found it easier to cheat electorally in rural areas. This was confirmed by a study by the Community Agency for Social Development, which 'overwhelmingly pointed to the ANC as the primary source of intimidation'. This was carried out mainly 'through manipulating people, using misinformation and threats regarding pensions and grants, interfering with access to meeting facilities, assaults and threats of physical harm', the chief target being 'poorer people'. Often this was quite open: Meshack Radebe, the provincial minister of agriculture in KwaZulu-Natal, spoke of how 'Zuma has increased grants, but there are people who are stealing them by voting for opposition parties. If you are in the opposition you are like a person who comes to my house, eats my food and then insults me.'[20] The ANC's problem, however, was that with urbanisation continuing apace in South Africa, this captured rural populace was steadily shrinking in importance.

Power in an ungoverned society

The great unknown in the ANC's conquest of power in 1994 was how an African nationalist party would deal with governing a modern urban society and a developed economy. This was a challenge that African nationalism had not had to face anywhere else in Africa. The answer is now clear: the ANC has failed to rise to that challenge. It has in general found the running of a modern state way beyond its capacities. It has not even managed to preserve an adequate power supply, that most basic essential of a modern society – even though it found, on attaining office, that it had a 25 per cent over-supply of electric power.

The towns and cities which the ANC controls are all in a state of advanced decay. This is true not just of Transkei towns like Mbizana and Mthatha, but even of Johannesburg. Despite the fact that it is still the hub of private sector investment, the city staggers from crisis to crisis. Its roads are marked by potholes and failed traffic lights, the city and suburbs by power cuts, water cut-offs and overgrown verges. The municipality seems incapable of billing its citizens correctly and city finances are a mess. The public hospitals don't work, policing is poor and crime is rampant. Prior to 1994 Johannesburg was undoubtedly Africa's premier city. In the main the city, like the country, is now un-governed.

The ANC-led provincial governments work equally poorly. The most potent symbol of this is the long-running scandal of the Limpopo provincial government's inability to deliver school textbooks to schools. The fact that the national minister of education, situated in nearby Pretoria, found herself unable to have any effect on the situation only emphasised the government's impotence. A study by the Centre for Development and Enterprise revealed that South Africa had the worst public school system in the entire developing world.[21] South Africa notably under-performed many poorer countries, suggesting that lack of resources was not the critical variable. The typical ANC excuse is to blame 'the legacy of apartheid', but this makes no sense: all these services worked far better under apartheid.

The national government doesn't really govern. Partly this is because many ministers – and this has been visible since the very outset in 1994 – devote little time and energy to their ministries. Probably the dominant ministerial activities since 1994 have been foreign travel and the observation of celebrations or rituals of one kind or another. There is a constant round of party events – conferences, rallies, *indabas, imbizos,*[22] national celebrations, commemorations, funerals and anniversaries. Even extremely minor events such as the launch of a new brochure or programme are used as an excuse for lavish parties. Previously sedate occasions like the opening of Parliament are turned into major jamborees, replete with dressed-to-kill partying. Ministers spend unconscionable amounts on luxury cars, first-class travel, bodyguards, private airplanes – and often on large newspaper adverts boasting of their activities and featuring large portraits of themselves. Inevitably, all this has been aped by provincial ministers and even by municipal officers. Far out in the wilds of Limpopo or northern Zululand one can find huge placard posters at the roadside featuring the smiling face of some obscure provincial minister accompanying banal announcements of local maintenance or improvement programmes. One is left in little doubt that the main point of the advert is the minister's (or mayor's) own ego.

Why ungoverned?

The government also doesn't govern because it cannot. In effect the 'transformation' of the civil service has destroyed it. Apart from occasional oases of expertise – usually in the treasury, central bank or tax collection service – the civil service has been stripped not only of competent personnel but also of its institutional memory. Instead it has become a free-fire field for 'cadre deployment' and every kind of political and familial nepotism and cronyism. One result has been colossal expenditure on outside consultants who perform many of the tasks that civil servants should but couldn't do. Second, the government has tried to get the private sector to do its work for it. A great deal of legislation – including everything to do with affirmative action and black economic empowerment – has been written in terms that require all manner of performance from the private sector and merely empower the minister to punish non-compliers. Similarly, mining legislation consists mainly of telling mining companies what to do in great detail under pain of dire punishment – and granting the minister large and vague discretionary powers so as to make the entire sector dependent on ministerial good will.

Third, the government doesn't govern because it simply isn't much interested in the job. Only a few, rare ministers such as the minister of health, Aaron Motsoaledi, appear to be driven by a passion for their work. Mainly, however, the focus of presidents and ministers alike is on the life of the ANC, its anniversaries, its rules and discipline, its national and regional conferences, its moods and its factions. Essentially, this is the body within which they have lived their lives, the body to which they owe their positions and power. And it is not just an organisation; it is a family, a history, an emotional home. Accordingly, they pay it far closer attention than anything in government. Ministers invariably give precedence to party meetings and occasions over state duties.

This tendency has reached an apogee under Zuma, partly because the defenestration of Mbeki showed what the penalties were for ignoring the balance of forces within the ANC or misjudging its factions and personalities. After all, Mbeki had forbidden the building of power stations and seen the country eclipsed by the catastrophe of major power cuts. He had also been responsible for hundreds of thousands of unnecessary deaths because of his refusal to allow anti-Aids drugs to be distributed to HIV sufferers. Mbeki had also supported Mugabe's regime of torture and murder next door. Yet the fact was that none of this brought him down. The ANC was willing to forgive or ignore all of it. What did for Mbeki was that he ignored the ANC's understood codes of conduct: he humiliated and expelled his popular deputy president, he ignored the rules of comradeship and solidarity – and he asserted his individual power against the most powerful factions, enraging them.

'In power – but still not governing'

In the early days after 1994 one frequently heard (usually from the left) the angry comment that the ANC might be in power but it still wasn't governing. The idea, usually, was that there was, somewhere, still a secret government of white bureaucrats and power-brokers. That paranoid vision is long gone and yet it remains relevant, for it continues to be true that the ANC is in power but doesn't govern. And most of the things that still work – the shopping malls, the supermarkets, the big companies – are run by a private sector still dominated by whites and Indians.

Zuma was determined not to make the same mistake as Mbeki. In any case, he was well aware that he could have been nothing without the ANC. Mbeki had always been a prince of the movement, a man who got the top scholarships, a man always marked for the top job. Zuma, on the other hand, came from the very bottom of black society. Thanks to the ANC he had made something of himself, had achieved basic literacy, had worked his passage. And when he was unfairly cast out by Mbeki he had fought his way, step by step, through the rules and institutions of the ANC in order to triumph.

So, in power, Zuma has paid most of his attention to the moods and factions of the ANC. He knows all the provincial committees of the ANC, who is a supporter, who not, who is buyable, who not – and he has a similarly encyclopaedic knowledge of the trade union movement and of ANC committees at municipal level. As one-time head of ANC intelligence he has naturally harnessed the security services in his aid. Zuma knows he has many enemies. That is normal; that doesn't bother him. He is a charming and friendly man who can be quite genial even with the Opposition leader. And he isn't an ideas man, so he doesn't aspire to the intellectual hegemony Mbeki pursued. Instead, he is a power man; he knows exactly what he needs to do in order to keep his balance, stay afloat and remain king of the castle.

So, in the last analysis the country is ungoverned because Zuma's only real objective is to maintain ANC dominance – and unity. Over and over again he has stressed that 'the unity of the ANC remains paramount. Unity is the rock upon which the ANC was founded.' As Anthony Butler pointed out, 'what Zuma is trying to say is that those who oppose him will be responsible for a potentially explosive ethnic division in the ANC.'[23] This is undoubtedly true: at all ANC gatherings the delegates from KwaZulu-Natal have made it abundantly clear that those trying to overthrow the first Zulu ANC leader since Luthuli are playing with fire.

And what is true of Zuma is true of his ministers too. The party comes first, with its need for constant factional activity. Typically, the minister is also the centre of a patronage network, finding jobs for family members, mistresses, clients from his local area and his tribal group. On top of which, of course, the minister is greatly preoccupied with trying to devise ways of using his official position in order to enrich him/herself. This isn't always just straight theft. It might be very complicated, including the setting up of dummy companies, the guiding of contracts towards particular tenderers, keeping certain key funders satisfied and so on. Certainly, there is no such thing as a poor ex-minister.

In the list of priorities, the business of government comes some way

after all that. And, given the fact that the civil service is broken and use-
less, it is not a particularly enjoyable or rewarding activity. So other activities are always more appealing. What is important is that the minister has
to be – and be seen to be – in charge and to be regarded as a VIP. This
might seem exaggerated but one could, for example, instance Stella Sigcau,
minister for public enterprises 1994–99 (appointed by Mandela despite her
openly admitted guilt of fraud) and then minister for public works from
1999 till her death in 2006. More than one newspaper commented that it
was impossible to think of a single thing that she had done in this 12-year
ministerial career. One could make the same point about many others.

Blacks can't govern?

The fact that the ANC has been proved incapable of governing a modern,
urbanised society is now widely accepted, not just by the Opposition and
minority groups but by most black journalists and, indeed, by the black
urban elite in general. The question is what to do about it. Many are held
by a primeval loyalty to the ANC, whatever its demerits. Some have joined
the Opposition, many others have despaired, retreating from politics altogether. But on top of all the inconveniences of having a government which
doesn't govern, many within the black intelligentsia feel humiliated. For
black majority rule in ANC hands has apparently proved correct all the
dire predictions made about black government by the old white right. Yet
there is no need to proceed from this to the mantra which Mbeki so hated
and feared, that 'blacks can't govern'. One has only to look at next-door
Botswana to see an impressive and democratic black government which,
in less than 50 years, has taken Botswana from being the poorest country
in the world to one which has overtaken South Africa in per capita income.

So the problem is not black government, it is ANC government. One
could make a persuasive case that the very nature of the ANC's history
and struggle has systematically unfitted it to govern. Moeletsi Mbeki, former President Mbeki's brother, seems to argue for this, saying that South
Africa's slowing growth rate is due to 'a comprehensive failure of governance'.[24] One could adapt the joke told in the USSR of the 1980s, when

many Soviet citizens gazed with admiration at Finland, the very model of democratic, modern prosperity just over the border, and concluded that the solution to the USSR's problems was to declare war on Finland and surrender immediately.

In the real world, such solutions are not available, which means that the tragedy of the ANC in power is likely to be ended in the big cities. Already a new generation of the 'born-free' urban young are increasingly impatient of the blunders of their elders. This cultural divide is likely only to grow. As the ANC gradually falls back onto its rural bases, inevitably it has taken on some of the socially regressive features of the old bantustan parties. This is, of course, most noticeable in its full support for traditional chiefs and its reliance on them as 'grands électeurs' but it is also reflected in the increasing use of religion and references to magic and witchcraft in ANC parlance.

Jacob Zuma has led this trend, becoming a priest in an African Zionist sect and making increasing reference to the ANC's God-given status. 'Even God expects us to rule this country,' he told an ANC rally in January 2014, 'because we are the only organisation which was blessed by pastors when it was formed. That is why we will rule until Jesus comes back.'[25] He also told the crowd that by voting ANC they could secure their place in heaven. When Zuma was booed by a section of the crowd after Bafana Bafana's 5–0 defeat at the hands of Brazil, the sports minister, Fikile Mbalula, explained that the booers were 'filled with evil' and 'infused with Satanism'.[26] Campaigning for the ANC in Cape Town in April 2014, Mbalula also declared that the DA-ruled Western Cape was 'governed by witches' and he called on ANC supporters to 'ask for tokoloshes to be called to chase the DA away'.[27] (This produced an angry rejoinder from the SA Pagan Rights Alliance, claiming to represent witches.[28])

Similarly, Cyril Ramaphosa warned young voters that 'If you don't vote the Boers will come back to control us.'[29] Angie Motshekga, the minister for basic education, called for prayers for matric students because 'nothing can defeat prayer … we will make sure that the kids are delivered from evil spirits'.[30] There were many invocations about the ANC having God on its side and Sindiso Mtenya, a Northern Cape ANC activist, even boasted that Oliver Tambo had told him that 'the ANC has its own God'.[31] In June

2014 the press carried reports that a senior (though, for legal reasons, un-named) cabinet minister who was divorcing his wife had accused her of witchcraft and casting spells on him.[32] In the same month it emerged that the SABC's chief operating officer, Hlaudi Motsoeneng, had received a wife (along with a cow and a calf) as a gift from Venda chiefs.[33] All of these prac-tices and rhetoric were typical of rural African society. They would once have been unthinkable in the ANC.

The 2014 election results confirmed this trend. In Nelson Mandela Bay (Port Elizabeth) the ANC fell to 49.17 per cent; in Tshwane (Pretoria) it fell to 50.16 per cent, in Johannesburg to 53.63 per cent and in Ekurhuleni (the East Rand) to 56.44 per cent. Given that, due to differential absten-tion, the DA always polls much better in municipal elections, and the ANC much worse, and given also the continuing trend to the DA and its proven track record of putting together electorally diverse coalitions, not one but several of these metropoles will be vulnerable in the 2016 local elections. The loss of any single one of them would be both symbolic and traumatic for the ANC. Moreover, the ANC has seen what happened in Cape Town where the DA first put together a multi-party coalition to defeat the ANC and then won the city on its own by a 2:1 majority. The lesson seemed to be that once the DA takes over, it is not easily shifted.

However, the DA, thanks to the increasingly erratic performance of its leader, Helen Zille, is clearly in a mess itself. But, if one assumes the party could put its own house in order, it seems only a matter of time before the ANC loses most of the major cities – and once lost, there will be no way back. The party will then stand ever-more exposed as a bantustan party, representative of all that is most backward in society.

The ANC knows that such a result would be a prelude to a general col-lapse and, accordingly, it is quite likely to cheat in order to stay in power. In that sense the party's widespread distribution of food parcels to voters in 2013–2014 and the use of the police to distribute ANC T-shirts in 2014 may only have been the first swallows of summer. Indeed, it seems quite likely that there was systematic cheating in 2014. How else to interpret the figures provided by the South African Institute of Race Relations which showed a 160 per cent turnout for those aged 80 and over? The only way to under-stand this was that many of the dead had voted. One should remember that many pensioners are falsely 'kept alive' so that their families can continue to receive their pensions, so the real turnout may have been nearer to 200 per cent. But such arcane oddities could happen only in the countryside. One doubts that they would long remain invisible or tolerated in the cities. As in the economic field, it is easy to surmise that things are moving quite rapidly towards a crunch.

CHAPTER SEVEN

The State's Repression of Economic Activity

I n the late 1990s I attended a public function in Pretoria at which I found myself surrounded by young black people, all of whom spoke with considerable excitement about 'the transformation of the public service', by which was meant the rapid Africanisation of the civil service at national, provincial and municipal level. One could understand the excitement, for this meant a large once-off bonanza of well-paid jobs, as huge numbers of white civil servants were made to take early retirement or otherwise got rid of. Inevitably, the young people I spoke to saw this as the model they hoped other organisations would follow too. It was difficult not to share their enthusiasm – until you reflected that no organisation could easily withstand such a large and sudden loss of skills and experience. In fact the result was disastrous, particularly since the turmoil and job turnover did not cease as nepotism, job-hopping and the insertion of political cadres continued pell-mell. Within a few years the civil service had been ruined, with the widespread loss of institutional memory so that employees no longer even knew what it was that they *should* be doing. Thus the post-apartheid state had unilaterally disarmed itself, making the government almost wholly impotent.

Much the same process was inflicted – as those young people had naively hoped – on all the state-owned enterprises (SOEs), resulting in the same disastrous torpor and inefficiency overtaking Telkom (telecommunications), Transnet (railways, ports and national transport), Eskom (electricity generation), Acsa (airports), South African Airways, Armscor and Denel (arms) as well as a multitude of other official bodies.

In both cases, the result was to suppress economic growth in the rest of the economy. The political class and the civil service took an ever-larger share of national income and yet produced next to nothing in return, acting merely as a drain on the productive private sector which paid the bulk of taxation. The SOEs were even worse. Because they were extremely badly run they hobbled other industries that depended on them (for example, the IT industry depending on Telkom). Because they pampered their managements and workforces, they were uneconomic and tried to recoup by price-gouging – for example, the rocketing price of electricity and airport taxes, the inflated costs of infrastructure projects, the sky-high port charges, and so on. These and other administered prices were a huge extra burden on the rest of society. And finally, of course, many of the SOEs still lost money and expected the national treasury to bail them out.

South African Airways, for example, is abominably managed – on average it gets through one CEO a year and they are often threatened with legal action after they are sacked. Not surprisingly, not only does SAA make regular annual losses, but it looks to the state to buy all its new planes for it – in 2013 it announced plans to buy an additional 23 wide-bodied long-haul aircraft for R60 billion. This, it said, was essential to its 'turn-around strategy' (every CEO has a new such strategy) – but the order had to be cancelled by the minister for public enterprises, Malusi Gigaba, in January 2014. The state-owned short-haul carrier, SA Express, is another money-sink. In 2011 the business almost collapsed due to poor management and thereafter each year's audit report has been qualified. This alone would sink a private company. In addition, however, its accounts show that in 2013 it had total equity of R264 million – less than half its accumulated losses of R594 million – as well as a R1.3-billion government guarantee. In October 2013 it announced that it planned to buy R9-billion-worth of new aircraft.[1] This order too seems certain to be cancelled by government.

All of which needs to be compared to the private airline, Comair, operating on the other side of the runway and flying to many of the same destinations. Comair buys all its own planes, has no government aid and always makes a profit.

It is the same with the other SOEs. All of them are badly managed and even Eskom – under apartheid a mighty, profit-making utility which always had a large power reserve – has been reduced to a crippled giant. It is poorly maintained and managed, unable to provide a steady power supply and desperately seeking funds from the state to pay its debts.

Thus the state-owned industries now represent a huge extra drain on the state. Collectively, they mean that the real position of state indebtedness is not 41 per cent of GDP, as is often stated, but over 57 per cent. And yet no end is in sight. By August 2014 the Treasury was being pressed to bail out Eskom and SAA to the combined tune of R300 billion – which it could not do without threatening the country's credit rating. Yet at the same time the yield on Eskom bonds (guaranteed by the government) had risen to 6.11 per cent and was only likely to go higher.[2] Borrowing at such rates is horribly expensive.

Lurking nearby is a monster which could sink the whole ship – the long-promised National Health Insurance system. The ANC and SACP have made this central to their vision though, to be fair, they do admit that the system cannot be introduced until the public health system is working properly again. Since there is no prospect of that being achieved under ANC rule – there aren't anything like enough doctors and nurses for such a system to work – this might seem to rule it out. But in the end the ANC always gives in to populist pressure and, probably, will go ahead with NHI regardless. Doubtless, the result would be to reduce the entire health system to a shambles, but there is also the question of cost – reckoned by the Actuarial Society of South Africa to be between R235 billion and R336 billion a year.[3] There is no prospect of this being funded except by further borrowing. If the cash is found by increasing taxes on the better-off there will be a further wave of emigration. If the health system is indeed laid waste, there will be a mass emigration of most doctors and nurses and many other qualified professionals. Either way, the country's tax base will be significantly reduced, making it harder than ever to see how further fiscal deficits (and growing debt) are to be avoided.

Faced with all this, finance ministers have continually promised to stick to spending targets and keep debt under control. However, as the KPMG economist, Lullu Krugel, put it after Pravin Gordhan's 2013 medium-term statement, 'Up until now the minister has not really managed to do what he has promised in terms of the deficit and that is why the ratings agencies are still punishing us about it. The intention is good, but the actual outcomes are not achieved. The pace at which borrowing is rising is frightening.'[4]

The government has declared that its central economic policy document is the National Development Plan devised by Trevor Manuel and his appointed experts. The Plan is bitterly opposed by the SACP and Cosatu but generally supported by business, the rest of government and the Opposition. This is, however, a fight over nothing. The NDP is very much in the tradition of other such ANC documents as the Freedom Charter, the Reconstruction and Development Programme and, indeed, the Constitution: they are adopted with great fanfare but then largely ignored. Thus there is no provision of any kind for the implementation of the NDP. When it was debated in Parliament the Cope leader, Terror Lekota, asked 'Who exactly is in charge of carrying this out?', a question met with howls of laughter from every party including the ANC. Manuel himself said it was 'up to society' as to whether the NDP was implemented, tantamount to throwing his hands in the air. The result is that the main economic policy document is wholly lacking in credibility and in practice the result is merely continuing drift. One could call this misgovernance or one could call it no governance.

No way to run a railroad

The problem about trying to re-organise the economy in order to maximise rent-seeking opportunities is that it is inimical to growth and to creating the conditions conducive to domestic or foreign investment. During the great commodity boom of 2002–2008 the problems were disguised: indeed, tax receipts were so buoyant that the state ran a fiscal surplus. But in 2009 all that collapsed. As tax revenues fell, the state lapsed into fiscal deficit. The government had meanwhile promised expenditure of several trillion rand on improved infrastructure, hundreds of billions of extra rands on its National Health Initiative and more still on free higher education and a new youth job subsidy. Yet a mere glance showed the virtual impossibility of increasing the tax take. The vast bulk of taxation is paid by some 1 000 companies and 2 million individuals. Many of the biggest companies responded to the advent of ANC rule by internationalising themselves, which suggests that in the event of higher taxation companies and individuals alike will evade, avoid or emigrate. Most companies responded to the downturn by building up sizeable cash balances both for prudential reasons and because of a lack of investment opportunities.

Businessmen are wary of criticising the government openly but actions speak louder than words and nothing speaks louder than the private sector's effective investment strike since 2009. In effect, we are now not far off the Zimbabwe or Swaziland situations. Though private business is careful not to criticise the Mugabe or Mswati regimes, in effect it has long since lost all confidence in their ability to govern. The result, in both these countries, is that the private sector has failed to produce a single new job in the last 25 years, and 70 per cent of the state budget goes on public sector salaries. This is a recipe for ruin: per capita income in both states is far below what it was a quarter of a century ago and both are in a state of financial collapse. Naturally, such a situation frightens off foreign investors and causes large-scale capital flight. Both Zimbabwe and Swaziland are very near the point of collapse.

However, as we have seen, no South African regime has ever successfully survived a prolonged investment strike, particularly if that includes FDI. By 2014 South Africa was itself moving nearer and nearer to the line of decision.

An inheritance squandered

The general business assessment of the current regime is probably best expressed in the following excerpt from an editorial in the *Financial Mail*:[5]

The South African government has become increasingly anti-business over the past two decades, as evidenced by gradually intensifying, successive rafts of legislation that either deliberately or carelessly seek to constrain or frustrate business. The enormous advantages and benefits South Africa gained over a century of capitalism remain resilient, but they are being gradually squandered.

Of course, the ANC did not set out to repress economic activity. This has happened because the party has overriding ideological objectives and because whenever it has been faced with the conundrum that if you do X it will constrain growth but cement your control and fulfil your political objectives, it has unerringly opted for the latter. This has particularly been the case since 2009 because of the ascendancy of the SACP within Zuma's coalition: all three economic ministries, finance, trade and industry and economic development, were held by SACP members. Moreover, Zuma himself was a lifelong communist – a fact he played down in office – and most of the senior ANC leaders (including Mandela and Mbeki) were communists for lengthy parts of their career.

Thus the awkward truth is that South Africa has what would have been known during the Cold War as a government composed of communists and fellow-travellers. Little wonder that the ANC government instinctively feels closest to Cuba, China, Russia and even North Korea. However, South Africa's communists have largely lost their bearings and their confidence. They do not analyse things in class terms; despite having a creed based in economic determinism, they have no knowledge of economics; and much of what they say is either voluntarist or racist or both. In 20 years they have not nationalised a single industry and theoretically, at least, have learned to live with the market economy which they inherited. But there was no disguising the fact that the government views businessmen, including foreign investors, simply as the class enemy and has no knowledge or sympathy with the logic of capitalism. It is hardly surprising that under these circumstances South Africa's capitalist economy has suffered.

The story of South Africa's economy since 1994 is one of decline towards lower growth, lower investment and higher unemployment. The problem which will thus have to be faced before long is whether the ANC's tolerance of capitalism will stretch to being willing to take the tough, even harsh measures required to restore health to the system. This will mean asking a lot from people who do not like the system or believe in it and many of whose actions have defied market logic. Moreover, tolerance of the system has been that for the goose that lays the golden eggs. If, by dint of their own policies, they manage to constrain the economy to almost complete stagnation, they could well decide to blame the goose and slaughter it.

One sign of the economic malaise produced by ANC rule is an increasingly serious balance of payments deficit, even in an era of low economic growth. In the past South Africa's attempts to accelerate growth rapidly ran into a balance of payments constraint, for South Africans have a high import propensity and once the purse-strings are loosened they will buy lots of German and Japanese cars, South Korean cell phones and TVs, and so on. In the past it used to be said that such constraints would kick in once the rate of growth went over 4 per cent. But in 2013, a year of 1.9 per cent growth, there was a huge balance of payments deficit. As Iraj Abedian put it, 'We have over the past three to four years undermined our export capacity.'[6]

As the 2014 election neared, the ANC, panicked by the advance of Julius Malema's EFF, introduced a whole raft of new populist laws, many of them incompatible with the NDP. As the *Financial Mail* commented, 'These measures will weaken property rights, reduce private sector autonomy, threaten business with harsh penalties, heighten policy uncertainty and undermine investor confidence. They represent what is arguably the biggest assault on business since the ANC came to power in 1994.'[7] No sooner was the election over than Zuma announced that the ANC was moving into a 'second transition'. In the first one, he averred, the ANC had been held back by regard for economic stability and the constitution, but now these restraints could be ignored as the ANC went flat out to achieve social and economic transformation. Clearly, the party now saw itself in a populist bidding war with the EFF. Nothing could be more destructive of economic growth and investor confidence.[8]

Surveying the situation in the wake of the 2014 election, the *Financial Mail* noted the many obstacles to growth. Quite apart from the crippling strikes which produced negative GDP growth in the whole first half of 2014, causing large job losses, the government still refused to put job creation at the top of its priority list. Policy was, Zuma averred, driven by a need to create 'an 'inclusive economy' which creates jobs, 'but more importantly it must reflect the demographics of the country'.[9] This obsession with demographic representivity was, of course, a luxury the country could not afford: it amounted merely to a demand to share unemployment around equally.

Second, it was noted that South Africa now had a 'reputation as a country in which employers have few rights'. The Production Management Institute reported that it had become 'so onerous' to employ people in South Africa that 'business is outsourcing, sub-contracting, automating and moving production offshore'.[10] One problem is that the corruption and lavish lifestyles of the new elite are on full display and this has fuelled a desperate and angry determination among workers not to get left behind in the race. The result is great labour militancy behind sheerly impossible trade union demands, leading JP Morgan Cazenove to warn that South African mines (and other employers) must compulsorily move away from a cheap labour model or continue on a path to 'self-destruction'.[11] Yet socially the imperative is for the opposite – for lots of cheap, unskilled jobs.

Moreover, the wide range of costs administered by government – road tolls, electricity, water charges, rates and so on – all 'severely outstrip' other forms of inflation.[12] In large part this was necessary in order to pay the vastly inflated salary bills of the public sector bureaucrats working in these sectors. Rob Davies, the communist minister for trade and industry, argued strongly for protectionism and autarchy but the effect of this administered price inflation was to undermine all his support to industry. Port charges – up to six times higher than in many of South Africa's competitors – were another major disincentive.[13] A Deloitte forecast of manufacturing competitiveness over the five years 2014 to 2019 found that 'almost every emerging market ... is expected to become more competitive by 2018. SA, however, is expected to deteriorate. Says Deloitte SA manufacturing industry leader Karthi Pillay: "We are losing ground in the battle to provide a business-friendly environment to local and global manufacturers".[14] A survey of international bankers found that while bankers in general saw over-regulation as their biggest risk, South African bankers saw political interference as their biggest risk.[15]

The great mining disaster

This over-regulation has, of course, been most notable in the case of mining, where government policies resulted in South Africa missing out altogether on the great mining super-boom of 2001–2008. I have written extensively about this and there is no need to repeat myself.[16] Suffice it to say that the general and complete mismanagement of the mining industry had, by 2013, resulted in lower investment, output and exports as well as a massacre of mineworkers at Marikana. It is difficult to see how the situation could be much worse.

Yet policy has merely become more restrictive since the 2002 Mineral and Petroleum Resources Development Act (MPRDA), causing further falls in investment. This Act, probably the most important the ANC government has ever passed, apart from imposing extremely stiff BEE obligations on the industry, removed ownership of the mines from the mining companies, offering in their place mining licences subject to very wide ministerial discretion. Because South Africa possesses the richest stock of minerals of any country on Earth, mining is the one industry in which it enjoys a large comparative advantage. It also earns the country most of its foreign exchange.

As the Bill made its way through Parliament the mining industry repeatedly warned that it would have a crippling effect since it placed companies in the situation where they might invest billions in drilling shafts or oil wells but in which they would have no security of ownership, with their licences subject to removal at a moment's notice. Moreover, they pointed out, the discretionary powers bestowed upon the minister were bound to open the door to large-scale bribery and corruption and even the straightforward instruction by government that BEE deals should benefit personnel directly dictated by the minister – as indeed happened in the Gold Fields BEE deal of 2010 in which the beneficiaries were simply given shares, thus diluting the value of all other shareholders' assets. The beneficiaries included the chairperson of the ANC, one of Jacob Zuma's lawyers, a convicted fraudster and a convicted bank-robber. This deal has been highlighted by the US Securities and Exchange Commission as involving bribery and corruption.

In 2014 further amendments to the MPRDA were passed, all strengthening the requirements placed on companies and greatly increasing the discretionary powers of the minister for mineral resources. The result was to considerably increase policy uncertainty. Moreover, the new amendments tried to force mining companies to assist in the beneficiation of minerals by prescribing that they should beneficiate a percentage of their production (prescribed by the minister), with equally prescribed qualities and timelines and at a prescribed price. The idea that one could thus force industrialisation was typical of the dirigisme of ANC policy.

There is open speculation that South Africa may now operate much like the DRC, with no mining rights conceded unless leading politicians get a cut straight into their (foreign) bank accounts. Twenty years ago South Africa was regarded as having one of the most impressive mining regimes in the world. In 2012 the Fraser Institute survey of mining countries rated South Africa 54th out of 93. In 2013 the rating fell to 64th.[17] This is amazing when one considers that South Africa has the greatest treasure trove of minerals on the planet.

In the utterly murky situation in which mining companies now exist it has become commonplace for the minister of mineral resources to grant prospecting rights to favoured companies (usually loaded with political and family friends) over areas where another company is already operating with a licence they thought valid. This has happened no fewer than 122 times to date.[18] Usually the interloper is expensively bought out without ever having to shovel a spadeful of earth. In effect such grants of rights amount to handouts granted by the state but paid by mining companies. This is, indeed, pretty much the DRC model, where miners have to expect to pay all manner of ex gratia payments and 'taxes' in order to keep going.

A good example of this piracy (the only correct word) was the grant of prospecting rights in 2013 to the Pan African Mineral Development Company (PAMDC) on land already being mined by the Australian company, Aquila Resources. Aquila found that there was no way to access any central register confirming who mined what and that they could get no help of any kind (or even any response at all) from the Department of Mineral Resources. This was hardly surprising. PAMDC was jointly owned by the governments of South Africa, Zimbabwe and Zambia. The company refused point blank to provide any account of its history, activities, plans or any financial statements. Moreover, it turned out that one of its directors was Thibedi Ramonja, director-general of the South African Department of Mineral Resources. Thus the regulators and the pirates were the same people. It would be quite surprising if monies accruing to PAMDC did not end up in private rather than government bank accounts.[19]

It is no accident that of the world's three biggest mining companies, BHP Billiton is on the verge of exiting South African altogether and has placed all its South African assets into a portfolio for 'second class assets'; Anglo-American has run down its holdings and Anglo Platinum has announced the sale of its flagship Rustenburg mines, while RTZ has slimmed down its holdings to just one titanium operation at Richards Bay. These three companies have been the major engines of investment in South Africa, and they are going.[20] Other major mining companies are also pulling back or out – Harmony, for example, has mothballed a shaft and shelved an expansion project on which it had already spent R1.4 billion.[21] In general, companies now find that there is a special discount which markets place on the value of South African assets, encouraging them to shuffle them off into separate companies or sell them altogether. Even more alarming, the new MPRDA Amendment Act is a huge disincentive for any new investors to come to South Africa. As *Business Day* reported, the new Act 'severely damages the case for any new entrant to the industry, who must now face the risk of tight export restrictions as well as cumbersome beneficiation requirements. New entrants also have to be "invited" to apply for [mining] rights to the minister, which gives the minister incredible power to determine just who may mine in this country.'[22]

So gross has the regulation and administration of the mining industry become that even an old communist like Raymond Suttner was simply revolted. His verdict on the Gold Fields BEE deal was that: 'In short, the poorest of the poor are not of any concern. The deal only relates to rewarding the "players", the people who are in the inner circle of the ANC leadership. This is just one instance, but it is a most glaring instance that exemplifies the erosion of any semblance of moral integrity once attached to the ANC. It has nothing to do with the ANC that once pledged to make "a better life for all".'[23]

South Africa's known mineral resources were valued at $2.5 trillion in 2013[24] but much remains to be prospected. It is quite staggering that an economy with such a unique natural endowment can be so mismanaged as to produce trade and fiscal deficits, mass unemployment, growing debt and the looming threat of IMF intervention. It is rather like watching a vintage and still working Rolls-Royce having its parts sold off, one by one, for scrap.

But the adventure has at least one more chapter. Initial research suggests that South Africa has one of the largest reserves of shale gas in the world – 485 trillion cubic feet – largely under the southern Karoo. Econometrix calls this 'a transformational opportunity for the South African economy and those who depend upon it for a livelihood'.[25] However, to the astonishment of potential investors, the government announced in October 2013 that it would take a 'free carry' of 20 per cent of all new oil and gas projects and also reserve the right to buy another 30 per cent at market prices. What this means is that the state would, without making any payment, simply be deemed to own 20 per cent of any new venture and then, if indeed large gas reserves are found, would be able to take control of the company simply by buying 30 per cent of the shares. So the private company would have to pay 100 per cent of all the prospecting and drilling costs only to see control pass to the state for a mere 30 per cent of the value.[26] In February 2014 the government added a further amendment to the effect that if the state deemed any mineral resource to be 'strategic' it could then buy it at below-market prices.[27] It would be hard to imagine a formula more likely to drive away investment. Sure enough, in September 2014 Sasol – which, in partnership with Italy's ENI, was exploring for oil and gas off the Durban coast – announced that they would cease all spending on the project until it was clear whether the government was really going to go ahead with this legislation.[28]

The collapse of manufacturing

Manufacturing industry has never been robust in South Africa but the ANC government came to power determined to expand it and to reduce

South Africa's over-reliance on mining. Partly this was because a strong manufacturing sector was seen as symbolic of the sort of country South Africa wanted to be; partly it was because it seemed the best way to generate jobs; and partly it was because the ANC/SACP saw themselves as the party of the working class and therefore wanted a strong industrial proletariat. The left has been particularly determined on this agenda and everything that communist ministers like Rob Davies and Ebrahim Patel did was focused towards that. Much of it was misconceived – for example the tremendous push to greater beneficiation of mineral products, despite the fact that the World Bank had over many years tried to persuade African countries that this was the wrong way to go.[29]

The World Bank argues that forward linkages to beneficiation will never work in competition with mineral-processing behemoths like China, the EU and USA. Nor will backward linkages (to engineering, services and higher education) in competition with such successful cases as Canada and Australia. Most African economies simply can't compete with such networks. The only sensible alternative is the creation of sovereign wealth funds which can be used for diverse purposes. In effect South Africa has refused to listen to any of this and continues, forlornly, to preach the doctrine of beneficiation and indeed, to try to force it upon mining companies by punitive taxation.

Not only has this failed, but the ANC government has presided over an unprecedented period of de-industrialisation. In 1994 manufacturing accounted for around 23

24 per cent of GDP. Twenty years later this had fallen to 11.1 per cent.[30] The combination of tariff liberalisation, high wage rates, a very high strike rate, and policies which inhibit both foreign and domestic investment have all played their part. Inevitably the stringent BEE codes are a major brake on both progress and profitability. Just how ridiculous the situation is may be judged from the fact that the state-owned freight and logistics group, Transnet, asked to be excused from the full force of BEE requirements for its expenditure of billions of rands on over 1 000 new locomotives.[31] Perhaps the key symbolic moment came in 2013 with the announcement by BMW that it had cancelled its plans for further investment in South Africa after a particularly prolonged and violent strike wave led by the

metalworkers' union, Numsa.[32]

Such a decision was bound to be massively influential. It is not just that soaring wage increases saw South African unit labour costs rise by 60 per cent between 2007 and 2013,[33] but that this occurred within the context of falling productivity. In many industries – led by the public sector – workers simply get away with whatever they can. Thus the number of workers absent on sick-leave more than quintupled between 2001 and 2013 and in the period 2009–2013 a whole one quarter of South African workers took their full maximum statutory sick-leave allowance.[34]

From a peak in 1993 labour productivity overall had declined by a stunning 41.2 per cent by 2013. Indeed, productivity is now down by nearly a third since 1967. This trend – strongly encouraged by the ANC's dependence on Cosatu – is simply disastrous. Nissan nervously notes that, despite all the subsidies paid by government, it now costs 20 per cent more to make a car in South Africa than in Thailand.[35] Such figures are rapidly driving new investment in that sector away from South Africa. According to Deloitte's 2013 Global Manufacturing Competitive Index, China is the number 1 competitive country for manufacturing and India will shortly join it at the top of the table. South Africa was ranked 24 out of 38 alongside bombed-out East European economies and oil-rich states like Saudi Arabia and the UAE – dreadful company.[36]

To a considerable extent this has been the result of allowing the Cosatu unions to rule the labour market, a decision made by Tito Mboweni when he was minister of labour. He was rewarded for this disastrous decision with the governorship of the Reserve Bank. Loane Sharp, a labour economist at Adcorp, a labour-contracting company, suggests that for market forces to be allowed to re-assert themselves in the labour market one would need to cut all public sector wages in half.[37] A situation in which the average public sector worker earns more than an entrepreneur is by definition ruinous.

The basic problem with South Africa's manufacturing industry has always been that while it could not compete with Europe on quality or productivity, its relatively high wage rates also made it uncompetitive with Asia. Unit costs are twice as high as in Indonesia, Malaysia or Taiwan and they are even slightly higher than in the USA.[38] True, some sectors have a local advantage in that they are producing directly for the local mining industry – but manufacturing in general enjoys no such advantage. The country's growing current account deficit in part reflects this weakness in manufacturing. The government response – trying to force businesses to become manufacturers – is as likely to work as trying to make water run uphill.

The suicidal combination of soaring wage levels with collapsing productivity is almost without international parallel. It can only be understood as a result of a strange combination of factors. First, Cosatu has since 1994 enjoyed a highly protected niche in which it has safeguarded the interests of a tiny labour aristocracy at the expense of the vast mass of the unemployed. Second, workers have exploited this new and favourable situation to get away with what they can. Third, the sight of elite-level corruption and the general atmosphere engendered by a frantic rush towards black self-enrichment have created a great emulative wave: crudely put, if there is a feeding frenzy, no one wants to be left out. This motive is prominent not only in the labour movement but in society at large, visible in the ubiquitous township protests demanding better goods and services. This does not happen in other African societies because there is a general consciousness that their countries are poor. Many South Africans, on the contrary, are convinced that their country is rich and that if one keeps up the pressure – just as the ANC did during the struggle – then in the end the walls of Jericho will fall and they too will benefit. Hence the common but utterly fanciful idea of 'an economic Codesa': that all that is needed is for business, labour and government to sit down together and make a deal by which everyone becomes richer. This is the South African equivalent of a cargo cult: if only one goes through the right procedures one's boat will come in.

How can anyone believe in anything so silly? The answer is an entrenched parochialism, born of the fact that South Africa is an isolated society at the southern tip of Africa, not much in contact with the rest of Africa, and thousands of miles away from all its main trade partners. It was this parochialism which allowed white South Africa to continue with legally entrenched discrimination long after it had been abandoned elsewhere. It is the same parochialism which allows the SACP to survive when communism elsewhere has collapsed. And, as a general rule of thumb, the lower down the social scale one goes, the greater the parochialism. Thus Afrikaner whites were far more parochial than their English-speaking peers, and today's ruling coalition is far more parochial than that. This parochialism is a blight on the country. It enables the ANC and SACP to dream of socialism in one country via the National Democratic Revolution, despite the fact that such notions belong in a museum of Soviet socialism the best part of a century ago. Comparisons with other middle-income countries, the views of the rating agencies, the IMF and the developed world are all impatiently dismissed. Africans from elsewhere in Africa enjoy visiting South Africa, but they often shake their heads and suggest that the locals are mad. There is a serious reality gap and when this is closed – as shortly it will be – there will be great expressions of pain, horror and indignation. What is really worrying is that this combination may lead to simple denial.

One can already espy this in many declarations of the SACP. Thus, for example, the declaration of the 7th Provincial Congress of the KwaZulu-Natal SACP (ie Nzimande's home province):

> The Congress unanimously agree (*sic*) with the notion that socialism
> did not fail, the people failed socialism.[39]

The problem, meanwhile, is that the situation is getting rapidly worse. The World Bank carried out a special study of South Africa's export competitiveness in 2013.[40] This sheds considerable light on the alarmingly weakened state both of South Africa's recent export performance and of its manufacturing sector. The Bank had been struck by the fact that since 2005 South Africa's total exports had grown in real terms at only 0.6 per cent per annum, or less than one tenth as fast as the 6.4 per cent average performance of other middle-income countries. Equally striking was the fact that this 0.6 per cent was only one tenth the 6 per cent growth rate targeted for exports in South Africa's own National Development Plan. Clearly, something was going badly wrong.

As the Bank's report says, actually countries don't export anything; companies do. So their analysis is based on an exhaustive study of 20 000 South African companies. They found that 93 per cent of all South African exports were accounted for by just 1 000 large companies, but that even these large companies were losing export momentum, creating fewer new products and not expanding into new markets. In the same period 2005–2013 there had been a dramatic shift in South Africa's export orientation so that the Rest of Africa was now its main market, having overtaken the EU.

This poor export performance lies at the root of South Africa's growing current account deficit and thus of its growing vulnerability to external capital flows, particularly since there is no end in sight to the budget deficit. The Bank put the current account deficit at 5.9 per cent of GDP in 2013 and a predicted 6.3 per cent in 2014 and 6.4 per cent in 2015.[41] While these two deficits continue, South Africa's debt can only increase. Its main hope of escaping from this debt trap is higher exports, particularly with a dramatically weakened rand. But if exports don't respond – and thus far they haven't – South Africa really is in trouble.

The Bank found that over half of all South Africa's exports were in the fuels/minerals/metals sector and that this sector had accounted for virtually all export growth since 2007. However, this growth derived entirely from higher commodity prices; the actual volume of minerals exported was flat.

Exports from the next sector, chemicals, metal manufactures and automobiles, had fallen in both volume and value since 2007. Indeed, export volumes from this sector were lower in 2013 than in 2001. This was despite the fact that automobile manufacturing was heavily subsidised by the state through the Motor Industry Development Programme (from 2013 the Automotive Production and Development Programme (APDP)), which has seen South African auto production double since 1994, constituting 6 per cent of GDP and no less than 12 per cent of total exports.[42] This is the one great success of the ANC's push for industrialisation. The Volkswagen and BMW plants are critical to this, with the Mercedes plant very much the jewel in the crown. Thabo Mbeki, when president, took enormous pride in the fact that South Africa was exporting something as sophisticated as Mercedes and BMW cars to the rest of the world. Conspicuously, there are no BEE shares in any of these companies (or in the Toyota, Nissan, Honda or Ford plants in South Africa). Mbeki reportedly tried to raise the subject with the then head of Mercedes, Jurgen Schremp, and was told 'Don't even think about it'[43] – advice he wisely took, since the ANC government knows it is fortunate to have such large investors and employers in the country.

Indeed, the motor industry is very much the prize exhibit by government of the virtues of protectionist regulation, and for protectionist ministers like Davies and Patel, a possible model for the future.

Most of South Africa's car exports are to the developed world. One might have expected that the general switch of export focus towards the rest of Africa would have enabled South Africa's somewhat crude but cost-effective manufactures (Defy white goods, Kenwood kitchen machines, house and garden tools, and so on) to thrive, but in fact this has not happened – a good indicator of just how repressed the manufacturing sector now is.

Finally there are the service sector's exports. Since this sector now accounts for 66 per cent of South Africa's GDP one might have expected it also to be a major export sector, but in fact the growth of exports in services has been far lower not only than in the other Brics countries, but also than in such other developing countries as Colombia, Thailand or Turkey.

Alarm bells are ringing. The performance of the big companies is slowing. Some export products – multi-ply paper, paperboard and bovine leather, for example – are simply disappearing. A worryingly large proportion of the country's exports are produced by the medium- or high-tech sectors and depend on considerable capital investment and small amounts of highly skilled labour. What South Africa needs is export industries which use large amounts of unskilled or low-skilled labour. Moreover, the dependence on highly skilled labour is a vulnerability given the somewhat rocky state of South African education.

But the greatest reverse came in October 2013 in the wake of a seven-week strike by Numsa in the motor industry. Numsa is an extreme-left union which treats employers as simply 'the class enemy'. And a Numsa strike is invariably violent. Like many unions, the lesson it learnt from being in the struggle was that violence works quicker and more thoroughly than a simple withdrawal of labour, so a Numsa strike always means that armed militants will go round threatening to kill any workers who do not stay away. The government made no move to intervene to stop the strike.

This was too much for BMW, which on 3 October issued the following statement: 'Any plans to expand our plant or capacity further have been put indefinitely on hold. Future decisions [on where new models are to be built] are being made where South Africa would have been in the running. Based on the current environment, we're definitely not. You could say things have changed.'[44] In particular, it emerged that BMW had been considering making its plant at Rosslyn (Gauteng) the single world producer of a new model BMW. But the Numsa strike, which had cost BMW 12.5 per cent of its entire annual production in South Africa, had resulted in Rosslyn being 'taken off the bidding table for that model',[45] a huge loss in high-tech investment, improved local skills and jobs. Even a former SACP member like Gill Marcus, then governor of the Reserve Bank, could not restrain herself from publicly mourning the effects of such ill-judged industrial action.[46]

Since BMW is the world's largest manufacturer of luxury cars and a pivotal part of the South African motor industry, this had some impact. In February 2014 Nissan confirmed that they had narrowed their search for a country in which to produce the new Datsun to just four (of which South Africa was one), but after extensive talks with government had decided against South Africa because labour unrest there effectively negated the subsidies they would receive under the APDP.[47]

South Africa's switch towards the African market in recent years has been very pronounced – for example 60 per cent of all its service sector exports now go to the rest of Africa. At the same time exports to the EU have fallen off a cliff: they were down 39 per cent in 2008/9 and even after a degree of recovery in Europe they were still 29 per cent down on the 2007 figure in 2013.

The World Bank suggests a number of reasons lying behind this poor export performance, including over-regulation and the lack of sufficient competition, and a transport infrastructure that is both expensive and poorly managed. Workers at South African ports, on average, are able to load 17 containers an hour, compared to a global average of 35 per hour.[48]

The combinations of poor management, low productivity and a turbulent trade union movement have resulted in South African port tariffs being 360 per cent of the global average.[49] This constitutes a tremendous disincentive for importers and exporters. At the same time there are worrying trends in terms of quality. For example, South Africa's iron and steel exports are more and more basic and low quality; while high-quality steels made up 40 per cent of exports in 2000, by 2012 this figure had fallen to under 15 per cent.[50]

Another problem that is strongly inhibiting export performance is a weak information and computer technology (ICT) sector. The paradoxical situation is that South Africa has Africa's most advanced telecom network but extreme regulatory constraints prevent competition in this sector, essentially to the benefit of the state-owned Telkom, which is a very poor performer. The result has been to throttle South Africa's once promising ICT sector. Whereas this sector was ranked 55th in the world in 2000, by 2012 South Africa had fallen to 98th.[51] This also results in higher than average telecom costs – for example South Africa's broadband prices are almost twice those of Mauritius, which is one of the reasons there has been a considerable outflow of financial services industries to Mauritius. This is a remarkable turn-around, given that the apartheid era bequeathed South Africa an impressive ICT sector, due to a combination of military invest-ment and domestic development forced by sanctions abroad. It is also another perfect example of the state's repression of economic activity: in effect the whole sector has been mortgaged to the need to prop up Telkom.

Even South Africa's great success in African markets recently is some-thing of a mixed blessing, for these markets often absorb relatively infe-rior goods (for example low-quality iron and steel) and they thus involve a degree of trading down compared to exporting to the highly sophisticated EU market. Most other countries find African markets extremely difficult. Such markets are characterised by poor transport, weak border manage-ment, weak logistics, very cumbersome fiscal regulation, poorly designed technical regulations and standards, plus various other non-tariff barriers such as import bans, permit requirements and licensing. Faced with this jungle of constraints, South Africa has benefited partly because of its sheer proximity to other African markets but particularly because of its local knowledge of how to overcome such constraints. This is all very well, but as the World Bank points out, while African markets are growing very rap-idly, the EU market is still 30 times bigger than the Rest of Africa market.

For all that, South African business has embraced the rest of Africa as both the new frontier and the promised land. The banks, SAB-Miller and retailers have been particularly aggressive in their expansion. Quite apart from sheer growth, businessmen are attracted by far looser labour laws and much cheaper labour costs. Indeed, labour economist Loane Sharp believes that 'over a ten-year horizon South Africa will become irrelevant to large companies' expansion plans ... Labour laws are moving in the wrong direction and becoming more and more conservative, not less. Labour costs are rising in SA at an extraordinary rate. If you include bonuses and overtime, they are growing at about 13 per cent p.a. – nearly three times the consumer inflation rate.'[52]

Inevitably, faced with figures like that, South African companies have been deciding *en masse* not to invest more in their home businesses. Instead they are either pushing investment flows abroad or simply letting profits pile up in cash: by 2014 the resulting cash mountain was estimated at R500 billion. Company treasurers have invested a good deal in the local stock market simply to preserve values – which is why the stock market has held up relatively well. The only other alternative has been to return more cash to shareholders as dividends. Thus in 2012–2013 for the first time in 30 years dividend growth in South Africa's equity market overtook earnings growth, the surest possible indicator of a collective investment strike.[53]

This in turn has slowed South Africa's growth to a crawl. The country's economy needs to grow at a yearly 4 per cent if it is to absorb school-leavers and other new entrants into the job market. But in 2013, when many other African countries were growing at 5–8 per cent, the South African economy grew by just 1.9 per cent. The South African Treasury forecast for 2014 was for growth of 2.5–3 per cent but the IMF repeatedly lowered its estimate, finally down to 1.4 per cent – a figure finally accepted by the Treasury in October 2014. Adcorp's Loane Sharp pointed out the consequences: 'The retrenchment rate is now at a 10-year high,' he said, 'while labour mobility rate is at 10-year low.'[54] Goolam Ballim of Standard Bank suggested that whereas the government forecast 3.5 per cent growth in 2015, the real outcome would be under 2 per cent. The problem, he said, chillingly, was that 'South Africa's latent productive capacity is being eroded and the country's potential growth rate has likely fallen below 3 per cent'.[55] Again, this is a measure of how effectively economic growth has been stifled by the government. Predictably, just as the figures above were released the government announced that unemployment had fallen, but the announcement was met with derision – nobody believed government figures any more.[56]

The tragedy of commercial agriculture

Simultaneously, a colossal tragedy was overtaking South African commercial agriculture. Already, as the number of farmers shrinks, the old days of large surpluses in agricultural trade are over and at best the country is roughly in balance. If the current attrition in the number of farmers continues there seems no doubt that the country will cease to be able to feed itself, with potentially explosive results.

The most rapid growth in agricultural exports over the recent period has been in exports to Africa – which are also much more profitable than exports to the EU. Now, with rapid demographic and economic growth throughout the rest of Africa, a once-in-a-century opportunity is opening up for South African agricultural exports. Indeed, South Africa's food exports to the rest of Africa were forecast to overtake its exports to Europe by 2020, but in fact this happened in 2012.[57] But, as Professor Nick Vink (Stellenbosch) pointed out, 'We are not witnessing additional investment into plant. SA farmers will expand only to meet demand from the SA market. They are not gearing up to serve the rest of the African market.'[58] John Purchase, CEO of the Agricultural Business Chamber, agreed with this assessment and said that 'farmers weren't investing in new expansion because of considerable policy uncertainty over water and land reform, the threat of further labour unrest and the near impossibility of getting any additional electricity supply connections on farms … Instead, given farmers' concerns over future land reform, they are diversifying their risk by investing in a big way in Mozambique and Zambia.'[59]

In 2014 the government struck another enormous blow at commercial farming by bringing in a new Restitution of Land Rights Amendment Bill which re-opened land claims for a further five years and even allowed claimants who had lost their case to start all over again. This prolonged yet again the complete uncertainty surrounding agricultural land ownership which had already lasted 20 years. Earlier, farmers had been promised that only claims lodged before the 1998 deadline would be valid – and even dealing with those will take the Land Claims Commission until 2029. The result is that farmers now have to live in a virtually permanent state of insecurity – which leads many to quit farming, and inhibits farmers from investing. Frans Cronje, Director of the South African Institute of Race Relations, termed the new Bill 'the beginning of the end for commercial agriculture'.[60] The new Act was expected to see a further 397 000 land claims worth R179 billion.[61]

But the budget for 2014/15 allows just R2.7 billion for these purposes and assumes this figure will not rise for the next three years.[62] Thus the new legislation is in the purest sense irresponsible: it deliberately promises what it cannot possibly deliver. The fact that this will create mayhem is simply less important than competing with the EFF's aim of carrying out Mugabe-style land seizures. Much the same can be said of the Agriculture Ministry's proposals, late in the election campaign, that 50 per cent of all commercial farms be expropriated by the state without compensation and given to the farm workers, with farmers obliged by law to stay on their farms and train workers in farm management. This proposal was clearly unconstitutional and unworkable as well as a major threat to food security.[63]

The SAIRR's Frans Cronje added that this Bill, together with the accompanying Protection and Promotion of Investment Bill (which allows the state to take over any property as 'custodian', which is not defined as expropriation and therefore does not merit compensation) 'could devastate the rural economy on a scale comparable to Britain's "scorched earth" policy during the Boer War'. He advised all commercial farmers 'to start making plans'.[64]

It would be difficult to put the problem of the state repression of economic activity more clearly. With food demand growing throughout the developing world, an agricultural bonanza beckons – and there is more unused arable land in Southern Africa than anywhere else in the world.[65] Yet despite that, South Africa, like Zimbabwe, has a steady policy of taking commercially farmed land out of production and (in effect) returning it to subsistence. Meanwhile, the old bantustan areas of South Africa remain, quite deliberately, without individual title to land and are sinks of persistent rural poverty. Under a different regime this would be a period of headlong investment and growth, of increasing employment, production and exports and of transforming the Transkei and Ciskei into booming agricultural economies. Better than that, such a boom would see South Africa ideally placed to lead the necessary transformation of agriculture throughout Africa. This enormous opportunity is being squandered.

However, things are worse than that. For most of its history South Africa has had a huge agricultural surplus to export. Under ANC governance this has been reduced to a situation where food imports and exports are barely in balance. Indeed, this is one of the major reasons for the deterioration of the trade balance, although government policy effectively ignores this crucial fact. Even worse is the fact that in the old bantustan areas of South Africa – where there are no white farmers and thus no land reform – agricultural support services have nonetheless been withdrawn, with the result that 'at most 20 per cent of the population are food secure'.[66] This is the real bottom line: under ANC rule more and more South Africans are going to bed hungry. No wonder the distribution of food parcels is an ever-more-present part of ANC election tactics, even at municipal level.

Thus the ANC government has, in general, had a strongly repressive effect on economic growth. It took only 14 years to so mismanage its power supply that a 25 per cent safety margin was gradually reversed by a policy of deliberately banning the building of new power stations. After all its boasts, the ANC had thus reduced South Africa to the enforced backwardness seen so widely elsewhere on the continent. Not only was the result strongly repressive of growth in all sectors of the economy, but the rocketing of power prices made many enterprises marginal, chasing away investment in power-heavy industries such as aluminium smelters and threatening many mines with closure.

Having, in opposition, campaigned for many years for disinvestment, the ANC in power has achieved disinvestment on a massive scale. The result, ever-higher unemployment, stands in violent contrast to the elite grab for resources and riches of every kind and the ever-growing inequalities which this produces. This is simply not a sustainable model. The only question is how and when it will collapse.

Such a collapse will, in South Africa's case, pose some very uncomfortable questions. Was Mandela a false prophet, was he the father of this huge failure? Was the ANC simply incapable of governing? Or was South Africa a particularly difficult case? Was there any way of preventing the ANC from collapsing into rent-seeking, gangsterism and the criminalisation of the state? And so on. Already, one notes, SACP stalwarts such as Ronnie

Kasrils and Jeremy Cronin have begun to devote much time to the question of 'where did it all go wrong?' Their answer – that South Africa missed the chance to advance towards socialism in one country at some point in the 1990s – is what might be expected. In effect, they hoped that a Communist Party elite would keep tight (and undemocratic) control so as to guide the transition to socialism. Instead, of course, they ended up with a sort of democracy which enabled a corrupt, unruly but genuinely popular African nationalism to misbehave in all the same ways that it has throughout the continent. A perspective which relied on a continuing denial of democracy is hardly worth considering.

More significant is the fact that even such stalwarts accept that things have gone completely wrong under a government in which they both participated and are now looking for alibis. What is not in dispute is that things have gone wrong; that the reasons lie some way back in the past; and that probably this means that they are irremediable. Both Kasrils and Cronin treat socialism as something which might have happened if only things had gone differently in the 1990s, but which is impossible now.

The continuing primacy of the land question

The ANC proceeded from the assumption that 30 per cent of arable land (a figure derived from the World Bank) must be redistributed to dispossessed communities or small African farmers. This target took no cognisance of the fact that farming is nowadays a very specialised activity and that many commercial farmers run quite sophisticated operations with computer-operated grain silos, extremely complex irrigation equipment, a keen knowledge of movements in commodities futures markets and so forth. There is no easy way that a subsistence African farmer or farm worker can take over and run a commercial farm; indeed, the number of people who even wish to do so is severely limited. On top of that the ANC government has abolished all the old privileges enjoyed by commercial farmers (such as freedom from paying rates) and made them subject to much more demanding labour laws, tougher restrictions on water use and so forth.

Moreover, agricultural protectionism has been abolished by South Africa but not by its competitors, and even experienced farmers with latifundia find it hard to compete.

Given all this it is not surprising that over 90 per cent of farms redistributed by the state to African communities fail and usually revert very quickly either to subsistence farming or to squatter camps. Finally, the state has effectively done nothing to prevent attacks on farmers and has meanwhile forbidden the farm commandos which were the farmers' main protection, so farming is also a dangerous occupation.

The result has been the dispersal of (white) commercial farmers to all points of the compass – Zambia, Mozambique, Nigeria, Congo-Brazzaville, Georgia, and so on, for all these countries greatly value the chance to acquire such experienced and productive farmers. Within South Africa the number of commercial farmers has shrunk from 60 938 in 1996 to 45 818 in 2002 and 39 966 in 2007.[67] Shrinkage has continued and it is predicted that by 2030 there will be just 8 000 commercial farmers. Up until now the effects have been cushioned by the remaining farmers getting better yields from a reducing acreage. But this cannot continue. After centuries in which South Africa was not only self-sufficient but a huge food exporter, by 2010 the country had reached a position where food exports of $6.8 billion were almost balanced by food imports of $5.2 billion.[68] This trend contributes heavily to the country's chronic balance of payments problem.

Worse, however, the government has not only extended the horizon for land claims almost indefinitely but has now also said that the timeline for claims can be extended back before 1900. The result is that in some provinces virtually every farm is under claim – for making a claim is free. In the end farmers get fed up holding off investment for years on end and just sell to get rid of the problem. The result is always the same: fewer productive farms. With most white farmers aged 50 and over, everything suggests that a calamitous drop in food security lies ahead.

In 2013 the government, scared by the Arab Spring, commissioned the National Intelligence Agency to see what South Africa could learn. The NIA reported that the key common factor behind the Spring was rising food prices.[69] Pretoria's response was to seek immediate consultations with

AgriSA about food security – to the delight of the farmers, who had been trying to interest the government in the subject for years. Of particular concern was the staple of white maize: South African farmers produce this at R2 200 a ton, while foreign imports cost R3 600 a ton, so the loss of self-sufficiency in this area would mean a price rise of at least 63 per cent.[70] Yet the only government initiative to result from this was, laughably, the proposal that sales of land to foreigners be forbidden. Indeed, the land affairs minister, Gugile Nkwinti, actually envisaged getting rid of even those foreigners who own land now.[71] This was a perfect example of ideology preventing a sensible policy response, even at the possible cost of regime instability or overthrow.

The various farmers' organisations are wont to point out that the ANC government has been lucky to date in that it has not yet had to deal with a major drought. But by early 2014 a localised drought in parts of the North West and Free State had produced a 50 per cent increase in maize prices, with knock-on effects in poultry feed, etc.[72] In fact the drought in the North West, along with the Northern Cape, was already in its third year, by which time it was the worst in over 80 years. Cattle and sheep farmers throughout the affected areas sold off their herds at depressed prices because of a simple inability to feed them. The farmers were highly critical because, contrary to all previous practice under apartheid governments, the ANC government had made no move at all towards drought relief, even though thousands of farm workers would be laid off, resulting in near-famine conditions for their families.[73]

The writing on the wall

The economy is in desperate trouble. Strong government intervention in both mining and agriculture has seen investment fall badly in each, while depressed demand and high wage demands made manufacturing increasingly vulnerable. Over the five years 2008–2013 manufacturing lost almost 300 000 jobs as the manufacturing sector shrank year by year.[74] The result, as the world recovered from the 2009 crisis, was a large and growing trade gap. If imports and exports in 2005 = 100, then by 2009 South African imports had risen to 103 and exports had fallen to 94. Then by 2012 exports had recovered to 110 but imports had risen to 140, producing a growing trade deficit.[75] Thus South Africa emerged from the crisis with a trade deficit of around 6 per cent of GDP and a budget deficit of about the same. A small amount of the fiscal deficit could be funded by local investment in government bonds but this still left deficits totalling around 10 per cent of GDP to be funded by foreign investments or loans. And with the government effectively repressing growth in mining, agriculture and manufacturing, this was a very big ask. Hence the growing crisis.

A particularly striking feature of the crisis is that it evolved in an atmosphere of complete public ignorance. When I gave an earlier version of this chapter to a conference in Oxford in April 2014 it was criticised by Professor Ian Goldin (who had had a lengthy career working as an economist for the South African government). He asserted that 'South Africa has one of the best managed economies in the world'. Similarly, the wage claims by the civil service unions noted above suggest that they are living in some alternative reality. However, those fantasies are clearly shared by their employers, for when the figures came in for the second quarter of 2014, economists were amazed to see that there had been a 155 000 jump in the number of jobs. It turned out, however, that almost all these were public sector jobs.[76] So despite everything the IMF and the Treasury had had to say about the urgent need to reduce the public sector salary bill, public sector employers had gaily carried on hiring as if there were no constraints.

It didn't stop there. In September 2014 the South African Treasury announced that R466 billion of guarantees had been extended to state-owned enterprises and that this was the absolute limit.[77] This left big questions unanswered as to how the state was going to fund the R225-billion deficit looming in Eskom, let alone the numerous other loss-making SOEs. The state was unable to sign off and publish the accounts for SAA and its junior line, SA Express, because they had deficits which could not be met. At the same time, Gwede Mantashe attacked business as 'unpatriotic' because it was holding over R500 billion in uninvested profits – without reflecting quite why there was such a protracted investment strike, let alone considering that such rhetoric was bound to lead to more capital flight. As the state moves ever closer to bankruptcy there is little doubt that this will become an increasingly sore point.

Despite all this writing on the wall the Zuma government announced that it would leverage state resources in order to create 'a hundred black industrialists', a peculiar priority for a government facing the imminent necessity for large spending cuts. Odder still, Tito Mboweni, a previous governor of the Reserve Bank, launched a campaign for the government to set up a state bank (which he would head), a cause quickly taken up by deputy president Cyril Ramaphosa. These were supposedly two of the more economically literate ANC figures, but it was hard to imagine where they thought the government would find the at least R100 billion required to capitalise such a bank.[78] Oddest of all, immediately following a trip to Moscow by President Zuma it was announced that South Africa had agreed that Russia would build a fleet of eight or nine nuclear power stations in various parts of South Africa at a cost estimated at between R500 billion and R1 trillion. No one could possibly imagine how this could be afforded.

For a while, no doubt, ignorance will continue to be bliss and one can enjoy believing that luxuries like a state bank are affordable or that 'South Africa has one of the best managed economies in the world'. It is rather like Captain Edward John Smith of the *Titanic* saying 'Icebergs? What icebergs?'

CHAPTER EIGHT

The View from the IMF

The IMF conducts annual country consultations under its Article IV. In 2012 the visiting IMF delegation expressed considerable shock at Pretoria's priorities. To be sure, a recession required Keynesian counter-cyclical public expenditure but this should have been on infrastructure in order to mop up some of the mountainous unemployment and to make the country more competitive ready for the upturn. Instead the government had borrowed massively abroad merely in order to give the money away to already overpaid public sector workers. As a result, the IMF warned, public spending needed to be completely 'rebalanced'. The IMF could hardly contain its horror at the government's complete disregard for the unemployed: 'Raising real public sector wages during the peak of the recession contributed to one of the largest job-shedding experiences amongst emerging markets during the global financial crisis.'[1] The fact that the IMF now evinces more concern for South Africa's unemployed than does its own government is no small measure of the ANC's journey since 1994.

Though expressed in diplomatic understatement, the IMF could not disguise its alarm. It 'urged the authorities to bring back the [public sector] wage bill to pre-crisis levels and cautioned that further slippage could erode the government's credibility at a delicate global juncture when rating agencies are questioning its ability to rein in spending'. The IMF warned that public sector pay did not need just to be stabilised but to be 'lowered'. It pointed out how the government wage bill in South Africa compared to its middle-income peers – Chile, Colombia, Russia, Israel, Poland, Thailand, Hungary, the Slovak Republic, Romania and Turkey:

- ❏ As a share of GDP (14 per cent) it was the highest of the entire group and more than twice as high as Chile (6 per cent).
- ❏ As a share of fiscal revenue it was, at nearly 40 per cent, by far the highest in the group and nearly twice the level of the Slovak Republic (21 per cent).
- ❏ As a share of government spending it was the second highest at 38 per cent, over twice as high as the Slovak Republic (18 per cent).
- ❏ As a share of the work force (22 per cent) it was by far the highest and four times as much as Colombia.[2]

Thus South Africa's 'bureaucratic bourgeoisie' is quite exceptional in international terms and constitutes a significant national handicap. No doubt the urge for primary accumulation is just as fierce in other African countries, but the fact that South Africa has much greater resources has allowed this veritable monster to feed and grow to a size seen nowhere else on the continent. The IMF, clearly shocked by what it saw, warned that the government was paying nothing like sufficient attention to the problem of mass unemployment which, it warned, was 'politically and socially unsustainable' and added that 'the government is finding it difficult to bring the public sector wage bill under control ... controlling the public sector wage bill now represents an important test of the government's political resolve and strength'.[3] It is, indeed, as if public sector workers existed on another planet. In 2000 their wages were on average 12 per cent higher than private sector wages. By 2010 their wages were 43.6 per cent higher on average.[4]

The idea that a government can lose control of the public sector it presides over and in fact be pushed around by public sector workers may seem odd at first sight but this situation is the result of a long period of misgovernance and, often, simply a lack of any governance. As we saw in Chapter Five, the South African Democratic Teachers Union is a vital part of Cosatu and thus of Zuma's ruling coalition. Sadtu has been primarily responsible for the collapse of educational standards in black schools since 1994 but no president or education minister has been willing to confront the union. Instead the government does whatever Sadtu says and even appoints its leaders to the cabinet.

Similarly, the police have almost completely escaped from official control. Torture and maltreatment of prisoners in police custody have skyrocketed to a level far worse than under apartheid. The number of civil claims against the police for rape, assault, corruption, wrongful arrest and the like doubled in 2012–13 and this is reflected in an ever-increasing figure for contingent liabilities (that is, liabilities depending on the outcomes of court cases) which quadrupled from R5.3 billion in 2006 to R20.5 billion in 2011–12, by which time it accounted for 32.8 per cent of the entire police budget.[5] But this is not the same situation as with Sadtu: police misbehaviour occurs not because the police union ordains it but because all meaningful discipline has broken down.

The government is perfectly aware that it has lost control of the police and is mainly concerned to hide this situation from the public. Thus its attempts to prevent Helen Zille from setting up a commission of inquiry into policing in Khayelitsha, the country's biggest squatter camp. Inevitably, when the commission finally met it heard repeated testimony to the fact that the police had largely given up bothering about this vast settlement where, as a result, vigilante justice rules and, on average, one person a week is burnt to death in a necklacing. No one had ordered the police to neglect Khayelitsha – they had just decided on their own to ignore this settlement of over half a million people. The commission heard that Khayelitsha was 'a dumping ground for incapable officers'[6] and even the police commissioner for the Western Cape, Arno Lamoer, had to apologise to Khayelitsha residents for the sub-standard policing they had to endure.[7]

Among the victims of this deliberate ANC policy to starve the sole Opposition-controlled province of policing[8] was the Cosatu general secretary, Zwelinzima Vavi, whose great-niece was murdered in Khayelitsha. Vavi bitterly declared that it had taken the police five days to inform the family of the girl's death and that after three weeks the police had done absolutely nothing. His family, he averred, were actively considering the alternative of vigilante violence because of the uselessness of the police.[9] Surveys show that Khayelitsha residents have far more confidence in taxi bosses than in the police to catch the culprits and punish them.[10]

The problem is nationwide. In Relela, Limpopo, in January 2014 the body of a 16-year-old girl was discovered. Her hands had been cut off before she'd been disembowelled, presumably for *muti* reasons. This triggered violent community protests against the lack of policing. The police responded to this with live ammunition, shooting three of the protestors dead.[11] In similar fashion the police in Durban were such a law unto themselves that they stormed the city and harassed motorists in pursuit of a pay increase, threatening to 'bring the city to its knees' by deliberately jamming all its arterial routes.[12]

What is true of teachers and policemen is true of many other public sector workers who can all hold the government to ransom and whose unions are a crucial source of support for Zuma. The government does not rule these groups; these groups rule the government. Why has this happened when it did not happen under apartheid? The key, as we have seen, is that the ANC regime is characterised not merely by misgovernance but by no governance. But nature abhors a vacuum and when that lack of governance became clear, these subaltern groups merely seized the opportunity presented to them. It will take a government of Thatcherite zeal and ruthlessness to dispossess them now.

The developing crisis

From the IMF on down commentators and analysts have come to doubt whether the government any longer has the ability to hold the line against the public sector unions. Standard Bank's chief economist, Kevin Lings, pointed out in 2012 that government expenditure had gone from 28.5 per cent of GDP in 2007–08 to 33.7 per cent in 2009–10 and that in just two years the government's own wage bill had increased by 40.4 per cent, while capital spending on infrastructure had essentially gone nowhere.[13] Indeed, each year South Africans got used to President Zuma making much the same budget speech, promising hundreds of billions in infrastructure investment – which never happened. The government was anxious that the money would be needed for other things and didn't quite have the nerve to borrow to invest.

This was understandable. As the ratings agencies downgraded South Africa's bonds, the cost of borrowing rose. In October 2012 the IMF warned South Africa about its rising public debt – by then 41 per cent of GDP. Once one included debt accumulating to the parastatals, it had already risen to over R1 trillion.[14] In fact, of course, a debt ratio of 41 per cent of GDP is not high, though it is rising. But what is striking is the diminishing willingness of foreigners to fund that debt. In 2011–12 the foreign debt stood at R116.9 billion out of a total of R1187.8 billion. But the projection for 2014–15 was foreign debt of R99.3 billion out of a total of R1694.9 billion.[15] By that stage debt service alone would cost R109 billion a year. The big drama was the steady credit downgrading. By January 2013 both Fitch and Standard & Poor's rated South Africa at BBB, Moodys at one notch above that. The agencies were quite frank, citing deteriorating public finances, rising levels of corruption and, as a result, rising levels of social and political tension. In effect, they successfully foretold Marikana.

However, within South Africa very few understood the significance of these trends and neither Jacob Zuma, most ministers nor ANC activists were among those who did. The result was that the feckless mood of *enrichissez-vous* continued to predominate at every level. The results were visible in the increasingly dire audit reports for government departments, provincial and municipal governments. The auditor-general, Terence Nombembe, became increasingly scathing about the sheer lack of response by government to his reports of runaway corruption. In May 2012 he pointed out that the management of supply chains, service delivery, human resources, the security of government information and the accuracy of government reports were all deteriorating.

These were essential pillars of rational democratic government and they were crumbling. 'Things are serious and they are even more serious than we thought they were. They are more serious because the people that are employed by the government to do the work are least prepared and equipped to do it. The situation is dire,' Nombembe said.[16] He had, for example, been shocked to find that R2.6 billion had simply vanished from the ministry of public works during the 2012–13 financial year. The minister, Thulas Nxesi (who was also the deputy chairman of the SACP) said he had simply no idea where it had gone.[17] Since Nxesi was the former boss of Sadtu and also extremely helpful to Zuma in explaining away the hundreds of millions of public money spent on Zuma's Nkandla home, he enjoyed complete impunity. In fact the real blame probably lay with Nxesi's predecessors, for he went on to reveal that the total sum lost by the department due to wrongful or wasteful expenditure since 2001 was R34.98 billion.[18]

Ivor Chipkin, director of the Public Affairs Research Institute, concurred: 'The organizational legacy of the apartheid period, compounded by policy choices in the 1990s, unwittingly weakened administrations that were working. It gave high levels of autonomy to a politicised senior management and a ruling party not worried that there will be electoral consequences for poor performance.' The result, he said was 'a perfect storm.'[19] Neren Rau, CEO of the SA Chamber of Commerce and Industry, commented that: 'The leadership is struggling to keep pace with the problems. They are too much and are accumulating too quickly. Some of the problems have long ago surpassed the solutions offered.'[20]

What this really boiled down to was that the whole national and local system of government and administration was simply unravelling under the weight of ubiquitous corruption, a ludicrously ill-equipped public service and a whole series of policy blunders. In 1994 the ANC inherited a going concern and, as Chipkin says, 'administrations that were working'. Gradually, the government has run down and exhausted this inheritance and it now seems virtually powerless to arrest the process of deterioration. Indeed, the promises made by ANC politicians seemed increasingly detached from reality. Thus in 1994 the ANC's slogan was 'Jobs, jobs, jobs'. But unemployment grew strongly. In 2009 at his inauguration Zuma promised an extra 500 000 jobs in a year. In fact there was a net shrinkage of jobs over that period. In 2011 Zuma promised a further 5 million jobs. These did not appear. In 2014 he promised a further 6 million jobs in five years. Meanwhile the National Development Plan talked of creating an extra 11 million jobs by 2030.

In fact, of courses, these promises of 6, 11 or more million jobs were the purest fantasy, as was the promised National Health Insurance scheme, which depended on such unobtainable factors as orderly public hospitals, enough nurses and enough doctors. Similarly, ANC left-wingers like Zwelinzima Vavi argued that the implementation of the National Democratic Revolution would result in the abolition of inequality and unemployment. This was nothing less than belief in magic. The experience of African nationalist regimes elsewhere in Africa suggests that South Africa has now entered a very late and dangerous phase of nationalist evolution in which politicians, disappointed with the reality of their own under-achievement, begin to search for sweeping and almost magical solutions – get rid of all the foreigners, seize the farms, nationalise everything, throw out the Asians, etc. The fact that Julius Malema has begun to market his set of magic formulae has naturally encouraged his ANC competitors to produce their own magic.

Inevitably, this situation causes frissons of anxiety among the minorities (especially Asians and Jews), but South Africa's ruling elite appears to be blithely oblivious to it, as also to the damage done to the investment climate. The ANC in the Western Cape has become increasingly open in its anti-Semitism – causing vocal protests even from old ANC stalwarts like Ben Turok, while in KwaZulu-Natal the Mazibuye African Forum found large support for its demand that Indians be excluded from all BEE and affirmative action policies. MAF's propaganda was incendiary and frequently referred to Africans working for Indians as 'slaves'. Malema held talks with the MAF in order to form a common front with them.

The budget presented in March 2014 was heavily symbolic and there was much protestation about how things had improved since 1994. More to the point, the budget suggested that the government had pretty much reached the end of the line. Each successive year the state had gone more and more heavily into the contingency fund[21] – and there was simply no notion of how the huge new burden of the NHI was to be borne. Even Pravin Gordhan admitted that the situation was unsustainable. The country, he said, faced 'an immense set of tasks and challenges' and it 'cannot just muddle through the next decade'.[22]

Yet the truth was that Gordhan was attempting to do exactly that, muddle through – for there was no sign of any willingness to attack this 'immense set of tasks and challenges'. 'Gordhan has been a soft finance minister,' pointed out the economist, Iraj Abedian. 'Under his watch the fiscal deficit has shot up, the currency has lost almost 30 per cent of its value, and he's been too accommodative on fiscal discipline. Unless SA has a tough-acting minister of finance, confidence will be difficult to rebuild.'[23] The financial journalist, Claire Bisseker, concurred: 'Something more has to be done because on current policies, SA's creditworthiness will keep deteriorating. Either government is going to make a far greater effort to implement sound macro policies, both to cut the fat and raise the growth rate, or concerns over SA's fiscal and social stability will continue to mount.'[24] In fact the ANC government has now fully exhausted the favourable momentum it inherited in 1994, has squandered and wasted its inheritance of competent, working institutions, has driven away investment, has acted in a host of ways to repress economic growth – and now finds itself trapped, as a result, in an unsustainable, low-growth scenario. October 2014 brought a new mini-budget by a new finance minister, Nhlanhla Nene, with even more severe warnings but again a virtual absence of remedies. To be fair, one may be sure the left in cabinet would be bound to block austerity measures and Zuma would not support them. Thus drift is not just the lack of reme-dial action: drift is official policy.

And yet the only way for South Africa to avoid IMF intervention would be for the government to pre-empt such an eventuality by carrying out IMF-style policies itself. That was exactly what Thabo Mbeki had done under the Mandela government in 1996. The policy worked – but Mbeki was never forgiven for it. So, everything suggests that the slide will con-tinue, ending with a further downgrading by the credit agencies. Should South African bonds descend to junk bond status the effects would be dramatic. International demand for South African bonds was strongly increased by the country's inclusion into Citibank's benchmark world government bond index in 2012. This led to an upward re-balancing of portfolios to bring them in line with South Africa's 0.44 per cent index weighting. As a result, net foreign purchases of its government bonds more than doubled in 2012 (R93.8 billion against R42 billion in 2011).[25] A further downgrading would, however, remove South Africa from that index, with commensurate results. Moreover, all manner of international pension and insurance funds are forbidden by law to trade in junk bonds, as are most tracker funds. The result would not only be a sharp rise in the cost of debt, but in absolute terms it might be difficult to fund the debt at all. The last stage of decay is where the markets simply refuse to accept one's paper.

Long before that, however, foreign investment would flee the country, accompanied by a huge volume of domestic funds. The rand would plummet, unemployment would soar and both the budget and trade deficits would rise. (Many of these features were already visible in 2013 – foreign purchases of South African bonds fell by 73 per cent in a year, and the rand collapsed by over 30 per cent.)[26] In June 2014 this produced further credit downgrades, with the rating left just one notch above junk bond status.

Probably the crucial point to watch is the budget for 2016–17. The finance ministry had originally promised to bring the budget deficit down to 3 per cent of GDP in 2015–16 but this target had to be repeatedly moved back. The improvement to a 4.2 per cent deficit in 2013–14 was entirely the result of accountancy changes, and the lower-than-expected GDP growth rates will make that hard to improve upon. There is no doubt at all that a failure to meet the 2016–17 target would trigger a further downgrade. Meanwhile, debt continues to climb – once one counts in the parastatals and local government, the total public debt will almost certainly surpass the 1994 level of 70 per cent of GDP by 2016.[27]

The other worry is the trade deficit. The rand's steep fall in 2013–14 was bound to worsen that deficit immediately and there is nothing automatic about exporters being able to take advantage of the cheaper exchange rate even after that. As the World Bank report cited above shows, there are serious problems in many export sectors but what probably matters most of all is the state's sheer repression of economic growth. It is simply no good expecting South Africa's mines, manufacturers or farmers to ramp up production to take advantage of a cheaper exchange rate if they are beset by uncertainties over ownership, labour troubles or anti-business policies. So the domestic investment strike looks likely to continue.

Again, one comes back to South Africa's heavy reliance on foreign capital. Currently, South Africa's savings rate is only 16 per cent of GDP and the country hobbles along with an investment rate of just under 20 per cent, with foreign capital making up the difference. But in reality an investment rate of 25 per cent is necessary to fund infrastructural spending alone.

Thus, although in theory the ANC and SACP would like to free themselves from reliance on foreign capital, in practice they have become more and more reliant on it: over the decade 2003–12 the country enjoyed net capital inflows of R1.2 trillion, a lot of which was used to repay debt.[28] Yet ANC leaders blithely continued to act as if they could afford to ignore the requirements of capital markets. The result is a disaster just waiting to happen. As Kevin Lings, the Stanlib chief economist, points out, 'Foreigners already own 30%–40% of our bond and equity markets and the concern will be when they feel their holdings are sufficient.'[29]

Should these trends continue – and currently they are continuing – it is just a matter of time before the government finds it impossible to fund either or both the fiscal and current account deficits. This would pitch the country into a debt trap from which it probably could not escape without IMF assistance. True, it might soldier on for a while on its own but this would not be viable for long. The multiple weaknesses of the post-liberation state, together with the general nervousness the ANC inspires in both domestic and foreign investors, more or less guarantee that. Yet for the ANC government to go cap-in-hand to the IMF asking for a bailout would, in effect, signal the final failure of ANC governance – the fate that Thabo Mbeki always feared. For the IMF would, of course, demand conditions for its support, the government would lose control of economic policy and inevitably part of the deal would be huge spending cuts, certainly in the public service pay bill and perhaps also in social grants. In addition there would, inevitably, have to be a liberalisation of the labour market which would give the *coup de grâce* to Cosatu and thus the SACP. And much more besides.

The temptation of autarchy

Almost certainly this would produce a split in the ANC between those willing to go along with IMF conditions and those who wanted South Africa to 'go it alone'. Already one can descry this division in government with communists like Rob Davies and Ebrahim Patel demanding a more autarchic policy, with a strong measure of protectionism. Indeed, to the fury of the EU, Davies has already scrapped all the investment guarantee treaties, provoking a stern lecture from the EU trade commissioner about the crucial significance to the South African economy of European and especially German investment and how such investment cannot be expected to continue without a protective treaty. Indeed, in the two days after the cancellation of the treaties with Germany and Switzerland, foreigners sold R2.95 billion of South African stocks and bonds.[30]

However, Davies blithely pushed ahead with a bill which provided sweeping grounds on which the state may decide to expropriate foreign assets, including the need to 'redress historical, social and economic inequalities' or to 'foster economic development, industrialization and beneficiation'. The need to avoid 'the unfair and inequitable treatment of investors' was jettisoned, as was all recourse to international mediation – on the grounds of the repeatedly stressed 'excellence' of the South African judiciary, which would decide all such cases in future. When one adds that the bill also scrapped the promise of full-market-value compensation in the event of expropriation, no one could really be blamed for seeing the bill as providing the means for the South African state to steal foreign assets, paying only bargain basement compensation for them.[31] On top of that, of course, the South African judiciary, in the words of one leading advocate, 'has been trashed'[32] so that quite routinely lawyers now advise clients to seek arbitration rather than go to court for fear of wildly prejudiced, unreliable or even bribed judgments.

The impression of complete South African fecklessness in regard to foreign investors was only strengthened by President Zuma's decision to stay away from the EU-Africa summit of April 2014 in solidarity with Robert Mugabe's refusal to go because his wife, Grace, was still on the EU sanctions list. Zuma was the only African head of state to act in sympathy with Mugabe and did so with an off-hand remark about how the EU should stop treating Africans 'as subjects'. Instead, a lower-level delegation attended. EU ministers professed themselves bewildered at this cavalier treatment. The EU ambassador to South Africa, Roeland van de Geer, spoke of the 'concern' over South Africa's investment climate which the move had given rise to. The EU, he pointed out, was not only South Africa's largest trading partner, investor and aid donor but it was also the biggest funder of

African peace-keeping operations, in which South Africa played a major part.[33]

De Geer was carefully diplomatic. His comments brought back to me, however, an off-the-record conversation I had had with a senior EU official in Brussels some ten years before. I had asked him how on earth European diplomats could take President Mbeki seriously, given his record on Aids and Zimbabwe. He laughed and said 'Mbeki certainly has his problems but he does at least speak decent English and has some idea as to how international relations work. You've got to realise how grateful for that you have to be when you meet other African leaders.'

The general impression of Zuma, I realised, was essentially that of a buffoon who didn't understand the implications of what he was doing and was simply far out of his depth at the helm of a G20 country. He had, after all, blithely promised the Russians that South Africa would order six new nuclear power stations from them at a cost of R1 trillion – with no indication as to where the money for this would come from. Corruption within his administration was out of control, as how could it not be when Zuma himself had had R246 million spent on his own house? Wherever one looked there were crooked deals. The government had paid a preposterous R1 billion for the Mala Mala private game reserve – in which, it emerged, David Mabunda, head of SA National Parks, had a personal stake.[34] Whatever the appeals for financial discipline or the promises to 'fight corruption', it seemed clear that the ruling elite would attempt to get away with whatever it could – and Zuma, heedless of the growing horror of international observers, would let it all happen.

Such impressions were hardly dispelled by the way that government returned, time and again, to the suggestion that foreign ownership of the main private security companies (ADT, Chubb, etc) was somehow 'a threat to national security' which could only be removed by forcing black ownership. It was originally minister of safety and security Steve Tshwete's attempt to push through such a measure that led British companies to remind the government with some force that an investment treaty protected their position.[35] In November 2013 this all came back with a bang when a Bill was presented to Parliament demanding 51 per cent local ownership of security companies. Given that this is an industry employing

2 million people and with an annual turnover of R50 billion, this was an attempt at a very large asset grab.[36] In fact it was guaranteed to produce the worst of all worlds because, on the one hand, the foreign companies were bound to use the ten years' grace granted them by the treaty change, and secondly, such an obvious attempt to steal profitable businesses was bound to do huge damage to investor confidence.

By March 2014 Parliament had actually passed the Private Security Industry Regulation Amendment Bill, which limited foreign ownership of security companies to 49 per cent. This prompted EU representatives to warn the government that the Bill was a clear infringement of the agreement signed by Nelson Mandela and John Major in September 1994, which protected such investments from nationalisation or expropriation.[37]

In addition, of course, the government's black economic empowerment policies have pushed away investors both domestic and foreign. The Nigerian billionaire, Aliko Dangote, issued a stern warning to the government in 2013 that BEE was pushing away even such investors as himself. Foreign companies have told government that 'billions were lost to communities' as a result of the policy[38] – and this was before government decided to make BEE equity ownership mandatory upon foreign-owned businesses. For domestic investors the terrifying fact was that many companies had operated BEE schemes which saw them effectively give away 26 per cent of their equity, thus diluting the holdings of all other investors. In many cases the BEE beneficiaries have since cashed in their chips, leaving such companies lily-white again. The government has made it clear that in that case it expects them to give away another 26 per cent of their equity. It is hardly difficult to imagine the effects of such policies on any rational investor. Similarly, President Zuma announced that the next phase of BEE would be to use government regulatory power to create a new class of black industrialists.[39] Leaving aside the fact that nowhere in the world have industrialists been created in that way, this presages an explosion of new legislation, codes of good practice and the like which will distort all normal economic relations in a way that can only offend rational investors.

It is doubtful if men like Rob Davies, Jeremy Cronin or, indeed, Jacob Zuma appreciate how irrevocable is South Africa's integration into the world political economy. Davies's abrogation of investment treaties effectively treats German, British and American investors as optional extras but South Africa can no more manage without such investment than it can fly. Similarly, when ANC ministers talk of 'forcing the private sector to invest' its R580-billion cash pile they simply have no notion of how impossible that is and of how mobile capital is. Johann Rupert early on warned Mandela that the government must realise that whereas labour was relatively immobile, capital could move in the blink of an eye.[40] But the point was not taken.

In effect ANC economic thinking has remained sunk in a sort of vulgar Marxist dark age, wholly inadequate to deal with capitalist economics in an age of globalisation. A good example of this stunted thinking was the attack by the SACP leader, Blade Nzimande, and his deputy, Jeremy Cronin, on Sasol's decision to invest $20 billion in Louisiana, USA, which they interpreted as a form of disinvestment in South Africa. Sasol was, they said, a South African company and should be investing in South Africa. 'The disinvestment trend,' said Cronin, 'went back to 1994. There has been a massive failure by monopoly capital to invest in the country. Between 20%–25% of our GDP has flown out of the country since 1994. Sasol is emblematic of the broader process.'[41]

There was no understanding here that Sasol is an international company with a majority of its shares held abroad and that this internationalisation of capital has long since changed the game. This is a bird that has flown long ago. There is simply no 'should' about where Sasol or other multinationals invest. One wonders if Cronin and Nzimande even realise that Sasol has been overtaken as South Africa's largest company by Naspers, thanks to its internet holdings in Russia and China. Similarly, some South African companies have begun to move their headquarters to Botswana or Mauritius (where MTN now bases itself), both free-exchange zones where business operates under far fewer constraints than in South Africa.

It was rather the same when each change at the top of the Anglo American corporation saw African nationalist demands that the next CEO must be a black South African. It is, in fact, some time since Anglo American was a South African company and one of the first benefits it got from its London listing was that the staff of its London HQ were beyond the reach of South Africa's affirmative action laws. Today, most of Anglo's assets are outside

South Africa, as are most of its investors. Nicky Oppenheimer, ensconced in his desirable landed estate in England, features prominently in the (British) *Sunday Times* Rich List. Much the same can be said of Billiton, SAB-Miller, Investec, Old Mutual and many other large, previously South African companies. Moreover, slow growth in South Africa, accompanied by much faster growth elsewhere in Africa, has seen many South African companies, led by the big retail chains and banks, invest heavily elsewhere in Africa. The consequence is a growing internationalisation of capital on every front. Even South Africa's biggest bank, Standard Bank, now has subsidiaries all over the world and is 20 per cent owned by the Industrial and Commercial Bank of China (ICBC). In effect this makes the nationalisation of such businesses increasingly difficult. If South Africa nationalised Anglo's, the more than two-thirds of its assets that are now abroad would escape the state's grab, just as Sasol's vast overseas assets would.[42]

The most important reason for this almost Neanderthal state of ANC economic thinking is that very few people in the government understand the true gravity of the situation. There is, for example, no sign that ANC ministers understand just how grave a threat to South Africa is the tapering down of quantitative easing by the US Federal Reserve or how significant it is that South Africa is the most exposed of what the IMF and *The Economist* refer to as 'the fragile five' (the others are Brazil, India, Indonesia and Turkey) – countries with large fiscal and trade deficits, dependent on capital inflows which could suddenly stop. Rian le Roux, chief economist of the Old Mutual Investment Group, said that the point of isolating the fragile five – and, according to *The Economist*, South Africa was the most fragile of the lot – was that they were 'off investors' radar screens and in need of structural reform'.[43]

The IMF warned of the same thing in October 2013, emphasising how urgent it was for South Africa 'to move ahead with planned structural reforms to boost growth and create jobs'. Its report spelt out South Africa's rapidly deteriorating situation. The savings ratio, which had been 15.5 per cent of GDP in 1995–2011, fell in 2012 to just 13 per cent.[44] That is, the savings gap between South Africa and other emerging markets had grown significantly over the last decade. The same sense of South Africa becoming an outlier on the downside emerged when exports were examined. Where

2005 = 100, South Africa was still stuck at 80 while both India and China were over 160. No other emerging market examined showed such a weak performance.[45] This led the IMF team to warn that while South Africa's total public debt of (then) around 55 per cent of GDP might not seem high, further analysis showed that 50 per cent might be a maximum sustainable level and that in fact sustainability might be as low as 35–40 per cent. This led the IMF to recommend that South Africa should aim to reduce public debt to 40 per cent of GDP, a large drop from the current 55 per cent.[46] Ominously, whereas in 2006 South Africa's gross financing needs (that is, funds needed from abroad) were 5.5 per cent of GDP, this figure climbed steadily to 11 per cent in 2009 and 12 per cent in both 2012 and 2013.[47]

All of this suggested that South Africa was becoming more and more dangerously exposed. But the real problem lay in the IMF recommendations for structural reform. The IMF blithely said that the National Development Plan needed to be implemented forthwith – a clear impossibility, not only because of SACP/Cosatu political resistance, but because there is no central planning office, no Gosplan, as it were. Secondly the IMF made it clear that South Africa needed, in short order, labour market reform, an increased supply of skilled labour (which could only be done via the large-scale immigration of foreign professionals), wage restraint (anathema to SACP/Cosatu), urgent improvement in education and training (which the teachers' union, Sadtu, would veto)[48] and various other steps, all of which would be resisted root and branch by major interests within the Tripartite Alliance.

Doubtless, successive finance ministers and Reserve Bank governors have done their best to warn the government of the stormy waters ahead, but anything like these structural reforms would be instantly shot down as 'neo-liberal' by the various veto groups within the ANC alliance. Yet, as the IMF warned, 'Limited reform progress leads to an unavoidable build up of vulnerabilities'.[49] What this boils down to is that these are measures that the IMF says South Africa needs in order not to go over the cliff, and the government has ignored them all. The only (and tell-tale) response one could discern in 2013 was a playing with figures reminiscent of Cristina Kirchner's Argentina.

The first thing that commentators noticed in 2013 was that despite sufficiently low growth to cause considerable job contraction, the jobs data issued by government signally failed to show any contraction. Indeed, according to official figures the post-2010 slowdown 'was accompanied by job creation unmatched since the pre-crisis boom years'.[50] No one sensible gave any credence to that. Next came a new way of calculating the budget deficit which, surprise, surprise, resulted in a sharp drop in the deficit. And then came a new way of calculating the trade deficit which, to further surprise, produced a sharp drop in that deficit too. Or did for a month: by December 2013 even with that adjustment, the deficit still soared to a new high.[51] The real problem here was that South African exports fell by 15 per cent in dollar terms in 2011–13. Partly this reflected low investment levels and the miserably low business confidence index, but it also had a lot to do with the collapse of mineral exports caused by strikes. Thereafter, surging wage rates caused the closure of many marginal mines and a consequent reduction in mineral production. The IMF, indeed, has decided that the stagnation which has seen South Africa under-perform its growth potential for many years has now seen a decline in that growth potential itself.[52]

As the jaws of the crisis fastened ineluctably, ANC politicians enjoyed making attacks on the credit rating agencies but in the real world, of course, this had no impact at all on either foreign or domestic investors – the audience that mattered.

The loss of economic sovereignty

In a sense the internationalisation of capital has already begun to deprive the ANC government of economic sovereignty, but having recourse to the IMF would complete the process. Nonetheless, the ANC would clearly not accept the loss at all easily. Cosatu and the SACP would realise that this would mean the end of the National Democratic Revolution and, quite likely, the end of them. They would be bound to resist as hard as they could. Above all, the bureaucratic bourgeoisie which has been the chief beneficiary and motor of ANC rule would realise that their feeding frenzy was coming to a close, and they could hardly be expected to accept that at all easily. Moreover, the ANC would, quite rightly, see this as a huge threat to its own continued political dominance. As Thabo Mbeki well understood, an ANC president who delivered the country into the hands of the IMF and World Bank would not lightly be forgiven, particularly since it would be seen as confirmation of his bugbear, that 'Africans can't govern'. This may seem absurd: many African states have survived IMF intervention and positively welcome the World Bank. But South Africa is not just any African state. It has a strong sense of its own exceptionalism and its governance by the ANC's Tripartite Alliance results in a series of self-imposed constraints which the IMF would be bound to dismantle. This is where the irresistible force meets the immovable object.

CHAPTER NINE

The Brics Alternative

Throughout its period in exile the ANC was tightly allied to the USSR and its foreign policy position reflected that fact. In the 1950s the ANC had celebrated Stalin's birthdays and supported the Soviet invasion of Hungary in 1956. In exile the ANC also supported the Soviet invasion of Czechoslovakia in 1968, maintained particularly close relations with Castro's Cuba and took the Soviet side in the Sino-Soviet conflict. The ANC found itself extremely comfortable in the world of what Moscow called 'actually existing socialism' in the People's Democracies of Eastern Europe. At the same time the ANC tried to develop a leftist Pan-Africanism very much in line with Nkrumah's original vision and also supported every 'progressive' left alternative to the existing American-led hegemony, such as the Group of 77's calls for a New International Economic Order in the 1970s, the rhetorical call for more South–South relationships and even the old Non-Aligned Movement (NAM) of the Bandung era which had sought to include Third World countries in an anti-Western alliance led by China, Vietnam, North Korea and various other radical Third World states which were anything but non-aligned.

In search of a foreign policy

When the ANC came to power in 1994 this was a world in ruins. 'Why couldn't the Soviet working class have just held on a bit longer?' was one of the sad-and-angry questions which Russian visitors of the early 1990s faced from SACP/ANC audiences.[1] The Cold War was over, the Soviet bloc was gone and Eastern European nations were now passionately anti-communist. This was a surreal experience for ANC activists who had sojourned for long periods in Moscow, East Germany and the rest of Eastern Europe. They had been comfortable in that world of 'People's Democracy', so comfortable that they hadn't even noticed that their host governments were bitterly unpopular with their own citizenry, who immediately took their first available chance to throw those regimes out. To the ANC's alarm their erstwhile hosts were soon revealed as corrupt and murderous. Some were killed, all were disgraced.

The ANC did not internalise any of this. Instead it came to power with its old dreams intact, quite unwilling to adapt to the real world of the 1990s. On the surface, and in good part due to Mandela, it accepted this new world, rejoining the Commonwealth and even partying on the Royal yacht, *Britannia*, during the Queen's visit of 1995. But at bottom the ANC remained anti-Western and especially anti-American. One only had to talk to ANC MPs to realise that they saw the US and the West in general as the enemy.[2] Under Mbeki this vision found expression in a series of initiatives. The discredited OAU was replaced by the AU (which was no better). There was much talk of the African Renaissance, the African Peer Review Mechanism on Governance and the New Partnership for Africa's Development (Nepad) and all of these found some (brief) institutional expression. Mbeki also tried to infuse new life into the Non-Aligned Movement, hosting a NAM summit. But NAM too had long outlived its usefulness and existed again only if South Africa paid its bills. There were also such ill-fated initiatives as the World Conference Against Racism, which ended in disastrous shambles. Mbeki also gave strong support to Mugabe's embattled regime, insisting that one rigged election after another was free and fair.

In truth Mbeki and his loyal henchmen, Aziz and Essop Pahad, conducted a foreign policy which might have been devised by radical students in the 1960s. It had little purchase on reality, ignoring the fact that Western countries, South Africa's main traders and investors, were still its most important partners. NAM, the African Renaissance and Nepad all collapsed and died with the overthrow of Mbeki. Thus 15 years into liberation the ANC had simply failed to find a foreign policy. It had wasted enormous international good will and achieved nothing. This was an extraordinary indictment of Mbeki, always seen as the movement's chief diplomat and international relations expert. Indeed, it was worse than that: thanks to his Aids denialism, his support for Mugabe and his peculiar mixture of paranoia and grandiosity, Mbeki ended up as an international leper, unable to land even the most junior UN job.

What all this made clear was that, in foreign policy terms, South Africa was simply adrift. It talked enthusiastically about South–South co-operation, but this was rather nebulous and anyway the other nations of the South were tough trade competitors. South Africa joined such loose forums as Ibsa (India, Brazil, SA) and Basic (Brazil, SA, India and China) with a view to adopting a common attitude to climate change, but this proved problematic because the various member countries would be so differently affected by such change.

There was one notable success. Mbeki was utterly fascinated by the Arab-Israeli problem. He would insist that his cabinet should spend whole days, even whole weekends, discussing the problem. Israel looked on in puzzlement: the only Middle Easterners asked to participate in these discussions were Palestinians or extreme left-wing Israelis. Clearly no solutions were going to come out of that. Gradually, it became clear that Mbeki's idea was that with South Africa now liberated, the next step was to focus on where another Western (and largely white) minority had managed to impose itself in the Third World – namely Israel. Thus the Israel–Palestine issue was seen as a re-run of the South African struggle. The Israelis were to be accused of apartheid, subjected to boycotts, sanctions and disinvestment and ultimately forced to hand over their country to an Arab majority in just the way that white South Africans had handed over to a black majority. Gradually this campaign achieved international traction. Apart from his struggle to maintain Robert Mugabe in power, this represented Mbeki's sole foreign policy success.

This was not much for a country which, as Hillary Clinton noted, saw itself as a world power. For South Africa's leaders saw themselves as the leaders of Africa, as leaders of the Third World, as leaders of the black race internationally – and in general, leaders of the world's progressives. It was an extraordinary inflation of ambition. Indeed, the South African ambassador to the US, Ebrahim Rasool (who has had more than his share of problems with the law) insisted that the country was 'poised to become a moral superpower'.[3] The reality was that South Africa was at best a medium power which was steadily being relegated down the list, as other countries overtook it economically and militarily: in 1977 its GDP ranked it 18th in the world, in 2012 it was 29th, in 2013 33rd[4] Yet South African politicians travelled the world claiming to have the key to solving the problems of Northern Ireland, the Middle East, and anywhere else torn by civil strife. South Africa maintained no fewer than 104 embassies abroad, plus 15 consulates, 84 honorary consulates, nine embassies to international organisations, and had accreditation to another 70 countries. And because every African country, no matter how tiny, felt it must have an embassy in Pretoria, South Africa entertained more foreign embassies (123) and representatives of international organisations (35) than any country save the USA.[5]

The emergence of Brics

Bric (Brazil, Russia, India, China), a notion famously invented by Jim O'Neill of Goldman Sachs, took life as an initiative by Vladimir Putin, who began ministerial meetings between the four countries in 2006, leading up to the first Bric Summit at Yekaterinburg, in the Urals, in May 2008. This was followed by another Summit in the same place in 2009 which produced a Joint Statement including demands for 'the reform of international financial institutions' to give more say to developing countries and 'a new global reserve currency' which should be 'diversified, stable and predictable': all of which was very much in line with Putin's already strong hostility to the dollar and the Bretton Woods institutions. The Summit also backed Brazil and India's demands for seats on the UN Security Council and demanded that in future the heads of international financial institutions must be appointed transparently and on merit (that is, not reserved for Americans or Europeans, as had been the case). This all reflected traditional Russian policy. Back in the 1980s Mikhail Gorbachev had pushed for a USSR–China–India grouping and had been happy to include Brazil as well. As any first-year student in international relations would have pointed out, Russia could not face America on its own and needed to generate an anti-Western coalition to do so.

The clearly anti-Western tone of this communiqué excited Pretoria, which quickly decided that this was a club it must join. All else apart, Nigeria was rapidly catching up on South Africa economically and challenging for African leadership. Acceptance into Bric would affirm South Africa's position as the leading African country. President Jacob Zuma lobbied hard, but he was pushing at an open door and South Africa was admitted as the fifth member of Brics on Christmas Eve 2010, allowing Zuma to attend the next Brics Summit in Sanya, China in April 2011. Jim O'Neill openly declared South Africa to be a quite inappropriate member, suggesting that Indonesia, Mexico and Turkey all had stronger claims.

The world financial crisis of 2008–09 greatly upped the ante, for the US responded to the crisis by quantitative easing – that is, printing money – which had the effect of devaluing the reserves of all other countries that were held in dollars, thus making the rest of the world pay a good part of the cost of the crisis. This lay behind the offer by Brics in June 2012 to pledge an extra $75 billion to the IMF, conditional upon reforms in the IMF voting system to reflect the new balance of world power. The G20 were quick to endorse the notion of such reforms. However, despite their talk of opening up the top positions of the IMF and World Bank, it was noticeable that the Brics nations failed entirely to rally round a Third World candidate when, in June 2011, yet another French citizen, Christine Lagarde, was named as head of the IMF – an early sign that Brics unity was more fragile than claimed.

It was with positive delight that South Africa joined Brics and embraced its implicit anti-Westernism, though from the outset Pretoria seemed to view Brics mainly as a way of pouring huge sums of money into African development – under South African leadership. Thus South Africa's representative, Mandisi Mpahlwa, happily told the Sanya Summit that 'we are now co-equal partners of a new, equitable international system' and invited the other Brics nations to join hands with South African companies to develop Africa, saying that $480 billion was needed in the next 10 years for investment in infrastructure alone.[6] None of Zuma's partners was undiplomatic enough to comment on this talk of 'co-equals', but it was noticeable that no money for African development was forthcoming.

South Africa's love affair with Brics

Similarly, at the Durban Brics Summit in March 2013 Zuma pushed hard for the establishment of a New Development Bank (NDB) and also a separate Contingency Reserve Arrangement (CRA), the latter to help states over balance of payments difficulties. Although Brics spokesmen laboured hard to insist that these new institutions were complementary to the IMF and World Bank (whose functions they clearly mimicked) and in no way opposed to them, Zuma was quite bluntly anti-Western: the CRA and NDB were, he said, 'necessary because the Bretton Woods institutions had never done anything helpful for African countries' – ignoring the many billions these institutions had poured into Africa over many decades – and that South Africa had joined Brics because the US and EU 'treat us like former subjects'.[7] Zuma also produced President Macky Sall of Senegal, president of a committee supervising Nepad, to present the Brics leaders with a list of 10 Nepad priority projects which needed to be financed. Again, there were no takers.

The full extent of Pretoria's anti-Western paranoia was revealed some weeks later when the UK announced that it was ending its aid programmes to South Africa and India because both countries were now much wealthier than they had been. Pretoria was livid and a senior official at its foreign office told the *Mail & Guardian* that the move was clearly an attempt to punish Brics members for setting up the NDB: 'Do you think it's a coincidence that both India and South Africa are in Brics? They're targeting Brics members.'[8]

This was much the same view as adopted by the SACP leader, Blade Nzimande, who greeted Brics positively, pointing out that powerful or ruling communist parties existed in all Brics members and that it was a blow against the West: 'The ideological foundations of the liberal offensive is that of seeking to permanently tie South Africa to Western imperialist interests ... [it] seeks to subject South Africa ... within the prism of the continued domination of Europe's and North America's economic and ideological interests.'[9]

South Africa's enthusiasm for Brics was in no way diminished by the fact that Russia and China are effective dictatorships. Indeed, officials from every level of South African government made their pilgrimage to Beijing and President Zuma himself repeatedly declared that South Africa must learn from China 'not just economically but politically'. Pretoria happily adopted the Sino-Russian line that virtually all opposition movements in Third World countries were really the work of Western imperialism. Like every anti-Western state, South Africa had been electrified when President George W Bush had quite calmly set forth 'regime change' (in Iraq) as a legitimate objective. Pretoria was also deeply shocked by the popular risings of the Arab Spring and the ease with which leaders it regarded as its allies, such as Gaddafi in Libya, were tossed aside.

This paranoid anti-Westernism was on full view at the Non-Aligned Movement's ministerial conference in Algiers in May 2014 where South Africa's foreign minister, Maite Nkoana-Mashabane, told her 119 colleagues that: 'We have recently observed with serious concern, concerted efforts to undermine democratic governance ... in most of the members of this movement by external forces through internal proxies [whose objectives] ... include regime change.'[10]

Nkoana-Mashabane also noted with pleasure the reconciliation between Fatah and Hamas: it was clear that this was what she regarded as a 'democratic' movement. Similarly, her reference to 'democratic governance' has to be understood in the ANC sense, namely that liberation movements such as itself represent democracy and that any attempt to vote them out of power represents an attempted reversal of democracy. The paranoid notion that Western imperialism was trying to effect regime change in 'most' of NAM's 120 members requires no comment.

South Africa thus entered Brics in a state of complete naivety, apparently unaware that each of its members had its own reasons for joining such a grouping, reasons which had nothing to do with developing Africa, let alone promoting South Africa's ambitions to act as the midwife of such development, to be Africa's representative on the UN Security Council and so forth. The alliance is peculiarly ideological. South Africa does little trade with Russia, while the other three Brics members are all major trade competitors. China may now be South Africa's biggest trading partner, but there is a huge trade deficit in China's favour and already China has completely wiped out South Africa's textile industry. The sole real focus of the alliance is its anti-Westernism and in particular its campaign against the dollar. This is not South Africa's fight. Putin may dream of the rouble one day becoming a reserve currency and China can think very seriously about the Chinese remnimbi in the same role, but no one imagines that the rand could ever play such a role.

There is, though, a peculiar symmetry to the way in which under apartheid South Africa's fortunes were bound up in a far larger international political economy and the way this has happened again now. To understand this one needs to follow the fortunes of gold.

Gold and international power

Britain adopted the gold standard in 1816, very much against the advice of David Ricardo. During the last three decades of the nineteenth century one country after another joined the gold standard group so that by 1914 the gold standard was nearly universal. Although of course a good deal of gold has always gone into jewellery the main holders of gold were the world's central banks which held over 8 000 metric tonnes. The outbreak of the First World War created a need for huge and inflationary spending on weapons and men and so the gold standard had to be abandoned and the printing presses churned out money. After the war, there was an attempt by the British to return to the gold standard which had to be abandoned. In other countries like Germany there was a frantic search for other means to support the currency, ending up with the Rentenmark. The USA maintained a gold-convertible dollar standard so that once Franklin Roosevelt had fixed the price at $35 per ounce the USA was pledged to redeem each

$35 with an ounce of gold. This in turn became the basis of the Bretton Woods system with all other currencies at fixed rates measured against the dollar, which in turn was valued against gold.

This system finally broke down in the 1970s with the adoption of a floating exchange rate by the USA in 1973, an example followed by the rest of the developed world. With that, gold was no longer exchangeable against the dollar and lost its place within the system. Thus the gold price was now free to oscillate like that of any other metal and it moved up sharply from $35 to nearly $200 in a matter of months.

The resulting situation is peculiar. On the one hand, gold is now said to have no place in the world's monetary system. On the other hand, the fact is that the world's central banks still hold gold reserves. They do so partly because gold is seen to have an insurance value – that is, its value tends to rise in times of crisis – and also, of course, the rising price of gold meant that many countries saw their reserves increase markedly in value. Moreover, it had been assumed that floating exchange rates would see continuous and minuscule adjustments of one currency against another, but this expectation turned out to be wrong. Instead currencies behaved much more like stock markets with wild swings of sentiment and a tendency to undershoot or overshoot by as much as 30 per cent. What this meant in practice was that central banks would use their reserves to intervene in foreign markets to stabilise their currencies. The result has been that in practice the world depends on managed floating rates.

Although gold's situation in this new system appears to be anomalous, the fact is that many people and cultures still see it as a historic store of value, and certainly gold retains a universal acceptance. In practice, ever since Bretton Woods the world has been on a dollar standard, which of course confers great advantages on the USA because the dollar is thus the international reserve currency of the world. However, American control of the world's financial system, exercised through the dollar's role and through the other Bretton Woods institutions, has come under repeated challenge. The rise of European capitalism in the 1950s and 1960s produced the world's largest internal market and a trading bloc actually greater in size than the USA.

The political expression of the European challenge was seen in the great political assertion of President de Gaulle. He deliberately attempted to undermine the rule of the dollar by accumulating gold reserves and by forcing the USA to redeem dollars into gold. This led to a sharp reduction in America's gold reserves, which had peaked in 1952 at over 20 000 tonnes. De Gaulle's policy was richly rewarded, of course, when the gold price soared after 1973 and French reserves were multiplied almost six-fold in value. Moreover many other European countries, although eschewing political Gaullism, nonetheless had followed in France's wake and quietly accumulated large gold reserves. In fact, this European challenge gradually subsided and the launch of the Euro created a second reserve currency widely used by the world's central banks in partnership with the dollar and the yen, although the dollar has remained the universal numeraire. In practice the USA has tended to keep a downward pressure on the gold price because it is universally recognised that a weak dollar means a higher gold price and vice versa. If the world is to retain confidence in the dollar as the world's international reserve currency, then there should be no perceived flight into gold. Thus despite the fact that gold is notionally irrelevant to the world's monetary system, in practice it continues to play a shadow role and each new challenger in turn to American power tends to express that challenge through upward pressure on the gold price.

Gold had soared to over $800 per ounce by 1980 and both the USA and other countries began to sell off some of their gold holdings, as did the IMF, partly in order to cash in on gold's high value but also, in the American case, to exert downward pressure on the gold price. The result was that by the 1990s gold had fallen back to as low as $250 per ounce and concern grew that un-coordinated sales of gold by many central banks were causing the value of gold reserves to fall for everyone. Accordingly the European central banks came together in 1999, to sign the Washington Agreement on Gold, otherwise known as the first Central Bank Gold Agreement (CBGA1). Under CBGA1 gold sales were not to exceed a total of 400 tonnes per year. This stabilised the gold price, particularly since the USA, Japan, Australia, the IMF and the Bank for International Settlement also associated themselves with the Agreement. Under CBGA2 (2005–09), gold sales were held down to similar levels and the CBGA3 (2010–14) foresaw this system extended into the future.

However, the world financial crisis of 2008–09 led to widespread panic and suddenly central banks not only ceased to sell gold but turned round and began to buy it again in large quantities. The first large buyer was Russia, which began to buy a steady 40–50 tonnes per year from 2007 on. In 2009, China bought 450 tonnes and India bought 200 tonnes. The next year Saudi Arabia bought 180 tonnes and Mexico bought 94 tonnes. Thus what was striking about this latter-day gold rush was that it was led by the central banks of emerging markets, particularly the Bric nations.

This in turn has evolved into what might be called a second-generation challenge to the dollar. This time the key challenger is clearly China, for the truth is that it is by far the biggest economy in the Brics group and has enormously greater reserves in its central bank, the People's Bank of China (PBOC). Occasionally boasts are made as to the total demographic or economic weight of the Brics group, but in reality Brics consists of one superpower (China), three medium powers (India, Russia and Brazil) and one small power (South Africa). Hence the peculiarity of South Africa's Brics membership: it is an alliance in which the South African rowing boat is towed behind the Chinese battleship.

Although gold buying has been notable since 2008 by many smaller emerging market nations, such as the Philippines, Thailand, Qatar and the states of the Commonwealth of Independent States (CIS) which groups the old members of the USSR such as Russia, Ukraine, Belarus and Kazakhstan, the big question remains the attitude of China towards gold sales. Publicly, Chinese officials have repeatedly insisted that they do not wish to diversify their mountainous foreign reserves of over $3.8 trillion into gold.

Nonetheless, everything suggests that China is building up its stock of gold. The fact is that the reticence of some central banks makes it difficult to be certain of who holds exactly what reserves. China has not told the world of any increase in its gold reserves since early 2009. Meanwhile, however, China has overtaken South Africa to become the world's biggest gold producer and all this gold – about 450 tonnes per year – stays in China. Indeed China forbids the export of gold. Secondly, China has been importing large amounts of gold through Hong Kong – more than 500 tonnes in 2012, and 1 158 tonnes in 2013. In addition, of course, it is perfectly possible that China is buying gold elsewhere as well, for there are always large sales of privately held gold and gold scraps. What we do know is that China clearly has a huge appetite for gold and that this seems to apply at every level of Chinese society, from individuals to banks. Thus Na Liu of CNC Asset Management calculates that China's 'apparent gold consumption' in 2013 actually exceeded 1 700 tonnes, over 500 tonnes more than had been reported. The PBOC admits to holding just 1 054 tonnes of gold but many speculate that the real figure could be 5 000 tonnes or more.

Ever since central banks began to purchase 400–500 tonnes of gold per year, from 2009 on, there has been a steady build-up of central bank gold reserves. According to the official figures of the World Gold Council (WGC) the 20 largest holders are as follows:

Top twenty gold holdings by country

Country	Tonnes	% of total reserves
1. USA	8 133.5	72
2. Germany	3 384.2	68
3. IMF	2 814	n.a.
4. Italy	2 451.8	67
5. France	2 435.4	65
6. Russia	1 094.7	10
7. China	1 054.1	1
8. Switzerland	1 040	8
9. Japan	765.2	3
10. Holland	612.5	54
11. India	557.7	7
12. Turkey	512.9	16
13. ECB	503.2	28
14. Taiwan	423.63	4
15. Portugal	382.5	83
16. Venezuela	367.6	71
17. Saudi Arabia	322.9	2
18. UK	310.3	12
19. Lebanon	286.8	24
20. Spain	281.6	25

Source: *Futures*, 28 August 2014.

It will be seen from the table that, despite their official protestations that gold is merely a 'barbaric relic', America and the major European countries all hold a substantial proportion of their reserves in gold, and that despite the legendary appetite for gold of Asian peasants, the big Asian countries, China, Russia, Japan and India, all hold a tiny fraction of their reserves in gold – except, of course, that if the true figures were known, China would probably already lie second only to the USA.

The real outlier here is China. The PBOC's reserves are about half held in dollars with another quarter in euros and most of the rest in a variety of other currencies, particularly the yen. The real question for the future is that of the renminbi. As China's economy grows to become the world's larg-est – which, according to the IMF, may already have happened – the obvi-ous question is whether the renminbi will displace the dollar as the world's reserve currency. Such an event would of course be an enormous blow not only to American prestige but in real economic terms as well. America has for many years been able to run large trade deficits without worrying that this would lead to a fall in the value of the dollar – although that is what would have happened to any other currency. Secondly America has run a large budget deficit year on year and has simply borrowed whatever it needed from the rest of the world, principally from China.

What this means in practice is that Americans have a budget which is appropriately sized for a large country but a taxation system appropri-ate to a small country. That is, all Americans, and particularly very rich Americans, have been able to enjoy the pleasures of low taxation while simultaneously enjoying the advantages of a large budget with all the ser-vices that brings. Should the dollar cease to enjoy its reserve status, all these advantages would be cancelled, which would mean a very rude awakening indeed for American taxpayers. Then again, all the major commodities – oil, gold, platinum, etc – are priced in dollars, which is clearly an advantage to the USA.

But perhaps the greatest demonstration of the advantages of holding the world's reserve currency came in the wake of the crisis of 2008–09 when the USA Federal Reserve embarked on 'quantitative easing' on a huge scale. What this meant was that the Fed simply printed many hundreds of bil-lions of dollars in paper money with which they flooded the American and world system in order to keep up demand during what would have other-wise been a huge international depression. The Fed was able to do this without paying any apparent price in dollar devaluation – an extraordi-nary privilege. But, if the renminbi were to replace the dollar as the world's reserve currency, all these privileges would vanish. Thus this would be a cataclysmic event for the world both economically and politically. It is as well to remember that the 2008 world financial crisis was ignited by a crisis in the US mortgage market. The much larger event of the dollar losing its reserve status would doubtless have an even larger impact on the world's economies.

Thus the great fear – perhaps one should call it the great suspicion – in the market, is that China had been secretly building up its gold reserves with a view to one day making a dramatic public announcement that its gold reserves now stand at some huge figure, well in excess of the USA's holdings. Such an announcement on its own would have enormous effects, driving up the price of gold and thus weakening the dollar. A further stage might then come in which China formally linked the renminbi to a gold backing. This would reinstate the gold standard first for the Chinese cur-rency and almost certainly would be followed by many other countries pegging their currencies to the renminbi and thus indirectly to the gold standard. This would completely capsize the dollar and America's loss of political and financial power would follow overnight.

The scary fact is that China could do this at any moment. With only 1.7 per cent of its reserves in gold, that figure could easily be multiplied by 30, 40 or 50 – and that without any change in the overall level of Chinese reserves. In practice, of course, any such move would be self-rewarding, just as it was for de Gaulle's France, because central bank gold buying on such a scale would inevitably drive up the gold price and thus increase the value of Chinese gold reserves. And the truth is that we only have a very vague idea of Chinese gold reserves and it is already quite possible that they are as large as those of the USA. Moreover, the relentless build-up of these reserves means that what China is aiming at is also the power to set the gold price. This would imply the complete overthrow of US financial hegemony.

The alternative to such a cataclysmic event is for change to proceed through the Bretton Woods institutions themselves. Thus for many years now the IMF has dealt in terms of SDRs (Special Drawing Rights) which are denominated in a basket of currencies which can be continually adjusted to reflect the changing size of the world's various economies. The renminbi is already part of that basket of currencies and it could be allowed to grow in size to reflect China's increasingly important role. This would be a smooth and easy transition but it would be essential that it was accompanied by China being allowed an increasingly important role in the IMF, the World Bank and the World Trade Organisation (the successor to the old GATT, born at Bretton Woods). China, seeing the logic of such a transition, has long campaigned for the replacement of the dollar by a revalued SDR.

Revising Bretton Woods

Even such a gradualist change would mean a major shift in the implicit bargain which Roosevelt drove at Bretton Woods, through his key representative, Harry Dexter White. It was an anomalous situation, for White was also a Soviet spy, who had fed information to Stalin throughout the war. Nonetheless, at Bretton Woods he forced through a deal – much to the distress of Keynes (representing the UK) and his deputy, Redvers Opie (who was my colleague[11]) – entirely in the interests of the US. First of all, both the IMF and the World Bank are headquartered in Washington under the watchful eye of the US Treasury, which is of course always the most powerful financial institution in that city, while the WTO is headquartered in Geneva. Secondly, the World Bank is always headed by an American and in return the IMF is always headed by a European, most commonly a Frenchman or French woman. This cosy arrangement reflecting a Euro-American hegemony is clearly way out of date in the world of the 21st century in which the Asian economies are dominant.

If the new balance of power were to be accurately reflected then a number of changes would have to occur. First, there would have to be a large change in IMF quotas, which in turn would mean that the increased quotas for Asian countries would be reflected in their increasing control of the IMF itself. This would come up firmly against the fact that the USA retains a formal veto over any changes in quota holdings, precisely in order to ensure continued American dominance within that institution. Quite clearly, that anachronistic arrangement would also have to go, and it would doubtless make sense for at least one and perhaps two of the three Bretton Woods institutions to be headquartered in Asia, probably in Beijing. After all, if Roosevelt believed that having the World Bank and IMF in Washington was important to guaranteeing ultimate American control of those institutions, why should Asians feel any different in future?

South Africa enthusiastically embraced the Brics war against the dollar, though without understanding even a tenth of its potential consequences. South Africa is a colonial construct, built by the British, and has grown to maturity under a US-sponsored hegemony. Would it really fit well into a new Chinese hegemony where China mainly looks to Africa for raw materials like a colonial power of old? South Africa's main trade and investment partner is the EU, a fact which would sit awkwardly in a new order ruled by Beijing. Moreover, rage as it may against the West, South Africa has embraced a multi-party system, free elections, free speech and a free media, all of which are anathema to Beijing. It is far from clear that a Chinese victory in the struggle against the West would really suit Pretoria.

South Africa has signed on to the anti-Westernism of Brics in large measure because it has got used to believing its own propaganda. The constant theme of both communist and African nationalist propaganda was that the IMF and World Bank were guilty of 'anti-African' behaviour because their aid was given on condition of reform – that is, the abandonment of the measures which had landed African countries in the debtors' court in the first place. Completely lost in this critique is the fact that developing countries end up borrowing from the IMF or World Bank precisely because they are often such bad credit risks that ordinary commercial banks won't touch them. Indeed, Africa has been extremely lucky that the Bretton Woods institutions have been willing to act as lenders of last resort. They have poured hundreds of billions of dollars into Africa when no one else would lend a cent. Be that as it may, South Africa and Russia have both enthusiastically embraced China's call to create what the Beijing People's Daily likes to call 'a de-Americanised world'. (South Africa's hostility has been duly noted in Washington, where, despite a lot of public verbiage to the contrary, it is often seen as an 'enemy country'.[12])

Would Brics help?

The significance of this to the question this book seeks to answer will be obvious. The attitude of the ANC government to the Bretton Woods institutions is clearly hostile and even if South Africa were to find itself in severe economic difficulties, it would clearly be loath to ask for IMF help. Yet everything suggests that the country is going to find itself in such difficulties. So what then? Without doubt Pretoria's first response would be to turn to its Brics partners for help.

Yet there must be considerable doubt as to whether this really constitutes a viable alternative. At its Durban summit in March 2013, we have seen, Brics agreed on a CRA (Contingency Reserve Arrangement) fund of $100 billion which would make funds available to fight 'currency shocks' and help countries over balance of payments problems. It was agreed that China would provide $41 billion, Brazil, India and Russia $18 billion each and South Africa $5 billion. In fact, of course, these were just notional amounts and whether any country will ever put any actual money into the pot will depend on whether the CRA actually starts to operate. And that was moot: India had arrived at the summit demanding co-ordinated intervention in world currency markets to protect Brics currencies. Brazil torpedoed this, pointing out that such interventions never worked and declaring that Brazil would have no part in any such initiative.[13]

At the same time the summit agreed in principle to set up a New Development Bank (NDB) with an initial capital of $50 billion. The irony that both the new Brics financial institutions were thus to use the dollar as their unit of exchange, despite all the rhetoric about displacing the dollar from its perch, went unmentioned.

By the time that Brics met again on the margins of the G-20 summit in St Petersburg in September 2013, everything had been agreed about the CRA – operation mechanisms, contributions, governance structure and loan-to-value ratios – all because this was something that China really wanted and the fact was, of course, that while the Brics had some $4.4 trillion in reserves, China alone at that point accounted for $3.2 trillion of this.[14] The fact was, as everyone knew, that it was China's deal and China was the elephant in the room. This became increasingly true after 2013 as all the Brics economies began to falter. China was still growing at 7.5 per cent p.a. but even this was sharply down on earlier performance. This caused the *Financial Mail* to comment that 'They are all in a bad place at the moment, and none looks well-enough positioned to bail itself out, let alone its partners ... Perhaps [Brics] was really just an alliance formed on the back of cheap money in the global economy caused by the US Federal Reserve. As the taps dried up ... their powers began to wane.'[15]

South Africa was enthusiastic about China's leadership – though, interestingly, China was now far less in favour of state intervention than South Africa was. Mandela had changed his mind about nationalisation of industry when he found that the Chinese no longer believed in it. Similarly, South Africa retained some currency controls and both the SACP and Cosatu openly bemoaned the fact that Mbeki had ever liberalised foreign exchange regulations. They wanted strong capital controls to prevent money from leaving the country. Yet the Chinese vice finance minister, Zhu Guangyao, observing that the difficulties of Brics countries were largely to do with their balance of payments, said that they could defend themselves either by hiking interest rates or by devaluing their currencies. Capital controls, though used in the past, were, he said, 'out of the question now'.[16]

However, in the run-up to the Durban summit South Africa had happily championed the idea of an NDB – to invest in infrastructure – which would be based in South Africa, perhaps even in Durban, Jacob Zuma's home base. China had suggested that the bank should have an initial capital of $100 billion. But South Africa did its sums and suggested $50 billion. Even so, the South African suggestion that there should be equal control of the bank by all Brics countries and that it should be in Africa because that was where most of the possible recipients of NDB loans would be, met with an icy Chinese response, particularly when South Africa also suggested that contributions to the NDB's capital should vary according to the economic weight of each Brics country (China had suggested $10 billion each).

This was too much for the Chinese. No bank should belong to its debtors, they said, and if China was going to be the main contributor to the bank's capital then China should have most control over the bank and it should be based in China. At which point, discussion stalled. As late as July 2014, South Africa's trade minister, Rob Davies, was still insisting that the NDB could well be domiciled in Johannesburg, although the Russian finance minister made it plain that as far as he was concerned the choice was between Shanghai and New Delhi. Given that the Russo-Chinese alliance is the *de facto* backbone of Brics, this actually settled the matter in favour of Shanghai.[17]

In the end the decisions of the Sixth Brics Summit, held in Fortaleza, Brazil in July 2014 merely emphasised how little purchase South Africa had. The new bank was indeed to be based in Shanghai. Its first president would be an Indian. The chairman of its board of directors would be a Brazilian and the chairman of its board of governors a Russian. All that was left for South Africa was an African regional office in Johannesburg. Moreover, it was agreed that, as the Chinese had wanted (and South Africa had not), the bank's capital was soon to be increased to $100 billion.

The uses and abuses of Brics

South Africa had happily approached the whole matter as an ideological one: surely all progressives wanted to make capital available to Africa and surely progressive South Africa would make the best hosts of such a bank? The Chinese, who understood perfectly well that they would be the inevitable paymasters of such a project, gave the South Africans a lesson in *realpolitik*. It was much the same a few months later when the Zimbabwean finance minister, Patrick Chinamasa, visited Beijing desperate for economic assistance – and got a dusty answer. China wanted value for money. Similarly, despite President Mugabe's all-out attempt to court China with his 'Look East' policy, the Chinese premier, Li Keqiang, did not include Zimbabwe on his African tour of May 2014.

In the end, the CRA and NDB were to go ahead largely as a result of the continuing stand-off in the IMF. Unlike the 5-member Brics institutions, both the IMF and World Bank have virtually universal membership (188 countries plus the Republic of Kosovo; only a few countries such as Cuba and North Korea don't belong). And the IMF has taken note of the pressure to increase the influence of developing countries; at its board of governors' meeting of 15 December 2010 it completed its 14th General Review of Quotas, doubling the value of all quotas to SDR477 billion ($725 billion). China would become the third biggest quota-holder after the US and Japan, while Brazil, India and Russia would all move into the top ten. This would also involve changes in the governance of the IMF.[18]

However, this reform was delayed by the failure of 47 IMF members, including the USA, to sign off on the new reforms. (Any quota reform has, specifically, to be agreed by the USA.) Indeed, in March 2014 the US House of Representatives failed to give its support to this deal, even though the USA would have been allowed to retain its veto. In large part the problem lay with the weak and indecisive Obama administration, but the problem was also simply that US legislators did not like the idea of diluting American power. As Birdsall and Kapur commented, 'The US is like an ageing parent: it is no longer willing to invest much in the family business, but remains averse to ceding control to its mature children. Resentful, the children are seeking opportunities elsewhere – to the detriment of the family firm.'[19] In addition, there was some resentment among Republicans at the perceived over-representation of the EU within the IMF and considerable cynicism about the fact that Christine Lagarde had no sooner left her job as France's finance minister to head the IMF than she moved to push huge amounts of IMF money towards saving the Euro.

A great deal thus hangs on the future of this IMF reform – scheduled to go through by 2015 at the latest. China has responded to this situation by making currency-swap arrangements with more than 20 countries, thus obviating the need for IMF liquidity support. India has followed with a $50-billion currency swap arrangement with Japan. However, the longer the US holds back, the more China and India feel they must build up a Brics alternative to the IMF – a bank that would also function as a bargaining chip. If, on the other hand, the IMF reforms go through, all the Brics nations save South Africa may well feel that they can achieve what they want within the Bretton Woods structures.

The key point to realise is that China and Russia are both great powers who see Brics as merely one instrument alongside others in their consolidation of great power status. And China, inevitably, will be the paymaster of anything that Brics decides. Thus the view of Brics from either Moscow or Beijing is rather different from South Africa's somewhat naïve vision, born of a great deal of rhetoric about the definitional preferability of South-South relations. In terms of that (delusionary) vision the Brics nations are part of a united front with a common determination to help the progressive states of the South led by South Africa.

Russia's push for continued great power status is largely a reaction to the traumatic loss of the Soviet empire which has left Russian nationalists desperately wanting to return to the old days when 'everyone was afraid of us' and furiously resisting the verdict that the US and the West were the winners in the Cold War. China's push is the more significant, for it is based upon the certainty that China will soon overtake the US as the world's largest economy.

South Africa's defeat over the setting up of a Brics development bank – and the deferral in setting up the CRA to 2015 – suggest that it might not be wise for Pretoria to assume that it can rely on aid from that quarter if it falls into a debt trap. Brazil's finance minister, Guido Mantega, let slip the hardly encouraging fact that the CRA was modelled on the Chiang Mai Initiative taken by Asian countries after the 1997 Asian financial crisis. Chiang Mai, which had the support of such heavyweights as Japan and South Korea, provided for an Asian alternative to the IMF: a $240-billion fund to support Asian currencies. Chiang Mai was launched with much fanfare but not a cent was ever paid out and the fund was a dead letter from the start. Once the countries involved realised that all loans would have strings attached and would involve potentially difficult relations between lenders and borrowers, enthusiasm for the project simply collapsed. It remains to be seen whether the same fate will overtake the promised Brics funds.

A perhaps similar model is BancoSur (the Bank of the South) originally proposed by the Venezuelan leader, Hugo Chavez, in 1998. Chavez and his Bolivian counterpart, Evo Morales, took up this proposal out of their discontent with the IMF and World Bank's predisposition towards market economics – they wanted a bank based on the principles of social-ist co-operation. Ultimately, the BancoSur was formally set up in 2009 by Argentina, Brazil, Venezuela, Bolivia, Ecuador, Paraguay and Uruguay, with an intended capital of $20 billion. But nothing ever happened – the bank has never made a loan and to this day no one can say how much each country is supposed to contribute. It would appear that BancoSur, like Chiang Mai, has been stillborn.

Such examples suggest one should be extremely cautious about the Brics financial institutions' future. Moreover, even if the Brics financial institu-tions become operational, there is still the question of how they would work. At Fortaleza it was agreed that each country should have one vote; that other developing countries might be allowed to join but that the Brics countries should never have less than 55 per cent control. Such arrange-ments could hardly overcome the fact that China was bound to be the dominant source of funds and thus have the dominant voice.

An alternative to an IMF bail-out?

There was also some suggestion that the NDB, unlike the Bretton Woods institutions, would make loans without conditionalities – though in fact a condition for being bailed out by the CRA was that a state must have an 'on-track' arrangement with the IMF.[20] But talk of conditionalities cut to the chase. Developing countries which have got into a financial mess have always resented World Bank and IMF conditionalities which rob them of some of their sovereignty. Yet how on earth would the NDB work without conditionalities? The point about imposing conditions is that a bank wants to be paid back and also wants to ensure that the debtor takes steps to get out of the mess that has brought them to the bank's door. If there were no conditionalities, how on earth to ensure that debtors repaid their debts or undertook necessary reforms? President Zuma talked happily of vast sums being pumped into African development, apparently as an act of charity, but it is highly unlikely that Brics lending would operate like that. If it did, it would soon go bust, as have South Africa's Land Bank and Development Bank: both have had to be recapitalised by the state.

On Pretoria's side is the fact that if South Africa needed to be bailed out it would present Brics with a crisis: if it failed to help one of its members, the association would surely collapse. But other questions crowd in. First of all, how can the NDB or CRA lend at interest rates which could well be higher than those charged by the IMF and World Bank? After all, China currently has a credit rating of AA- and the other four Brics members are all at BBB-, which is to say that they have a much higher cost of capital than the Bretton Woods institutions, so if they are not to lose money on every loan they make, they have to reflect that higher cost in higher interest rates. The point is that the Bretton Woods institutions are backed by the strong economies of the EU, Japan and North America so, logically enough, they have lower interest rates and it is a matter of the haves lending to the have-nots. But the NDB and CRA are backed entirely by developing countries in a somewhat fragile state: the idea seems to be lending to the have-nots by those who don't have very much.

Second, the Bretton Woods institutions are dominated by the world's democracies, whereas Brics is dominated by the authoritarian alliance of China and Russia. Brics makes no pretence of being democratic. Typically enough, at Fortaleza no mention was made of Russia's grab for Crimea or the fact that this had earned Russia expulsion from the G-8. The Summit issued lengthy commentaries on the state of the world but effectively said nothing about the Russian attempt to destabilise Ukraine. Yet most commentators were in little doubt that Russian willingness to set up the NDB stemmed in good measure from its fury at the $17-billion IMF loan to the anti-Moscow regime in Ukraine.[21] What Russia wants is an international bank which lends in line with Russia's foreign policy, not against it. The NDB may have started on the basis of equal votes for all but this is hardly the way that Russia or China normally behave.

Third, South Africa's expectation of large loans to Africa seems unrealistic, and particularly so if these are to be without conditions and at low interest rates. The NDB is supposed to lend to build infrastructure and the World Bank estimates that there is currently an infrastructure deficit of at least $1 trillion in developing countries.[22] In effect such loans would simply become grants, for as the online magazine, *The Diplomat*, put it, 'debt repayment from recipient states will be a challenging job for the NDB'.[23]

How likely is this? China gives considerable aid to various African countries but India, Brazil and Russia normally don't do so. Moreover, by 2014
all three of those countries, as well as South Africa, were suffering low or
even negative growth. Any move to give or lend large amounts of money
to Africa would quickly be met in those countries with suggestions that
the money could be better spent at home and a consequent determination
to lend only with strings intended to make sure the money gets repaid.
Frederic Neumann, Head of Asian Economic Research at HSBC, concurs:
'I doubt that Brics funding will be a free cheque. Lending will have strings
attached, which is intolerable to receiving countries.'[24]

So, quite clearly, if South Africa were to get into economic difficulties
and turned to Brics, the question would quickly come down to what China
would do. All one can say with certainty is that China has been careful thus
far never to get itself into a lender-debtor relationship of that kind and, if
asked for help, would measure such a request against its wish to advance
Chinese interests in Africa. It would hardly commit funds merely out of
friendship or goodwill – as the Russian Chinese expert, Mikhail Kapitsa,
puts it, 'The Chinese never befriend anyone for a long time.'[25]

It is difficult to see why China should advance the large sums that South
Africa might require. Indeed, the Chinese have been pulling back somewhat in their recent dealings with Africa. 'There was a lot of enthusiasm
and momentum [in 2013]', says Clement Kwong of Long March Capital
(Beijing). 'That momentum is definitely reined in by a new level of risk
aversion and caution.'[26] The reason is simply that China has now had quite
a few failed investments around Africa and has become nervous about
committing large amounts of capital. There have, in particular, been problems where the Chinese have bought mines and become employers, for the
Chinese tend to have a fairly robust view of value-for-money wages and of
worker discipline. In one Chinese-owned coal mine in Zambia in 2010 the
Chinese management actually fired on protesting workers, injuring 11 of
them. In 2012 the same workers killed the Chinese mine manager.[27]

China's biggest African deal to date, a $2-billion oil-for-infrastructure
bargain with Angola in 2004, has not been a roaring success – but if South
Africa hits a debt crisis it could well need a lot more than that. The only
precedent is the Chinese loan to Venezuela, initially negotiated in 2008

by President Hugo Chavez for $20 billion, to be repaid in oil. By July 2014 this debt had risen to $44 billion and more and more of Venezuela's oil output was mortgaged to pay for the loan – at that date, some 600 000 barrels of oil a day, a problematic figure since Venezuela's oil production is declining and the more that is sent to China, the less there is to export for cash elsewhere.[28] Thus the loan arrangement has turned into an arrangement whereby China is sucking 220 million barrels of oil a year out of Venezuela's falling production and the country's entire economy is increasingly mortgaged to China. This is not, perhaps, an appealing model for South Africa.

At which point one should note that the new Brics institutions are quite small: according to Unctad calculations, even after a decade the NDB could only lend $3.4 billion a year, compared to the $61 billion that the World Bank was expected to lend in 2014.[29] The NDB hopes ultimately to have a capital of $100 billion; the World Bank already has $223 billion.[30] What this means is that in a crunch the CRA might be of some use to South Africa, but any really large-scale help would inevitably require a major decision by China. However, the CRA rule is that South Africa could only borrow up to twice its own contribution, namely $10 billion.[31] Since even to get into that position, South Africa has to chip in with $5 billion, that would mean only $5 billion of real new funding. This would not conceivably be enough. South Africa's needs would probably be at least as big as Venezuela's.

How likely would this be? A really big loan – like that to Venezuela – would see China enter into a virtually colonial relationship with South Africa, one which would provoke a good deal of unfriendly world attention. From China's point of view it would be unnecessary as well as unwise. For a start, China has a huge debt crisis of its own – by June 2014 it had debts amounting to 220 per cent of GDP, a figure then rising by 18 per cent of GDP a year. It appeared that Beijing was meeting the immediate crisis simply by printing more money, but this is hardly sustainable.[32] This is not a situation in which China is really going to feel like extending large new loans to other countries – unless, of course, such loans, as in the Venezuelan case, are actually just a means for procuring necessary mineral imports on acceptable terms.

In August 2014 President Robert Mugabe of Zimbabwe made a special trip to China, desperately seeking a large loan. The Zimbabwean economy – badly managed and looted – was steadily contracting and even the Zanu-PF government was scared. Mugabe had drawn up a new national plan called ZimAsset which required funding of $27 billion. Since Mugabe's 'Looking East' foreign policy had for some years already involved a whole-hearted embrace of China, he felt safe in requesting an initial loan of $10 billion. After protracted talks this came down to $4 billion. However, the Chinese pointed out, Zimbabwe already owed China $700 million and was not even servicing that loan. They couldn't even begin to think of any more aid until loan repayments began. Once Mugabe agreed to that they agreed to $2 billion of investment in infrastructure projects, though in every case they had to be linked to future earnings from mineral resources. As Zimbabwe's finance minister, Patrick Chinamasa, put it: 'You will not come to China to ask for money to invest in a project that won't pay for itself. That would not make economic sense.'[33] And sure enough, as soon as Mugabe returned home, Zimbabwe repaid $180 million of its Chinese loan. With hundreds of millions of Chinese still earning less than $2 a day, the People's Republic is interested in solid business propositions, not charity.

This does not mean, as is sometimes suggested, that South Africa, searching with increasing desperation for a 'Get out of Jail' card, might find that the only way to get Chinese money would be to allow China to buy up South Africa's mines. What China wants is to be able to buy large amounts of minerals from South Africa – and that it can do now, without any need to own mines. In Beijing in 2012 President Zuma pointed out to (then) President Hu Jintao that South Africa's enormous trade deficit with China was 'unsustainable', and implored the Chinese to address it.[34] Absolutely nothing happened because South Africa simply doesn't produce more of what China wants or needs. The only way South Africa would be able to repay a large Chinese loan would be the Venezuelan way – by exporting free an ever-larger share of its mineral production, thus squeezing its exports to others. This might be unacceptable to South Africa. Here one might note, though, a strange similarity. Venezuela has the world's largest oil reserves. Despite (or because of?) that, it has been so spectacularly badly managed that it is heavily in debt and has not even managed to invest sufficiently to maintain production in its oil industry. South Africa has the world's most valuable mineral deposits. Despite or because of that it has become heavily indebted and has not even managed to maintain its mining industry ...

So, if South Africa desperately needs loans and wishes to avoid the IMF, Brics is not really an alternative and, probably, nor is China. It really comes down to the fact that the NDB and CRA are primarily instruments for the projection of 'Chinese soft power',[35] since China is unlikely to need either bailing out or development finance, whereas all its other Brics partners might well need both. If the Chinese did make a loan, it might come at a significant price.

However, experience elsewhere in Africa – in Zimbabwe, for example – suggests that there are few limits to the greed and fecklessness of the new black elite, so that one cannot be sure that the ANC would not, as it were, take the Venezuelan road if that was the only way to keep the cash-flow coming. The ANC now only works as a result of systematic corruption, looting and patronage: to a large extent it is a federation of patronage lords, even of warlords. So the revenue flow absolutely has to be maintained so that those patronage networks can be maintained and so that ANC cadres can continue to enjoy the (corrupt) fruits of office. No doubt similar considerations motivated Venezuela's enthusiasm for a Chinese loan. But that very example shows that this is no way out of anything: by 2014 Venezuela was facing depression and hyperinflation – and, as a result of spending its loans on anything but the needed investment in oil production, it was now facing slumping oil production while sitting on top of the world's biggest oil reserves.[36]

Thus the example of Venezuela suggests that accepting Chinese loans is probably just a stage on the road to ruin and that ultimately reality has to be faced and corrective measures taken. It is worth pointing out that while China might be willing to make such loans, it not only wants its pound of flesh but in fact has no real sympathy with governments that get into such a mess. The Chinese, after all, would never accept such loans themselves. Nor would China itself ever allow trade unions to dictate its labour market (or any other) policy; it would also not long tolerate loss-making state industries which were a burden on the state; and China is used to making fearsome demands on its own consumers in order to keep capital investment high.

So while South African policy makers may well have been comforting themselves with the thought that if the worst comes to the worst, Brics will bail them out, this is probably a delusion. What is possible is a bail-out by way of Chinese loans which would, in practice, simply mean prolonging an untenable situation even further, making the final mess even harder to sort out. At the end of such a rake's progress one would still come back to the IMF, conditionalities and all.

CHAPTER TEN

The Impossibility of Autarchy

South Africans, living in some isolation at the tip of a continent with which they don't interact much, are prone both to parochialism and South African exceptionalism. They are not only slow to accept that other countries have lessons for them and tend to believe that they are special, different, even 'the people of the miracle'. On top of that they have forever before their eyes the example of the apartheid government which successfully paddled its boat against the international currents for over 40 years, which firmly legislated itself into the position it wanted and was able to re-order the entire country in terms of its ideology.

All of this bred what can only be termed 'the illusion of autarchy'. The fact that it was achieved in the context of an ever deepening integration of South Africa into an international political economy – as I attempted to show in *How Long* (1977) – passed most South Africans by. Yet in the end it was those international factors which were decisive. Had the struggle against apartheid been left merely to the ANC and its guerrillas, the apartheid regime would still be in power today. Or, to put it another way, the soaring price of oil and gold enabled the Soviet government and the apartheid government to survive until the end of the 1980s. Had those prices stayed at their 1970 levels, both regimes would have fallen far sooner.

Since 1990 South Africa's integration into that international political economy has deepened enormously. With the end of apartheid, sanctions were lifted, the barriers to investment fell away, the tariff regime was liberalised and people from all over the world flocked in to trade, to invest and simply as tourists. South African trade grew exponentially, foreign exchange regulations were loosened, money flowed in and out and South Africans themselves travelled abroad in ever greater numbers. The result is that South Africa today is more vulnerable – and more sensitive – to international factors than ever before. Despite that, the illusion of autarchy persists, and nowhere more powerfully than on the left. Communist ministers like Rob Davies (trade and industry) and Ebrahim Patel (economic development) continually push for protectionist policies of every kind and even attempt to kick-start local industry with 75 per cent local procurement rules, force mining companies to beneficiate their minerals locally, and so on. Similarly, the ANC left and the EFF both talk in terms of sweeping nationalisation of industry, the enforced take-over of commercial farmland and the expropriation of assets without compensation.

In October 2014 the SACP made its objective of greater autarchy quite explicit:

> It follows that a critical pillar of a second radical phase of the NDR must be to regain a greater degree of national economic sovereignty. Amongst other things this must mean breaking out of South Africa's semi-peripheral positioning within the global imperialist system. In practice this will require a 'relative de-linking' from the dominant global economic powers – including through sub-Saharan regional development, and the development of alternative economic alliances, as in BRICS. Critical also is the challenge of re-industrialisation so that economically we move up the global value chain.[1]

None of this works or can work. Already de-industrialisation under the ANC has halved the size of the manufacturing sector. The intensification of ANC policy foreseen in the document above would doubtless have the effect of shrinking that sector even further – the exact opposite of the 're-industrialisation' it is hoping for. The objective of a 'relative de-linking' from the world capitalist system would simply intensify the domestic investment strike, accelerate capital flight and interdict the steady inflow of foreign capital essential for the economy merely to stand still. It would, in effect, be a recipe for a complete economic breakdown even in the short term. In practice the left either ignores the importance of foreign investors or even sees them as the enemy. Often it speaks as if it would be possible to build socialism in one country in South Africa, even though that failed even in the far larger and more self-sufficient USSR. This is another example of 'magical thinking'.

The basic argument even in *How Long* (1977) was that South Africa was deeply integrated into a world political economy and that this was in the end decisive in forcing the abandonment of the antique ideology of apartheid. Today, South Africa is far more deeply integrated than ever before. That it could 'break out of its semi-peripheral positioning within the global capitalist system' – apparently by dint of simple voluntarism – is no more likely than that it could change its geographical position on the map of the world.

The Zimbabwean example

Nonetheless, faced with the necessity of an IMF bail-out, the left may insist that South Africa attempts to go it alone. In effect they will reach the same moment that Robert Mugabe did in Zimbabwe in October 1999 when he told the IMF to 'shut its mouth'. (He later said the IMF was 'the devil'.) Ever since then Zimbabwe has had to manage without IMF loans and this is what tipped it into its frantic pursuit of autarchy. It would seize the white-owned farms, it would forcibly 'indigenise' commerce, mining and industry, and it would ignore foreign investors and international markets. Fifteen years on, the failure of those policies is apparent to all. Zimbabwe's per capita income is now far below its 1965 levels, many have starved, many have fled, huge numbers are unemployed and, even so, the country has been forced to abandon its own currency and use dollars and rands instead. At the time of writing its economy continues to contract and another great outflow of desperate migrants into the rest of Southern Africa has begun.

Despite Mugabe's obviously ruinous strategy, the ANC has instinctively supported him, allowing him to get away with one rigged election after another. Moreover, radical African nationalists are still attracted by Mugabe's bare-knuckle confrontation with the West and against whites. Hence the EFF slogan in the 2014 election: 'Mugabe, not Mandela, was the True Liberator'. So, without a doubt, when South Africa finds itself face to face with the IMF, there will be powerful voices within the ANC as well as within the EFF, SACP and Cosatu, all demanding that South Africa too should follow the Mugabe example and tell the IMF to go to hell. If that were to happen, South Africa too would find itself on the road to an attempted autarchy. Without doubt such a confrontation would privilege populist initiatives of every kind and South Africa too would see forced indigenisation, much tougher 'land reform' and perhaps nationalisations too. Thus the fear, often-voiced by many abroad and by whites at home, that South Africa will follow the Zimbabwean road to ruin.

Why South Africa can't be like Zimbabwe

It would be impossible to follow such a road for long, for there are vital differences between the two countries. Consider the Zimbabwean example. Its economy has always been primarily agricultural and 80 per cent of the population lives in the countryside. The only towns even of moderate size are Harare and Bulawayo. If disaster strikes – as it did after the farm invasions which began in 2000 – and there is a build-up of urban unemployment added to distress in the countryside, then there are two safety valves. First, every African in Zimbabwe has some relatives living on a farm or on tribal trust land where they can scratch a subsistence living. If things get really bad it is usually possible for the unemployed to return to that subsistence plot and scrape a living by running a few chickens and harvesting a crop of mealies. This is a life of extremely thin commons – often semi-starvation – but it is something. It reflects the fact that a large proportion of Zimbabwe's population lives on the margins of the international economy. Secondly, perhaps as many as 3 million Zimbabweans have flooded into South Africa and more into Botswana, Zambia, Mozambique, Britain and Australia. Even now, this outflow of desperate migrants continues.

South Africa is very different. Only a third of the population – a fraction in continuous decline – lives in the rural areas and the entire life of the country revolves around six large cities – Johannesburg, Ekurhuleni (the East Rand), Pretoria, Cape Town, Durban and Port Elizabeth – and three smaller ones, East London, Bloemfontein and Pietermaritzburg. Some 20 million people live in these cities, their number increasing all the time, and that urbanisation is irreversible: there is no circumstance in which these urban dwellers will return to a rural existence. All these people are wholly integrated into the international market. Secondly – and crucially, there is no country further to the south: after Cape Town all you get is water and the South Pole. So in an emergency South Africa's urban citizens can't flee south like their Zimbabwean counterparts did and do. They would be locked in and that would greatly increase the stakes above anything seen in Zimbabwe. These two reasons alone guarantee that South Africa simply could not survive taking the 'Mugabe option'.

Already, we have seen, the ANC is losing its political grip over this critical urban population. Cape Town already belongs to the DA and the 2016 local elections could well see Port Elizabeth, Pretoria and Johannesburg join the Opposition column or, if the balance of power is held by the EFF, cease to have any stable majority. Indeed, only Durban is really safe for the ANC: it is no accident that the country has largely been ruled from Durban since 2009. It is not clear how the ANC can retain much authority as a national government if it loses these major metropoles.

To this mix one should probably add a new socialist party likely to be created by dissident trade unionists, particularly from Numsa, though probably with support from Zwelinzima Vavi and left activists indignant with the ANC and SACP tolerance of and involvement in corruption. Such a party would provide competition for both the ANC-SACP and the EFF. Its main significance would probably lie in further fragmenting the left electorate at just the point when the ANC can least afford it.

However this political evolution is happening just as South Africa is likely to be hit by a major economic crisis. The exact form of this crisis is hard to predict because – as Marx was quite right to suggest – a regime crisis takes many different forms simultaneously.

Scenario I. Accepting the bail-out

If South Africa is forced towards an economic bail-out it is likely that some fraction of the ANC will join the EFF in refusing to accept IMF conditionalities, a stance which would also be adopted by the new Socialist Party (SP), though it will doubtless choose another name. Given the growing significance of ethnicity within the ANC, it is possible that any split could be along tribal lines with the currently dominant Zulu bloc taking a rejectionist position because of the presence of the (mainly Zulu) SACP within its ranks. But it could just as easily be a Zulu rump that supported the recourse to the IMF, with non-Zulus siding against. The main point is that this deeply divisive event will impact on a party already riven by incipient tribal tensions.

If enough ANC MPs refused to join with the EFF in rejecting the loan, we would see the emergence of a rump ANC–DA coalition which would have the unenviable job of carrying out the measures dictated by the IMF in return for its loan. The DA may have dreamed of power but its reality would be very uncomfortable. The government would have to liberalise the labour market, with Cosatu and the SACP resisting every inch of the way. Public service salaries and numbers would need to be cut, despite the furious resistance of the entire bureaucratic bourgeoisie. Politically 'deployed' but incompetent ANC cadres would have to be rooted out of the civil service and the parastatals if they were to operate efficiently despite their reduced staff numbers. The privatisation of at least a few state industries would lead to job losses and provoke the furious resistance of the well-paid bureaucrats who man them. And so on.

Being part of such a government would be no fun. Cosatu and the SACP would know that they could not survive the liberalisation of the labour market, let alone the abandonment of the National Democratic Revolution. Without doubt they – together with the ANC left, the SP and EFF – would launch mass strikes and bitter protest actions to 'defend the revolution'. These strikes would undoubtedly involve violence and, if this were not enough, the SACP might well decide that it must re-launch Umkhonto we Sizwe to try to defeat the government. Thus the DA-ANC government would face an all-out confrontation – and it would do so with an army and police that are ragged and corrupt remnants of the forces they once were. Although many within the government would be squeamish, there would be little real option but to attempt to crush all extra-legal resistance, even though their opponents would argue that they were emulating the apartheid regime of old. Large numbers of left-wing resisters might indeed end up dead or in prison and attempts would be made to liken them to Mandela, Sisulu, *et al.* Thus this confrontation would also mean South Africa painfully confronting its own history and perhaps looking at it in a new light.

Clearly, the ANC-DA government would have to be very determined to win what might, at times, resemble almost a civil war. One problem is that under Helen Zille the DA has moved more and more in an ANC direction and shown a heightened sensitivity to all the ANC's bugbears. In such a guise the DA would simply lack the guts and nerve which the new situation demanded. But new leaders would emerge within such a struggle and the rhetoric of both sides would escalate. It is ironic to think that some members of the DA recoiled from the party's 'Fight Back' campaign of 1999 because it made them a little uncomfortable. In the battle to make South Africa market-friendly – which is what the struggle would fundamentally be about – they would find themselves fighting back quite literally, as would the rump ANC. How could they do otherwise? It would be impossible to allow the wild men of the EFF and the violent left to take over.

If the new government won this huge social confrontation South Africa would be a rather different place at the end. It would be somewhat battered but far better equipped to take its place within a competitive international market economy. The fight thus engendered would have been so bitter that there would be little prospect of the two wings of the ANC re-uniting, so the change of regime would likely be permanent. The result would be a new version of the 1930s Fusion government led by Barry Hertzog and Jan Smuts. This time it would be a fusion of the DA with the pro-market fraction of the ANC. This would mean a decisive break with the Freedom Charter – but the more that was true, the more the new Fusion party would insist that it was loyal to that Charter, which is so helpfully vague that it can be interpreted in many different ways. Of course, this would be ridiculous.

Clearly, a document produced by a handful of white communists in 1955 is utterly out of date and of no use to a modern party. But the new Fusion party would need all the fig leaves it could get and would insist that it was the true heir of Mandela, the Freedom Charter and so on. In this way it would hope to provide a political home for many of the apolitical and even some of the defeated left.

Naturally, this Fusion party would be attacked by its opponents as sell-outs. The refusenik fraction of the ANC which had teamed up with the EFF would be less likely to fuse with Malema's group and would proclaim itself the 'true' ANC. Its prospects would be uncertain but the EFF would doubtless flourish as the inheritor of the intransigent tradition of the old anti-apartheid struggle. If the Fusion party had a plurality but not a steady majority it would doubtless change the electoral system away from its currently strict proportionality towards a more majoritarian system – in order to favour itself and keep the radicals out.

Scenario II. Why (most of) the ANC would refuse an IMF bail-out

However, it is at least as likely that a majority of the ANC will join the EFF and SP in refusing an IMF bail-out and conditionalities. Whereas the scenario adumbrated above is hardly devoid of excitement, such a choice would mean almost nothing but excitement. In that case the country would in effect take the 'Mugabe option'. But why should it do such a thing when South Africa is so clearly different from Zimbabwe and when the Mugabe model has so evidently failed?

There could, of course, be no economic reasons for such a decision. The reasons would be psychological and political and they are compelling. As we have said, for the SACP and Cosatu an IMF bail-out would be a death sentence and they could be expected to fight an all-out battle to refuse it. The ANC would not only have much the same reservations about the IMF but would know that accepting a bail-out would be a huge public confession of failure. After all, the apartheid government never had to ask the IMF for help – any more than it allowed the electricity supply to fail.

It would thus mean a public admission that the whole era of liberation launched in 1994 had ended in failure. This would cause all manner of agonised soul-searching. Had Mandela been a false prophet after all? Or had later ANC leaders betrayed his promise? When had everything started to go wrong? If the pursuit of the National Democratic Revolution had resulted in this catastrophe, did that mean the whole strategy was wrong? Again, some painful history would have to be reviewed.

For some time now the ANC's critics have claimed that the party is leading South Africa towards failed state status and the sight of the country losing its economic sovereignty would cause many of those critics to feel vindicated. The ANC, for its part, has become increasingly sensitive to the question of failure. Anyone who suggests that the ANC government is failing is immediately attacked as a racist and an 'Afro-pessimist' (optimism being presumed to be a patriotic duty). There is no doubt that the ANC was badly shaken by its loss of ground in the 2014 elections, the emergence of the EFF and the continuing advance of the DA. It kept its post-mortems confidential but its hyper-sensitivity to criticism – even to banal cartoons – suggested considerable anxiety at the now quite clear prospect of political and governmental failure. Acceptance of an IMF bail-out would confirm all those fears.

Moreover, there will be many left and far-left voices which will counsel South Africa to take the Mugabe route – some of them South African voluntary exiles who now support the revolution from a safe distance. For an IMF deal – a submission to the imperatives of the international market – would mean the end of many dreams. It would mean the acceptance that socialism in one country is not a dream but a cul-de-sac (and, almost certainly, a nightmare). It would mean the end of Afro-Marxism, of the aspirations of Cosatu and the SACP, let alone the various further-left fractions beyond that. It would mean the end of the National Democratic Revolution and also of the National Development Plan. The intelligentsia born of the United Democratic Front, the mass movement of the 1980s, and of the Anti-Apartheid Movement have all accepted the *Marxisant* logic of the NDR and have hoped that any failure by the ANC would lead to a still-further-left alternative. But now they would face the prospect of the country making a sharp correction towards the 'Washington consensus' centre – leaving them all politically marooned, even orphaned. Oddly, per-haps, many people find it even harder to abandon their dreams than they do to accept cuts in their standard of living, so one could expect much passionate contestation.

Going for the Mugabe option

All of these reasons make it more likely than not that an IMF bail-out will be refused, at least initially. The system is complicated by the fact that the electoral system gives all power to the party bosses who can simply sack MPs if they fail to toe the line. If there was a pro-bail-out majority in the ANC this would not prevent an insurgency against it by the SACP and Cosatu, because for them this would be a survival issue. If, on the other hand, there was an anti-bail-out majority within the ANC those who dis-sented would simply stay very quiet for fear of losing their seats. Their opposition would be palpable, nonetheless, and would doubtless grow as the implications of 'going it alone' became clear.

The initial decision by an ANC or ANC-EFF government to go it alone and refuse an IMF deal would doubtless be accompanied by much revolu-tionary rhetoric and there would be cheering from Cuba, Venezuela, North Korea and some radicals in the West. But by the same token the public refusal of a bail-out would itself be taken as a very bad signal by the mar-kets and it would soon tip the ANC (or ANC-EFF) into a sort of denialist populism. (Whether it liked it or not, and whatever the formal arrange-ments, a refusal of an IMF bail-out would put the ANC into an *implicit* coalition with the EFF.) There would be a tidal wave of capital flight (the imposition of further exchange controls would not stop it), together with a further currency collapse and the emigration of many skilled workers and professionals, causing the deterioration of key services. Unemployment would increase rapidly and the debt crisis would worsen as lower eco-nomic growth and a growing interest bill made the budget impossible to get back into balance. The rand's fall would have the immediate effect of increasing the trade deficit. The country would thus find itself deep within a debt trap. It would be obvious that things were getting worse and that there was no way out without external help. The combined effects of the crisis would produce seething urban discontent which could well tip over into xenophobic riots.

On top of that, of course, an EFF-ANC government would undoubtedly attempt to blame the crisis on the whites and on foreign capitalists. This might trigger some degree of expropriation and forced 'redistribution', though in fact, of course, the real emphasis would be on creating rent-seeking possibilities for members of the political elite and their friends and relatives. Such things would, by then, be in increasingly short supply and many of the bureaucratic bourgeoisie would be facing ruin. In the 2014 election the EFF promised a doubling of all social grants and also a 50 per cent pay increase for all civil servants. Such pledges are and would be sheerly impossible but, despite the deteriorating financial situation such a government would face, the urge would exist to carry out at least some (unaffordable) increases in both those directions. There would doubtless be similar pressure for the immediate introduction of the mooted National Health Insurance scheme, though, again, this would be wholly unaffordable and without doubt would trigger a further surge in the emigration of doctors, nurses and other medical technicians, the country's most mobile professionals.

Even so, one would expect there to be many voices – not only those of African nationalist ideologues but those of many white and Indian *bien pensants* – which would, at least initially, welcome the idea of a forced and large-scale redistribution of wealth. Unfortunately, this too is a dead end. Of course there are a small number of white billionaires who could be targeted. But it would quickly be found that they had already taken precautions against this by putting a large portion of their wealth off-shore. Similarly, the nationalisation of industry would quickly reveal that many of the companies concerned have built up large-scale interests off-shore and would manage to make these immune to nationalisation so that a government grab would only secure whatever residual assets they had left in South Africa. Even then, of course, there would be the insoluble problem of managing such assets. This requires all manner of technical skills that the government simply doesn't possess. The probability is thus that the companies thus seized would quickly run into crippling management problems, some of which would lead to them closing down completely. This was, after all, the fate of many profitable and technically advanced farms which, a few years after redistribution, were bankrupt and overgrown with weeds.

The reason why initially such changes would be welcomed is that the fact of South Africa's great inequalities has weighed heavily upon the country's 'conventional wisdom' intellectuals. For some time now it has been common for such folk to issue striking appeals for the hyper-wealthy to give away some of their wealth. This marks out those who issue such appeals as progressive, forward-thinking and unselfish – though it is notable that none of them divest themselves of any of their own assets. But this is all kindergarten stuff. The reasons for South Africa's inequalities are (a) the market economy, (b) the dreadful education system which prevents most young Africans from gaining the means to advancement, and (c) the super-imposition on the old class structure of a new, wealthy and completely unproductive elite. The ways of changing all this include the de-fanging of the teachers' union and the eviction from power of this new parasitic class. But no one is willing to envisage either of those measures.

However intolerable the inequalities are, there is simply no political will to do anything which would really change the situation. No one feels comfortable about abandoning the market entirely, let alone union-breaking. And the whole meaning of 'liberation' is that there should be this new parasitic elite feathering its nests, so no one wants to act against 'liberation'. Instead intellectuals waste their time on symbolic appeals to a few individuals who have long since placed their assets beyond reach. The debate over inequality in South Africa is thus fundamentally dishonest. Those who wish for greater equality refuse to will the means. In practice the only hope for less inequality is headlong economic growth.

Back to the land

Without doubt the decision to go for the 'Mugabe option' would entail a drastic acceleration of 'land reform', that is to say the taking of more and more commercial farmland out of production. In the 2014 election the ANC proposed taking 50 per cent of all commercial farms and giving this to the workers, without any compensation for the farmers – thus already moving the party a lot closer to the EFF ambition of complete land seizure without compensation, on the Mugabe model. Even the sheer existence of an EFF-ANC government would panic many farmers into emigration, but any attempt to carry out such 'land reform' proposals – let alone any nationalisations of industry – would plunge the country into a far greater crisis. For, quite quickly, it would bring the very real possibility of the government being unable to feed the cities. Both nationalisations and 'land reform' would see major falls in production and exports, increasing the trade deficit. They would also entail the formal abandonment of the national consensus which produced the constitution, for many of the new initiatives would be unconstitutional.

'Land reform' has an explosive potential. As we have seen, South Africa under ANC rule has already seen a dramatic deterioration from the old agricultural export surplus to a situation of food trade being barely in balance. Any proposal to carry out even the proposed ANC 'reforms' – let alone anything the EFF might demand, or the 'spontaneous' land invasions they might encourage – would undoubtedly produce a major crisis in commercial agriculture and a sharp rise in the food deficit. With the trade deficit already soaring, the government's ability to import extra food would be very limited and before long one might well see food riots in the major cities – which would, of course, inevitably and quickly turn into xenophobic riots. In May 2008 such riots cost the lives of 62 people and saw nationwide unrest. Xenophobia has remained only just beneath the surface and ever since 2008 it has frequently erupted in more localised violence. Indeed, the experience of urban unrest in South Africa is that once mob violence erupts it turns very quickly in a xenophobic direction, whatever its preceding cause.

The loss of central control

As may be seen, the creation of an ANC-EFF government (or merely an ANC government which takes the turn to a Mugabe direction on its own) would soon find itself trying to implement a wholly impossible and, indeed, ruinous set of policies. For one must remember that, even without the EFF, the ANC has on its own embraced a series of policies (expropriation without compensation, the 50 per cent seizure of commercial farmland, the NHI, forced demographic representivity in the workforce, etc) which are already far down that road – and the ANC's official policy is now for a much more radical 'second transition'. While what it euphemistically terms 'land reform' might be the match that ignites the gunpowder, it is clear that there are many other such ignition points once the government embarks on such a road. All of these lead ineluctably towards large-scale urban unrest and a growing loss of central government control.

At this point it is germane to recognise that the South African state is already anaemic and rickety. The average calibre of cabinet ministers is extremely low. Many of them seem to suffer from acute paranoia; some believe in witchcraft. In addition, there is very little co-ordination amongst the absurdly high number of ministries and no really strong drive from the centre. Moreover, few ministers have sufficient economic knowledge to understand how serious the situation is. When the ratings downgrades of June 2014 took place – a crucial step on the road to ruin – Goolam Ballim, Standard Bank's chief economist, remarked on the absence from public discourse of any sense of urgency. 'It's like a real life showing of *Home Alone,*' he said. 'There are no adults in charge.'[2] This is not a government which could withstand a major crisis.

Indeed, the lesson of the May 2008 xenophobic riots was that the ANC government is incapable of dealing with large-scale urban unrest. This was why many terrible acts of violence were allowed to continue for days in major South African cities and why none of the perpetrators were ever punished. Similarly, the government has been powerless in the face of thousands of township protests over poor service delivery, municipal corruption, and so on. In part, this is because both the police and the army are now mere shadows of what they once were, racked by brutality, corruption and incompetence. But the ANC is acutely aware that the old apartheid National Party government also had the greatest difficulty in dealing with township violence, despite its then highly effective security forces. The ANC government lacks such security forces and is in any case desperately concerned not to appear as if it is acting in the same way as the apartheid government. The combination of these disabilities paralyses action. Yet the brute fact is that violent urban discontent is a constant under both ANC and apartheid governments. And the lesson of history is that no government is really able to cope with it.

If South Africa reaches that point it will be obvious to any neutral observer that the government has effectively lost control and that the need for external help has become impossible to resist. However, the government will hardly be composed of neutral observers and would likely continue in denial for a while longer. This, at least, is what happened in Zimbabwe. There one saw African nationalism enter into a prolonged denialist rage in which the very reality of economic factors was disregarded. Prices or exchange rates or farm ownership or the currency were fixed by government fiat, quite regardless of the effects on production or the sheer impossibility of maintaining those prices or rates. In the end the central bank was printing notes for 100 trillion Zimbabwe dollars before the sheer nonsense of it all collapsed under market forces.

If the ANC or ANC-EFF government continued to deny market realities – as it would for a while – then South Africa would be at the crossroads. Most probably, reality would break in and the government would ultimately go running to the one bank willing to lend to it – the IMF. The problem would then be that the IMF's conditionalities would have to be carried out by a government which disliked and disbelieved in them, trying to sabotage them at every turn. However, the record is that reform programmes carried out under such circumstances do not work. They only work when host governments really believe in and embrace the reforms. So South Africa would probably end up taking the IMF's money but then sabotaging the reform programme.

As can be seen, this ends in queer street. Obviously, no other bank would be willing to lend until South Africa had a clean bill of health from the IMF, and this it would not get. The scenario ends in another negotiation with the IMF, this time imposing even tougher terms with provision for an immediate cut-off of funds if reforms were not carried out. In other words, at the end of this lobster quadrille South Africa would always still face the fundamental choice of accepting the IMF-sponsored reforms fully or not. There would, no doubt, be a great amount of verbiage talked about how South Africa would get out of the crisis on its own, that it needed no help and so on. These would be just words and in fact the government's position would become weaker with each failed reform.

In the end the government would either have to buckle and carry out the reforms or it would have to do a Mugabe and throw the IMF out. If the latter happened then things would become harder and harder to predict, for the chances are that the central government would progressively lose all control. This has, after all, happened in many other African states where the government ends up controlling only a strip between the presidential palace and the main (get-away) airport. At that stage the government might even face a situation in which it faced the unravelling of the deal which created South Africa in 1910. The question which South Africa's provinces would then have to face would be whether they were prepared to go down with the ship or strike out on their own. At the very least one would expect the whites-only *Boerestaat* of Orania in the Northern Cape to enjoy mushrooming growth and, probably, other Oranias to be founded elsewhere. By that stage the central government's ability to prevent such initiatives might be very frail indeed.

Thus, if the government (whether ANC or ANC-EFF) did take the Mugabe option it would quickly discover that it was a brutal cul-de-sac which South Africa could simply not survive. The real question is how far down this road to ruin such a government would travel before it reversed itself or collapsed. One cannot be sure that the political elite would react rationally to that choice. Africa is full of examples of political elites who grind their countries down until they are riding on bare tyres, then on the wheel rims, then on axles and so on. Even by 2014 Zimbabwe's rulers were loath to admit that they had taken a fundamentally wrong road with the farm invasions in 2000. But as we have seen, South Africa lacks the safety valves which enabled the Mugabe regime to hold out so long.

Recognising reality

Those who regard the above as merely an apocalyptic vision have the advantage that history never turns out exactly as predicted. But they should ponder the following. Time after time foreign investors, via the medium of the credit-rating agencies, have urged on the South African government the absolute necessity of 'reform'. By this is meant labour market liberalisation, relaxation of immigration rules for skilled foreigners, return to a balanced budget, large cuts in the public service salary budget, ceasing to throw money away on loss-making state-owned industries and a sharp improvement in educational standards in order to produce a more skilled labour force. In practice all these realities have always been simply denied, for each of them would mean offending some key element within the ruling ANC alliance. In practice the reality that matters is the maintenance of the ruling ANC alliance in its present condition.

In the long run there is simply no denying these market realities, but if they are not to be imposed on South Africa by the market's *force majeure* then the only way to avoid that is for the ANC alliance to reform itself and carry out all these changes itself. Hence the question: does anyone really believe in the ANC's ability to thus reform itself?

Ultimately, there is only one way out. That lesson can either be understood in advance, rationally; or it can be learned very painfully after inflicting lasting harm on the country. The real question thus becomes: how quickly will the lesson be learnt? The longer the elite holds out, the more capital, key professionals and international credibility it will lose, making it that much harder to repair the damage later.

The ratings agencies and foreign investors keep up their demands for the above reforms because they cannot believe that they are that difficult to carry out. After all, they have seen dozens of countries accept this logic, whatever their previous policies. Why should South Africa find it so hard? This ignores the whole emotional temper of ascendant African nationalism, its parochialism and its belief in entitlement, victimhood and South African exceptionalism. These are all very strong ideological forces, so what is in prospect is a major trial of strength.

Facing the inevitable

Thus one way or another, a regime crisis – and almost certainly a regime change – is inevitable. Either South Africa will end up with a DA-ANC Fusion government committed to observing market realities; or there will be an ANC or ANC-EFF government which takes the Mugabe option, after which the latter will either hurriedly reverse itself in order to guarantee its own survival, or the country that was so painfully patched together in 1910 will disassemble.

Either way, we are now pretty much at the end of the 'liberation' period. In the most important sense, this is a very sad end to a whole historical epoch. From the days of the early nineteenth century on South Africa saw the birth of a liberal conscience which hoped to see the abolition of all discrimination and the inclusion of black people as full citizens. Despite endless vilification and many setbacks, this current gradually grew in strength and in the twentieth century was strengthened by many socialists and communists, all equally struggling for the same liberation, a current finally made real by the growing strength of African nationalism. It was a very hard and long struggle and the author played his own tiny part in it, espousing this cause from my teenage years on. In the end I came back to live in South Africa to see that liberation through.

What is now clear, just 20-odd years later and beyond any reasonable doubt, is that 'liberation' has failed, that the regime it has produced is quite incapable of governing South Africa as a free, democratic and functioning country. More and more things just don't work. This not just rhetorical hyperbole. Around 80 per cent of state schools don't work, and nor do many state hospitals. The electricity supply has failed and the new power stations necessary to fill the gap are both many years late and many times more costly than they should have been – a sign of comprehensive management failure. The civil service, the police and many of the local municipal bureaucracies clearly don't work. By July 2014 it was reported, for example, that every single municipality in the whole of North West province was bankrupt, victims of the usual ANC looting.[3] There is a growing trade deficit but the government has decided to tax mineral exports.[4] Similarly, the one great growth industry – tourism – stands to be throttled by ludicrous new immigration restrictions.[5]

Throughout the economy the consequence of the disastrous failure of education is an ever-growing shortage of skilled labour of every kind yet the state's restrictions on the admission of skilled professionals ensures that this cannot be met. As a rule of thumb, anything controlled or touched by the ANC – 'the liberation movement' – works very poorly or doesn't work at all.

On top of that, abuses of democracy pile one upon the other. Crime and insecurity rack the land, the economy fails, unemployment and inequality grow. The very integrity of the nation state is increasingly at stake. It is a commonplace to find people of all races who say things were better under apartheid. Inevitably, some whites feel thus confirmed in their old contempt for all things African, but much sadder and more important is that this turn of events risks confirming many Africans in their lack of self-esteem, in their anxiety that the white supremacists might have been right after all. It is this agonised sense of threatened inferiority, almost of self-hatred, that lies behind many of the most passionate black panegyrics against whites. The worse the sense of failure, the more passionately the 'liberated' ego needs to vent itself. This is strictly Frantz Fanon territory. No one has written about it better. It is quite common among such outpourings to find anti-white racism, anti-Semitism, a hatred of Asians, sexism, homophobia – every and any prop for desperately threatened egos.

The ongoing failure of South African 'liberation' – and there is no end yet in sight – will be a trauma for the black world as a whole. In 2010 the UN General Assembly proclaimed 18 July to be Nelson Mandela International Day, a bizarre (and failed) attempt to declare a sort of universal public holiday.[6] This had, of course, been pushed by an ANC government desperate to capitalise on Mandela's legacy. But where does all that lead if the whole experiment of black rule in South Africa fails? There is, of course, a considerable recrudescence of white racism in South Africa fuelled by a very deep anger at this failure. The internet is full of inexcusable racism, insisting that black people are and always will be genetically inferior. This is sometimes expressed by people who say they bitterly regret their previously more liberal opinions. But failure is racially divisive on both sides and there is no shortage of equally furious black racists.

Of course, the white supremacists were and are wrong and it is not true that 'Africans can't govern'. What has gone wrong in South Africa is a mixture of things. First, the whole long history of oppression suffered by the

African people. Then a wrong turn in the 1950s saw the seduction of the African nationalist leadership by the communists. The ANC thus became committed to the SACP-written Freedom Charter – a piece of impossibilism which has haunted the country ever since – and then to hopeless and self-defeating armed struggle. This led to nearly 30 years of jail and exiled bitterness.

The result was that what re-emerged into the light in the early 1990s was a badly wounded black persona, full of complexes and grievances, and this has been working itself out in grandiloquent style since then. Everyone hoped for better, of course, but history is not to be denied. It was the same after the Anglo-Boer War. The English-speakers hoped that Afrikaners would now settle down as happy compatriots in a united South Africa, but Afrikaners were driven by many of the same ghosts of inferiority, by the memory of the concentration camps, the bitterness of defeat and 'a century of wrong'. It took Afrikaners several generations to work through that inheritance. It will take Africans at least that long.

Unfortunately, perhaps, we are now all part of a globalised world and these passions cannot be worked out in such ignorant defiance of the international political economy as was once true. Globalisation ensures that the costs of such dysfunctional behaviour are now very much higher. If, in the 1930s, a South African textile or other industry was mismanaged or wages were too high, it could stagger on in the local market. Today, such an industry would quickly be annihilated by Asian competition. Similarly, a country – like South Africa – which tries to tax its exports, deliberately prevents the inflow of skilled immigrants or ignores investors' wishes will quickly be punished. South Africa's tragedy is that it has always been governed by the last century's ideology – by segregation into the late twentieth century, by an amalgam of Marxism and 1960s African nationalism well into the 21st century.

The country is set up for a huge and obvious failure. This, sadly, has got to take place. It really is true that South Africa is a place where things have to get worse before they can get better. So its inevitable failure is not really such bad news. Ever since 1994 South Africa has lived in a sort of dream world in which it was possible to believe six impossible things before breakfast.[7] We have seen all considerations of merit and ability to do the job disregarded in the cause of affirmative action. The highest good in this new society was 'transformation' in which people were pushed to the front of every queue on account of their gender, skin colour or political persuasion. Everything which could be termed 'anti-transformation' was racist, sexist or reactionary. Indeed, even the words 'merit' or 'standards' were, bizarrely, seen as racist. Demographic representivity was seen as a good in itself. No society in world history has succeeded on this basis.

Everywhere there was a huge amount of pretending. One had to pretend that people who were hopeless at their jobs were good at them. That South–South trade was a good thing, even if it meant the annihilation of the South African footware and textile markets by the Chinese. That black economic empowerment was not just corrupt crony capitalism. That South Africa's steady decline on every sort of index was due to the 'apartheid inheritance'. That corruption under apartheid was just as bad as under the ANC, though the rankings of Transparency International told a very different story. One had to refrain from pointing out that many cabinet ministers were obvious buffoons or thieves. One had to pretend that the dislocation of the black family was simply due to apartheid, even though it had worsened considerably since the end of apartheid. One had to pretend that the state, the economy and the country were not failing. And so on and on.

What the assertion of these values and this optic amounted to was a belief that South Africa could live entirely within its own bubble. Along with this went a belief in South African exceptionalism, that this was somehow a 'miracle country' where everyone else's hard-earned lessons did not apply. This was ridiculous and in a world of globalisation it couldn't possibly last. Not that the author wishes to sing the praises of globalisation or the free market. But in the modern world no state can defy market forces completely and nor can it defy the rules of rationality as practised elsewhere. It doesn't matter whether one likes this or not. Market forces are simply like the weather and you have to accommodate them, have to be market rational. If one learns nothing else from the collapse of communism, one must at least learn that.

What this all means is that the 'liberation era' is almost over, by which I mean a period in which the ANC ruled mainly according to its lights as a 'liberation movement', without much regard to the constraints of the real world beyond. It is difficult to argue that it used these 20 years well. That period has seen a deterioration of the whole national infrastructure – roads, railways and ports. It has seen the virtual collapse of public health facilities in many areas and it has seen a large and steady fall in educational standards. The government stood by and did nothing while an Africanist ideologue all but destroyed a major national asset, the country's third-best university, the University of KwaZulu-Natal. The government has also provoked a vast outward movement of the country's best brains and skills and it has made it all but impossible to replace these via immigration. It has seen a steady decline in its ratings on almost every major international index.

These are not just the signs of a country that is not succeeding. The problem is more fundamental than that. The government not only does not believe in appointments on merit: it actively denounces such a practice as 'racist'. Worse still, the once-liberal Opposition DA agrees. One simply cannot run a modern market economy on that basis. The same is true about hobbling companies and other institutions with black empowerment and affirmative action schemes which the country's international competitors would never apply. Moreover, the ruling party is steadily becoming a bantustan party based on chiefly patronage, exhibiting all the cultural signs of rural backwardness. No modern country has succeeded under such a party. The government took over a public electricity provider in rude health with 25 per cent spare capacity and the cheapest electricity in the world. In 20 years it has reduced that to a shambolic wreck unable to provide a reliable electricity supply even at extremely high cost. Many of the major corporations which once invested in the country are fleeing. One could go on.

The big question about ANC rule was whether African nationalism which had elsewhere conquered only poorer agrarian economies and societies would be able to cope with the challenges of running a modern industrial economy. Twenty years of ANC rule have shown conclusively that the party is hopelessly ill-equipped for this task. Indeed, everything suggests that South Africa under the ANC is fast slipping backward and that even the survival of South Africa as a unitary state cannot be taken for granted.

The fundamental reason why the question of regime change has to be posed is that it is now clear that South Africa can either choose to have an ANC government or it can have a modern industrial economy. It cannot have both. As this choice becomes more pressing, the ANC will pretend that only a few white capitalists want anything different from them, but the fact is that the overwhelming mass of South Africans of every colour cannot imagine – and certainly do not want – a future in which they are not part of a modern industrial society. As the pressures for regime change increase the ANC will certainly be tempted to rig elections to prevent change – it has already begun to do so – but the longer the movement attempts to hold back the huge majority which wants a different future, the more likely it is to be swept away altogether by the tide of change.

As the era of 'liberation' fades, one has to hope that South Africa will recognise the obvious good sense of making the best use of the human capital that it has. This may seem elementary, but it has not yet happened in South Africa. When the whites ruled they tried to manage without allowing Asians to contribute all they could and actually trying to deprive Africans of their citizenship. Now that Africans rule they are trying to limit the contribution of whites and Asians. Neither regime treated those of mixed race fairly. We are still waiting for a truly non-racial inclusivity. It is encouraging that the Democratic Alliance has made steady gains in every election since 1994, for it is by far the most inter-racial party – though, of course, it is equally striking that African nationalism is beginning to erode while the party for which almost all whites vote is gaining. The tragedy is that under its present leadership the DA has abandoned its decades-long commitment to merit, not race. This betrayal of principle is likely to be treated harshly by future historians.

The problem that South Africa faces is that on the basis of all past experience it seems likely that a protracted further period of ANC rule will see continued national decline, a possible debt-trap and even threats to the integrity of the country. The real questions are two. First, will the ANC lose power soon enough for all these disasters to be avoided? And second, if the ANC's decline does continue, will the party be willing to accept democratic defeat? What one can be sure of, whichever of the above scenarios play out, is that as the long dream of liberation fades and practical problems press in ever more urgently, the future will be a whole lot less ideological than the period since 1994. As Franklin Roosevelt said during the Depression, ordinary Americans were not all that concerned to debate capitalism and socialism. What they really wanted was 'a chicken in every pot'. South Africans are no different.

This book is an exercise in political economy. I was happy to leave the argument here but many people with whom I discussed the book's ideas told me that the perspectives I held out were deeply depressing. Observing that I am by no means depressed, they demanded to know why. Let me start with Jan Smuts's observation that 'South Africa is a country in which neither the best nor the worst ever happens'. The wisdom behind this, even in Smuts's time, was that the multiracial nature of South African life prevented any group from having its own way completely. In the era of universal suffrage this has only become more true.

This book arrives at the conclusions it does through what I hope is objective economic, social and historical analysis. I am not, in any case, a Cassandra who enjoys the prediction of disaster. I have always found that however dire a prognosis one may reach, if it makes realistic and rational sense it is always better to face the truth and deal with things as they really are. But it is also why I am more optimistic than many. However much the ANC may resist an IMF bail-out, many countries (including Britain) have had to go through that experience. They all survive it and some, at least, are the better for it.

Secondly, South Africa has had six presidents in the last 25 years. That, plus Mbeki's eviction when he tried to overstay his welcome, make it all but certain that South Africa will not fall prey to the phenomenon of the president-for-life which has done so much to destroy democracy elsewhere in Africa.

Third, although this analysis highlights a huge failure of governance by the ANC, it also suggests that the penalty for that will indeed be a regime change of some kind. That is surely as it should be if accountability matters.

Finally, it seems to me that a fundamental fact of South African history is that the struggle for black liberation temporarily empowered a radical left elite without real roots in the black majority. That is, the situation is rather like Portugal after the overthrow of the fascist regime of Salazar and Caetano by the Armed Forces Movement led by Major Otelo de Carvalho and Major Vitor Alves, both men of the revolutionary left. After more than 50 years of fascism, there briefly seemed to be the possibility that Portugal would lurch straight from the far right to the far left. But before long the underlying sociological realities asserted themselves. Portugal was, after all, a Catholic European country. In 1976 Mario Soares, a social democrat, was elected as president and thereafter the Portuguese were left with the familiar choice between Christian Democrat conservatives and social democrats.

South Africa too endured almost 50 years of apartheid rule and, mainly because of its resolute rejection of even the most modest reformism, the SACP was able to gain ground within the African nationalist movement. There was strong resistance to this – Robert Sobukwe split away from the ANC to form the Pan Africanist Congress in protest and even though Albert Luthuli, the ANC leader, accepted the alliance with the SACP, he himself was a Christian liberal who abhorred violence. Nonetheless, by 1961 a leftward version of the ANC became dominant, launched the armed struggle and by 1994 had come to power.

Yet this version of the ANC is actually strongly at variance with majority black opinion, let alone the opinion of the minorities. The evidence of all the opinion surveys is that support for the SACP has never risen above 2 per cent; that black, white and coloured South Africans are all overwhelmingly Christians; that most black opinion is socially conservative (far more so than white opinion), wanting the return of the death penalty, disliking abortion, taking a somewhat traditional view of women's role, gay rights and so forth. Moreover, such surveys showed that a large majority of black opinion wanted consensus, not inter-racial conflict, and would like to see a solution backed by whites and the business community.

In that sense the whole ANC experiment is top-heavy. As we have seen, in power the ANC has actually become more chiefly, more tribal, a giant federation of political bosses held together by patronage, clientelism and concomitant looting and corruption. This has created a political regime which is quite incapable of managing and developing a modern state. It may take great social convulsions to change that because the groups now in power will not easily let go of it. Indeed, had they played their cards more cleverly they might have consolidated their rule. But in fact they have done the opposite. The result is an imminent crisis on many fronts. So, somewhere out ahead of us lies a regime change towards a form of governance which is closer to South Africa's underlying sociological realities. My own hope – supported by a certain optimism – is that, as in Portugal, this will ultimately see the consolidation of liberal democracy here in South Africa too.

Notes

CHAPTER 1

Then and Now

1 National Security Council document 1969, Foreign Relations of the United States, 1969–1976, Volume XXVIII, Southern Africa, Document 17.

2 GM Fredrickson, *White Supremacy: A Comparative Study in American and South African History*, Oxford University Press, 1980.

CHAPTER 2

KwaZulu-Natal, the World of Jacob Zuma

1 The best source on Mandla Gcaba and S'bu Mpisane is, inevitably, the Durban morning paper, *The Mercury*, together with the *Sunday Tribune*; but see also *The Witness*, 11 February 2013; *Sunday Sun*, 29 December 2013; *The Citizen*, 12 May 2008; *Sunday Times* (Johannesburg), 25 May 2008.

2 See the Mandla Gcaba Archives at *City Press*; 'Keeping it in the family', *Mail & Guardian*, 19 March 2010; *The Witness*, 16 May 2008; 'An empire built on controversy', *City Press*, 4 June 2011; 'Gcaba sued over R4m house', *IOL News*, 22 August 2010.

3 *City Press*, 4 June 2011.

4 *Daily Maverick*, 11 February 2013; *The Witness*, 16 May 2008; *The Times*

The Witness, 16 May 2008; *The Times* (Johannesburg), 20 March 2011.

5 *News24 Archives*, 11 January 2001.

6 Court testimony of Inspector Siyabonga Shange, *News24 Archives*, 11 January 2001.

7 See, for example, 'The rise and fall of Shauwn and S'bu Mpisane, Durban's Teflon Couple', *Daily Maverick*, 11 February 2013.

8 See, for example, 'Constable with a fleet of supercars', www.dispatchlive.co.za, 8 February 2013; 'Mpisanes give away homes, furniture', *Independent on Saturday*, 22 March 2014; 'Mpisane pays R5.6m to have cars returned', *City Press*, 2 August 2013.

9 *Sunday Tribune*, 24 April 2011.

10 *Daily News*, 11 July 2011.

11 Private source, interviewed in Durban, 20 January 2009.

12 See N Claude, 'Mayhem in the Midlands', *KwaZulu-Natal Briefing*, November 1997; C Goodenough, 'Richmond follow-up', *KwaZulu-Natal Briefing*, February 1998; C Goodenough, 'Who killed Sifiso Nkabinde?', *KwaZulu-Natal Briefing*, March 1999.

13 See RW Johnson, *South Africa's Brave New World. The Beloved Country Since the End of Apartheid* (Allen Lane/Penguin, 2009), p 62, for more detail.

14 Private information.

15 *Mail & Guardian*, 7–13 December 2012.

16 See R Guha, *Gandhi before India* (Allen Lane, 2013), especially pp 403–11, 428–9, 437, 444,

448–9, 454, 472, 478, 500.

17 See Johnson, *South Africa's Brave New World*, pp 122–30.

18 Interview with Jacob Zuma, 15 April 2008.

19 See M Gevisser, *Thabo Mbeki. The Dream Deferred* (Jonathan Ball, 2007), p 38.

20 Private information. The emissary, Mendi Msimang (then the ANC Treasurer), visited the Judge-President of KZN, Vuka Tshabalala, and pointed to Squires's name, which Tshabalala immediately agreed to.

21 See Johnson, *South Africa's Brave New World*, pp 544–50.

22 I have covered these events in greater detail in *South Africa's Brave New World*, especially chapters 12, 13 and 15.

23 Profile of Mandla Gcaba, wordpress.com. weblog, 20 October 2009.

24 See Johnson, *South Africa's Brave New World*, especially pp 545-555; also 'Manipulation, trumped-up charges, selective prosecutions, honey traps, hoax emails and abuse of power paved the road to Mbeki's Waterloo', http://152.111.1.87/argief/berigte/citypress/2012/03/29/CP/5/p5lead.html.

25 *The Witness*, 25 March 2011.

26 *Mail & Guardian Online*, 6 June 2014.

27 Dr Van Zyl Slabbert, who was at the same table, told me this. He also told me that at the same dinner he received a message that Jacob Zuma was waiting to see him in the car park. He hastened outside where Zuma explained that this was the only way to have privacy. Everywhere else there were informers and microphones. He had, he said, determined to bid for the presidency and asked Slabbert if he would be willing to give him the benefit of his advice. Slabbert readily agreed. I don't know whether his offer was ever taken up but the fact that he sought the help of Slabbert (who was thought to be close to Mbeki) shows how widely he cast his net.

28 Interview with Jacob Zuma, Cape Town, 15 April 2008.

29 Gevisser, *Thabo Mbeki*, p xli.

30 Johnson, *South Africa's Brave New World*, p 555.

31 There were, however, continuous ethnic rumblings amongst the ANC in exile. See S Ellis, *External Mission: The ANC in Exile 1960–1990* (Jonathan Ball, 2012).

32 See Johnson, *South Africa's Brave New World*, especially pp 560–72.

33 Memo of 2009 to the National Prosecution Authority, *News24*, 12 October 2014.

34 In what follows I have relied heavily on *City Press*, 17 July 2014. On MRDI see *New Age*, 24 July 2013; *M&G online*, 7 October 2011;

eNCA, 14 July 2013.

35 *City Press*, 14 July 2013.

36 *City Press*, 31 August 2014.

37 Hulley is claiming not to have been a director in order to avoid a R1.5-billion suit. However, another of the directors, Thulani Ngubane, has filed an affidavit saying that Hulley was 'an active director'. Hulley now faces perjury charges which could lead to a fine of R100 000 and being struck off as an attorney. See *Mail & Guardian*, 8 February 2015, together with various other articles in the *Mail & Guardian* Hulley file, http://mg.co.za/tag/michael-hulley.

38 On Huang see *Africa-Asia Confidential*, vol 4, no 5, 2014; *IOL*, 20 August 2012; *News24*, 22 June 2014; and *M&G online*, 7 January 2011.

39 *Sunday Times*, 22 June 2014.

40 *News 24*, 22 June 2014.

41 *City Press*, 27 July 2014.

42 *Business Report, Sunday Independent* (Johannesburg), 18 July 2010.

43 *Business Report, Cape Times*, 21 July 2010.

44 *Mail & Guardian*, 25–31 October 2013.

45 *The Witness*, 29 January 2014; *IOL News*, 23 October 2012.

46 *Sunday Tribune*, 24 April 2011.

47 *The Witness*, 25 March 2011.

48 *Ibid.*

49 *Noseweek*, August 2014.

50 *Mail & Guardian*, 18–24 June 2010.

51 *Ibid.*

52 *Ibid.*

53 *Ibid.*

54 Selebi was receiving money directly from criminal bosses. See, for example, *M&G online*, 6 and 9 October 2009.

55 *Mail & Guardian*, 15–21 November 2013.

56 See under 'The ANC: party of the bantustans', p 135.

57 *Mail & Guardian Online*, 25 July 2014.

58 See, for example, http://mg.co.za/tag/thuthukile-zuma.

59 *City Press*, 27 July 2014.

60 *Sunday Times*, 4 May 2014.

61 *City Press*, 23 March 2014.

62 *Sunday Times*, 29 December 2013.

63 *Business Day*, 20 October 2014.

64 *Sunday Independent*, 16 February 2014.

65 *Mail & Guardian*, 16–22 May 2014.

66 *City Press*, 18 May 2014.

67 *Ibid.*

68 *Business Day*, 26 March 2014.

69 For all these references and many more see G van Onselen, *Clever Blacks, Jesus and Nkandla* (Jonathan Ball, 2014).

70 *City Press*, 4 May 2014.

CHAPTER 3
The ANC Under Zuma

1 Johnson, *South Africa's Brave New World*, especially chapter 2.

2 Such a situation is not just African: one could observe similar processes at work in many of the ex-Soviet republics once communism collapsed.

3 *Mail & Guardian Online*, 14 January 2009.

4 A byword for corrupt politics: the system of political patronage that ran New York City in the 1800s.

5 All data from Independent Electoral Commission, Election Report, 2009.

6 See, for example, Sunette Bridges, 'Free State – The private kingdom of Premier Ace Magashule', 23 May 2014, http:// sunettebridges.co.za/free-state-private-kingdom-of-premier-ace-magashule/; 'ANC-versus-ANC man lays charges against Magashule', *City Press*, 12 February 2013; 'Magashule tackled on corruption', *IOL News*, 26 February 2013; 'Ace Magashule's Potemkin Villages of the Free State', *Daily Maverick*, 6 March 2013; 'Magashule in denial about the state of the province', DA MPL Assistance Network, 25 February 2014, http://www.dampl.co.za/2014/02/magashule-in-denial-about-the-state-of-the-province/.

7 *Mail & Guardian*, 26 June–2 July 2009.

8 See, for example, 'David Mabuza shrugs off Malema's "cheap politicking"', *City Press*, 22 January 2014; 'Benadie (Mpumalanga DA leader) says Mabuza is corrupt', *Barberton Times*, 8 April 2014; 'The indomitable David Mabuza, still the king of Mpumalanga', *Daily Maverick*, 10 April 2012; 'Murder, lies and corruption: Mbombela and the bequeathal of the ANC's "Family" War', sacsis.org.za, 9.9.11, http://sacsis.org.za/site/article/744.1; 'Mathews Phosa denies vendetta against David Mabuza', *Citizen*, 25 November 2014, 'Mabuza, Phosa go head to head', *News24*, 1 February 2015.

9 *City Press*, 27 March 2014.

10 Chris Vick, 'They never fought for us', *Daily Maverick*, 6 September 2014.

11 *The Star*, 8 September 2014.

12 Lawrie had been busy on this project not long before he died in October 2011 and discussed his findings with me.

13 *City Press*, 23 December 2012.

14 *Mail & Guardian*, 18–22 December 2009.

15 In 2010 Nyanda's Director-General reported fraud by Nyanda to the tune of R70 million. She was immediately sacked but took legal action. Nyanda was then removed from his cabinet post, only to be re-appointed as a counsellor to Zuma. 'Nyanda Inc makes millions from govt', *Mail & Guardian*, 29 January 2010; 'Siphiwe Nyanda makes millions from govt', mybroadband.co.za, 30 January 2010; 'Siphiwe Nyanda and unlawful tenders', mybroadband.co.za, 18 March 2010; 'Nyanda's company got R68m Gauteng tender – DA', PoliticsWeb, 18 March 2010; 'Nyanda report gets mixed reactions', www.ITweb.co.za, 13 August 2010; 'DA: govt must get R50m out of Abalozi', *Times Live*, 4 November 2010.

16 *Sunday Times*, 31 January 2010.

17 *The Sowetan*, 1 October 2012.

18 *Sunday Times*, 16 May 2010.

19 *City Press*, 20 August 2014. Nontuthuzela 'Pankie' Sizani was charged with 30 counts of fraud and money laundering. The *Mail & Guardian* of 2 September 2014 reported that Equal Education had expressed concern at the way that the case was being repeatedly postponed. The first postponement, for a year, took place when Sizani claimed to have a medical condition which could not, however, be disclosed to the court or the public. Equal Education protested at 'ongoing delays which have thus far prevented justice from being done'.

20 *Mail & Guardian*, 22–28 January 2010.

21 *Business Day*, 5 August 2010; *Cape Times*, 25 January 2010.

22 *City Press*, 20 February 2011.

23 'Mbeki hits back at interference comments', *Mail & Guardian*, 18 September 2008, http://mg.co.za/article/2008-09-18-mbeki-hits-back-at-interference-comments.

24 For more on the Guptas see *News24*, 2 May 2012 and *M&G online*, 7 May 2013 and 20 December 2013.

25 See *Mail & Guardian Online*, 31 March 2013; *Sunday Independent*, 2 March 2013; *City Press*, 13 March 2011.

26 Quoting Koki Khojane, a Cosatu shop steward. *City Press*, 5 May 2013.

27 See *Mail & Guardian Online*, 3 May 2013.

28 Secretary-general's *Report to the Third National General Council of the ANC*, Durban, 2010.

29 All figures from Independent Electoral Commission, Municipal Results, 2011.

30 www.ifp.org.za, 20 October 2013.

31 Even Anthony Sampson, Mandela's biographer, once acidly dismissed Inkatha to me with the remark that 'Zulus are bloody stupid'. But such stereotypes are common.

32 *Sunday Independent*, 25 March 2012.

33 See www.iol.co.za, 7 May 2012.

34 *Sunday Independent*, 6 May 2012.

35 *Mail & Guardian Online*, 9 September 2012.

36 Gaston Savoi is on trial for multiple charges of corruption, fraud, money-laundering and racketeering in both the Northern Cape and KwaZulu-Natal. He also seems to have similar cases to answer in Namibia and Uganda. He protests his innocence.

37 His office did not deny the charge and it seems to have been this amount which he repaid. See www.drum.co.za, 19 April 2012; *City Press*, 16 July 2011; www.iol.co.za, 2 August 2011; *Mail & Guardian Online*, 21 November 2013 and also the *Wikipedia* entry on Zweli Mkhize.

38 *Business Day*, 18 December 2014.

39 See R Pithouse, 'Twelve bullets in a man's body, twelve more in a collective fantasy', www.opendemocracy.net, 29 August 2013; also *IOL News*, 19 March 2012.

40 *IOL News*, 6 February 2014.

41 *Business Day*, 10 April 2013.

42 On Vavi–Nzimande tensions see *The Sowetan*, 18 September 2012; *Business Day*, 13 March 2013; and the *Daily Maverick*, 14 December 2013.

43 *Sunday Independent*, 26 February 2012.

44 *City Press*, 9 September 2012.

45 *Mail & Guardian*, 13–19 July 2012.

46 *Business Day*, 26 June 2012.

47 Nzimande joined fellow cabinet member Siphiwe Nyanda as a long-term resident at the 5-star hotel. See I Davidson, 'ANC defence of luxury hotel stays desperate', *PoliticsWeb*, 19 July 2010.

48 See *Mail & Guardian Online*, 4 April 2014; also R Munusamy, 'Dlamini v. Vavi: only one will survive', *Daily Maverick*, 7 April 2013, and on the delayed congress see www.iol.co.za, 3 November 2013.

49 See www.terrybellwrites.com, 14 September 2014; 'Hands off Cosatu!', *Amandla*, no 30, April–May 2013.

50 *The Times*, 9 April 2014; *Business Day*, 9 April 2014.

51 *Sunday Times*, 23 March 2014.

52 *Ibid*.

53 *Sunday Times*, 14 September 2014.

54 *Sunday Independent*, 27 April 2014.

55 *Ibid*.

56 *Ibid*.

57 *Ibid*.

58 *Ibid*.

CHAPTER 4
Manguang and After

1 *The Times*, 18 July 2012; *Business Day*, 12 December 2012.

2 *Sunday Times*, 13 May 2012.

3 *Sunday Times*, 13 May 2012, and *Sunday Independent*, 7 November 2012.

4 *Sunday Times*, 13 May 2012.

5 *Sunday Times*, 1 July 2012; *Sunday Independent*, 1 July 2012.

6 *The Times*, 19 September 2012.

7 *Ibid*.

8 For Thandekile Sabisa (anti-Zuma) against William Ngozi (pro-Zuma), *Business Day*, 14 August 2012.

9 *Business Day*, 6 August 2012.

10 *Sunday Times*, 14 October 2012.

11 *Business Day*, 22 November 2012.

12 *Cape Times*, 19 November 2012.

13 *Sunday Times*, 17 June 2012.

14 *The Times,* 6 December 2012.

15 *Sunday Times*, 9 December 2012.

16 *Sunday Times*, 16 December 2012.

17 *Sunday Independent*, 23 December 2012.

18 *Sunday Independent*, 16 December 2012.

19 *Business Day*, 27 June 2012.

20 *Mail & Guardian*,14–20 December 2012.

21 *Mail & Guardian*, 30 November–6 December 2012.

22 *Ibid*.

23 *City Press*, 2 December 2012.

24 *Sunday Times*, 17 March 2013.

25 *Sunday Times*, 15 December 2013.

26 *Sunday Independent*, 29 July 2013.

27 *Business Day*, 16 July 2013.

28 *Sunday Times*, 21 July 2013.

29 *Business Day*, 30 May 2013.

30 *Business Day*, 31 May 2013.

31 *Business Day*, 12 March 2013.

32 *Mail & Guardian*, 20 May 2011.

33 *Sunday Independent*, 10 March 2013.

34 *Sunday Independent*, 2 June 2013.

35 *Sunday Times*, 18 August 2013.

36 *The Times*, 22 April 2013; *Sunday Times*, 9 June 2013.

37 *Sunday Independent*, 17 March 2013.

38 *Business Day*, 30 September 2013.

39 Mpho Ramakatsa, one of the six ANC members who successfully got the Constitutional Court to nullify the ANC provincial conference of 2012 and dissolve the provincial committee it elected, has also laid criminal charges against Magashule and a series of businessmen and officials. See 'ANC-versus-ANC man lays charges against Magashule, others', *City Press*, 12 February 2013. See also Sunette Bridges,

'Free State – The private kingdom of
Premier Ace Magashule', 23 May 2014, http://
sunettebridges.co.za/free-state-private-
kingdom-of-premier-ace-magashule/.
40 *Mail & Guardian Online*, 7–13 June 2013.
41 *City Press*, 21 September 2014.
42 *Sunday Times*, 14 July 2013.
43 G van Onselen, 'Is Jacob Zuma a dictator?',
Business Day, 29 September 2014.
44 *Sunday Times*, 23 June 2013.
45 See IOL News, 8 December 2013; also
Aislinn Laing in the *Telegraph* (London),
9 December 2013.
46 *City Press*, 13 December 2013.
47 *Mail & Guardian*, 28 March–3 April, 2014.
48 All figures from *Independent Electoral
Commission*: 2014 National/Provincial
Elections.
49 All figures from Independent Electoral
Commission.
50 *City Press*, 3 November 2012.
51 See *Sunday Times*, 11 May 2014.
52 *Business Day*, 4 August 2014.

CHAPTER 5
The New Class Structure

1 See I Filatova and A Davidson, *The Hidden
Thread* (Jonathan Ball, 2013), especially
pp 219–46.
2 Cited in D Steward, 'Jan van Riebeeck', FW
de Klerk Foundation, 4 April 2014.
3 *City Press*, 8 January 2014.
4 News24, 26 January 2014.
5 See, for example, http://www.
engineeringnews.co.za/article/
can-south-africas-manufacturing-
sector-rise-again-2014-10-31-1;http://
www.citypress.co.za/business/
sa-ranks-8th-worst-unemployment-rate-list/.
6 *L'Afrique Noire est Mal Partie* (Editions du
Seuil, 1962).
7 In May 2014 the Auditor-General told the
Swazi government that he was suspending
the right of civil servants to salary advances
'due to cash-flow problems', so this process
may have run to its limits. See 'Swaziland:
Lower reserves and cash flow problems',
Moonstone, 9 June 2014.
8 *Mail & Guardian Online*, 14 September 2012.
9 *Business Report, Cape Times*, 3 July 2013.
10 *Mail & Guardian*, 13–19 September 2013.
11 See 'Driving Ms Mbete. Part I', www.inside-
politics.org; and Tony Leon, 'Parliament will
battle under Baleka Mbete', *City Press*, 22 May
2014.

12 *BizNews.com*, 12 June 2014.
13 *Business Day*, 2 May 2013.
14 *Mail & Guardian*, 23–29 August 2013.
15 *The Times*, 17 October 2013.
16 *Business Day*, 7 December 2013.
17 Justice Pillay headed a three-man
commission which was originally appointed
by Premier Nosimo Balindlela for 6 months,
extended to 9 months, to look at financial
abuses in the Eastern Cape government.
They produced 12 huge volumes plus a
100-page executive summary. It was utterly
damning. The accused then took suit against
it and Justice Daylan Chetty set the whole
report aside on two grounds – first that
the extension to 9 months had not been
separately proclaimed and was thus invalid;
second that the commission had not given
those it found guilty the right of reply. The
Premier first opposed this but she then
joined COPE and then the DA and ceased to
be Premier, clearly convinced that the whole
Eastern Cape was a den of corruption. The
point to note is that Justice Chetty set the
report aside on technical and procedural
grounds, but without even contesting the
veracity of those 12 volumes. See *Mail &
Guardian* 18 May 2009.
18 *Business Day*, 14 December 2012.
19 *Fin24*, 6 December 2012.
20 *Sunday Independent*, 28 July 2013.
21 *The Times*, 5 September 2013
22 *Sunday Times*, 5 May 2013.
23 IOL News, 28 May 2013.
24 *Financial Mail*, 20–25 September 2013.
25 *Business Day*, 22 May 2013.
26 *Mail & Guardian Online*, 26 July 2013.
27 *City Press*, 27 January 2013.
28 *The Times*, 30 January 2013.
29 *Sunday Times*, 3 February 2013.
30 Parliamentary reply by the Minister for the
Public Service, Ms Lindiwe Sisulu, *Hansard*,
21 June 2013. By the end of 2013 the number
of ministers had risen to 36.
31 *Ibid*.
32 *TimesLive*, 3 September, 2014; *IOL News*,
18 February 2014.
33 *City Press*, 20 July 2014.
34 *Financial Mail*, 14–19 February 2014.
35 *The Times*, 16 September 2013.
36 *Hansard*, 21 June 2013.
37 *Business Day*, 25 October 2013.
38 The government's own assessment is that 80
per cent of government departments did not
even comply with minimal requirements such
as the submission of plans to the Department
of Public Service and Administration. *Cape
Times*, 12 September 2013.

39 Christo Luus, 'South Africa's growing public debt', www.financialmarketsjournal.co.za/15thed./publicdebt.html.
40 BUSA press statement, 23 February 2011.
41 *Mail & Guardian Online*, 11 November 2011.
42 Luus, 'South Africa's growing public debt'.
43 *Mail & Guardian Online*, 25 October 2012.
44 Ministry of Public Service and Administration: 'Government and labour unions agree on three year salary adjustments', 31 July 2012.
45 *Business Report, Cape Times*, 20 February 2013.
46 *Ibid.*
47 *Fin24*, 29 January 2010.
48 *Business Report, Cape Times*, 8 January 2014.
49 *City Press*, 27 April 2014 and 1 June 2014.
50 *City Press*, 27 July 2014.
51 *The New Age*, 22 May 2014. Overall South African state schools were ranked 148th out of 149.
52 See Greg Marinovich, 'The cold murder fields of Marikana', *Daily Maverick*, 8 September 2012.
53 *Cape Times*, 15 May 2014.
54 *Business Day*, 4 February 2014.
55 *Business Day*, 12 October 2013.
56 *The Times*, 3 October 2013.
57 *The Times*, 3 April 2014.
58 *Sunday Times*, 14 July 2013.
59 *Mail & Guardian*, 31 January–6 February 2014.
60 *Sunday Independent*, 26 January 2014.
61 *Mail & Guardian*, 21–27 September 2012.
62 *Business Day*, 14 May 2014.
63 *Sunday Independent*, 15 September 2013.
64 *Sunday Independent*, 7 July 2008.
65 *Ibid.*
66 See PM Baker, 'Arrest after failure to pay maintenance', www.capetownlawyer.co.za.
67 *Ibid.*
68 *Business Day*, 23 December 2013.
69 *Mail & Guardian*, 24–30 January 2014.
70 *Business Day*, 24 October 2013.
71 *Mail & Guardian Online*, 5 January 2014.
72 http://www.thoughtleader.co.za/sandilememela/2009/09/11/judge-blade-not-by-the-car-he-drives-but-by-the-contents-of-his-head.
73 *Business Day*, 2 October 2014.

CHAPTER 6
Culture Wars

1 *Business Day*, 30 August 2013. WSU paid its staff a R48-million bonus in 2013 despite the university's bankruptcy, the highest staff labour unrest and the lowest pass rate in the country.
2 *Sunday Independent*, 19 July 2008.
3 See RW Johnson, 'Liberal institutions under pressure: the universities', in RW Johnson and D Welsh (eds), *Ironic Victory. Liberalism in post-liberation South Africa* (Oxford University Press, 1998).
4 *Mail & Guardian*, 11–16 April 2014.
5 *The Citizen*, 4 June 2014; *Public News Hub*, 30 May 2014.
6 *City Press*, 6 July 2014.
7 *Mail & Guardian Online*, 23 August 2013.
8 *Mail & Guardian*, 29 August–4 September, 2014.
9 Interviews with Arthur Konigkramer, Durban, 24 and 26 October 2012.
10 *Cape Times*, 18 October 2013.
11 *Mail & Guardian Online*, 23 August 2013.
12 *City Press*, 3 August 2014.
13 *Business Day*, 28 February 2014
14 *City Press*, 17 August 2014.
15 *Business Day*, 18 March 2014.
16 *Business Day*, 10 April 2014.
17 A number of ANC ministers then insisted that the press was forbidden to print further photographs of Zuma's homestead – an extreme extension of the chiefly principle. The press responded by printing fresh pictures of it.
18 *Business Day*, 18 February 2014.
19 *Sunday Times*, 20 April 2014.
20 *Cape Times*, 10 April 2014.
21 Centre for Development and Enterprise, *Mathematics Outcomes in South African schools. What are the facts? What should be done?* (2013). According to the 2001 Trends in International Mathematics and Science Study, South African schoolchildren came bottom in maths and science knowledge in a survey of 21 middle income countries. Given that the major reason for this is the poor quality of teachers, it is likely that such findings would be true across all subjects.
22 An *indaba* is usually a rural retreat lasting several days at which issues are discussed in a discursive fashion, with no actual decisions made or binding agreements reached: in a word, a talk shop. An *imbizo* is somewhat similar but invites community participation. Usually this means that villagers are treated to addresses by the President or ministers; these are held to be major occasions when the movement meets the masses. Again, they are purely talk. Typically, a good deal of food and drink is consumed on both of these occasions.

23 *Business Day,* 29 June 2012.
24 *Business Day,* 23 October 2014.
25 *Mail & Guardian,* 14–20 March 2014.
26 *Ibid.*
27 *Cape Times,* 9 April 2014.
28 *Ibid.*
29 *Cape Times,* 11 November 2013.
30 *Mail & Guardian,* 14–20 March 2014.
31 *Ibid.*
32 See *Sunday Times,* 1 June 2014.
33 Department of Women, Press statement of 19 June 2014.

CHAPTER 7

The State's Repression of Economic Activity

1 *Business Day,* 24 October 2013.
2 *Business Report, Cape Times,* 12 August 2014.
3 *Mail & Guardian Online,* 3 May 2013.
4 *Business Report, Cape Times,* 24 October 2013.
5 Tim Cohen, 'An example to all', *Financial Mail,* 27 September–2 October 2013, p 10.
6 Cited in *Business Report, Cape Times,* 3 January 2014.
7 *Financial Mail,* 11–16 April 2014.
8 See, for example, Dave Steward's commentary on Zuma's Inaugural Speech, De Klerk Foundation, 27 May 2014.
9 *Financial Mail,* 23–28 May 2014.
10 *Ibid.*
11 *Business Day,* 19 May 2014.
12 *Ibid.*
13 *Ibid.*
14 *Ibid.*
15 *Business Day,* 16 May 2014.
16 On the disastrous Minerals Development Act and its effects, see Johnson, *South Africa's Brave New World,* especially pp 403–26.
17 *Financial Mail:* Special Report on Mining, 31 January 2014.
18 *Business Times, Sunday Times,* 6 October 2013.
19 *Ibid.*
20 It is the same with Sasol, now run by a Canadian. Under fire for only spending on maintenance for its assets in South Africa, company spokesman Alex Anderson stressed Sasol's commitment to 'the Southern African region', which mainly meant investment in Mozambican gas. *Sunday Times,* 6 April 2014.
21 *Business Day,* 1 September 2014.
22 *Business Day,* 7 April 2014.
23 *Mail & Guardian,* 25 September–3 October,
2013.
24 'Mining and minerals in South Africa', southafrica.info, 14 February 2014.
25 Econometrix (Pty) Ltd, *Special Report on Economic Considerations Surrounding Potential Shale Gas Reserves in the Southern Karoo of South Africa.* See Executive Summary, point 3.
26 *Business Day,* 11 October 2013.
27 *Legal Brief,* no 3456, 19 February 2014.
28 *Sunday Times,* 14 September 2014.
29 R Grynberg, 'Facets of value', *Africa in Fact,* issue 20, March 2014.
30 R Poplak, 'Manufacturing consent', *Africa in Fact,* issue 20, March 2014; *Financial Mail,* 4–10 September 2014.
31 *Business Day,* 25 October 2013.
32 See pp 163-4.
33 *Business Day,* 1 November 2013.
34 *Business Day,* 30 October 2013.
35 Poplak, 'Manufacturing consent'.
36 *Ibid.*
37 *Business Day,* 11 November 2011.
38 For full table of unit labour costs see *Financial Mail,* 11–16 July 2014.
39 SACP, Moses Mabhida Province, 13 January 2015, 'Moses Mabhida Province speaks from a successful congress'.
40 World Bank, *Economic Update on South Africa: Focus on export competitiveness* (2014).
41 World Bank, *Economic Update on South Africa,* fig 1.3, p 15.
42 'South Africa's automotive industry', www.southafrica.info, 7 February 2014.
43 Private source.
44 *Business Day,* 4 October 2013.
45 *Business Report, Cape Times,* 3 October 2013.
46 *Ibid.*
47 *Business Times, Sunday Times,* 9 February 2014.
48 World Bank, *Economic Update on South Africa,* p 36.
49 *Ibid,* fig 2.3, p 34.
50 *Ibid,* fig 2.5, p 35.
51 *Ibid,* p 36.
52 *Business Day,* 17 October 2013.
53 *Ibid.*
54 *Business Day,* 11 February 2014.
55 *Financial Mail,* 14–19 March, 2014, p 29.
56 *Business Report, Cape Times,* 12 February 2014.
57 *Financial Mail,* 6–11 December 2013, p 32.
58 *Ibid.*
59 *Ibid.*
60 *Legal Brief,* issue no 3454, 17 February 2014.
61 *Financial Mail,* 14–19 February 2014.
62 *Cape Times,* 4 April 2014.

63 See Gugile Nkwinti, 'Farmers can retain 50 per cent ownership of their land', Department of Rural Development and Land Reform, Final Policy Proposals on 'Strengthening the Relative Rights of People Working the Land', 21 February 2014; and FW de Klerk Foundation, '50/50 down on the farms', press release, 9 April 2014.

64 *Legal Brief*, issue no 3456, 19 February 2014.

65 See Hugo Ahlenius, 'Current and potential land use in Africa' (UNEP/GRID-Arendal). http://www.grida.no/graphicslib/detail/current-and-potential-arable-land-use-in-africa_a9fd

66 *Financial Mail*, 2 May 2014.

67 http://www.daff.gov.za/docs/statsinfo/Abstract2013.pdf

68 www.southafrica.info/business/trade/export/agriculture-030212.htm, 29 September 2013.

69 *Financial Mail*, 8 August 2013.

70 *Ibid*.

71 *Business Report, Cape Times*, 13 August 2013.

72 *Business Report, Cape Times*, 7 Jan 2014.

73 *Business Report, Cape Times*, 28 February 2014.

74 *Financial Mail*, 10–15 January 2014, p 14.

75 IMF: South Africa 2012 Article IV Consultation, Staff Report, fig 8.

76 *Business Day*, 1 October 2014.

77 *Business Day*, 18 September 2014.

78 Even a year before, Nedbank, the smallest of the four big clearing banks, had a market capitalisation of over R100 billion. *Moneyweb*, 11 March 2013.

CHAPTER 8

The View from the IMF

1 IMF, South Africa. Staff Report for the 2012 Article IV Consultation, p 11.

2 *Ibid*, fig 5, p 15.

3 *Ibid*, p 16.

4 *Mail & Guardian*, 25–31 October 2013.

5 *Business Day*, 12 October 2013.

6 *Cape Times*, 20 February 2014.

7 *Cape Times*, 2 April 2014.

8 *Ibid*.

9 *Cape Times*, 4 February 2014.

10 *Business Day*, 4 February 2014.

11 *Ibid*.

12 IOL News, 26 August 2012.

13 K Lings, 'Analysis of the 2012/13 Budget', *Stanlib Insights*, February 2012.

14 National Treasury: Report on Public Debt Management (2012), p 2.

15 *Ibid*, p 12.

16 *Business Day*, 7 May 2012.

17 *The Times*, 3 October 2013.

18 *Mail & Guardian*, 29 September 2014.

19 *Ibid*.

20 *Ibid*.

21 The contingency reserve, R42 billion in 2010, was down to R3 billion by 2013/14. *Financial Mail*, 28 February–5 March, 2014.

22 *Ibid*.

23 *Ibid*.

24 *Ibid*.

25 *Financial Mail*, 1-6 March 2013.

26 *Business Day*, 6 January 2014.

27 *City Press*, 2 March 2014.

28 *Financial Mail*, 15–20 November 2013.

29 *Business Day*, 8 March 2013.

30 *Business Report, Cape Times*, 3 November 2013.

31 *Business Day*, 16 January 2014.

32 Private communication.

33 *Business Day*, 4 April 2014.

34 *Financial Mail*, 4–9 April 2014.

35 For the full story of Tshwete and the security industry, see Johnson, *South Africa's Brave New World*, pp 255–56.

36 *Business Day*, 5 November 2013.

37 *Sunday Independent*, 16 March 2014.

38 *Business Day*, 1 November 2013.

39 *Business Day*, 4 October 2013.

40 Interview with Johann Rupert, Cape Town, 28 July 1998.

41 *Business Day*, 29 August 2013.

42 Even back in 2002 the *Financial Mail* reported 90 per cent foreign ownership of BHP Billiton, 70 per cent for Sappi and Anglo's, and 50–70 per cent for Harmony, Anglogold, Angloplats, Goldfields and Impala Platinum, *Financial Mail*, 25 January 2002.

43 *Business Report, Cape Times*, 31 October 2013.

44 IMF Country Report no13/303, *South Africa: 2013 Article IV Consultation*, p 29.

45 *Ibid*, p 25.

46 *Ibid*, pp 30–31.

47 *Ibid*.

48 *Ibid*, pp 13–30.

49 *Ibid*, p 2.

50 *Financial Mail*, 28 February–5 March, 2014.

51 *Business Day*, 2 December 2013.

52 *Business Day*, 27 January 2014.

CHAPTER 9

The Brics Alterative

1 Source: Irina Filatova.

2 Not long before his death in October 2008,

Billy Nair, an ANC MP, told me that the ANC had, sadly, not been able to legislate through what it wished since 'that would have meant US Marines landing on the beaches'. This sort of paranoid fantasy was (and is) widespread.

3 *City Press*, 10 August 2014.

4 *Financial Mail*, 17-22 January 2014.

5 Figures from Department of International Relations and Co-operation, Pretoria, May 2014.

6 From 'Statement by Ambassador Mandisi Mpahlwa of South Africa at People's Friendship University, Moscow, 18 May 2011.'

7 *Sunday Independent*, 31 March 2013.

8 *Mail & Guardian*, 3–9 May, 2013.

9 Blade Nzimande, 'Brics: A critical platform to advance and deepen the National Democratic Revolution?', *Umsebenzi Online*, vol 10, no 10, 4 May 2011.

10 *Cape Times*, 30 May 2014.

11 Redvers was, like me, a Fellow of Magdalen College, Oxford and, like me, had been Senior Bursar. I remember our conversations with pleasure. He died in 1984.

12 This opinion has been ventured to the author by sundry Americans. In addition, Edward Snowden revealed that the USA spied on South African diplomats at the 2009 G-20 summit while *The Guardian* has revealed that British intelligence has penetrated the computers at Pretoria's foreign ministry. In addition the US NSA seems to have maintained regular surveillance of the South African embassy to the UN, its New York consulate and (doubtless) its embassy in Washington. *Sunday Times*, 18 May 2014.

13 *Moneyweb*, 26 March 2013; *Fin24*, 2 September 2013.

14 *Brics Post*, 28 August 2013.

15 *Financial Mail*, 11–16 April 2014.

16 *Mail & Guardian Online*, 5 September 2013.

17 *Business Report, Sunday Tribune*, 12 July 2014.

18 IMF Fact Sheet. IMF Quotas, 1 October 2013.

19 Nancy Birdsall and Devesh Kapur, 'World Bank, IMF influence fades', *Business Day*, 1 April 2014.

20 *The Guardian*, 27 August 2014.

21 *Forbes Magazine*, 28 July 2014.

22 *The Diplomat*, 28 July 2014.

23 *Ibid.*

24 *Moneyweb*, 11 September 2013.

25 Cited in Sergey Radchenko, 'Brics: A strange political partnership', *PoliticsWeb*, 2 April 2012.

26 *Business Day*, 4 June 2014.

27 *Ibid.*

28 *Economonitor*, 28 July 2014.

29 *Business Day*, 15 July 2014.

30 *Business Day*, 28 July 2014.

31 Charles Simkins, 'The New Development Bank and the Contingency Reserve arrangement', *HSF Briefs*, 5 August 2014.

32 *Business Report, The Star*, 3 July 2014.

33 *Mail & Guardian Online,* 5 September 2014.

34 *Business Report, Cape Times*, 29 April 2014.

35 Simkins' phrase. See Simkins, 'The New Development Bank and the Contingency Reserve arrangement'.

36 *Economonitor*, 28 July 2014.

CHAPTER 10

The Impossibility of Autarchy

1 SACP, *Going to the root – a radical second phase of the NDR – its context, content and our strategic tasks* (Cape Town, 29 October 2014).

2 *Financial Mail*, 13–18 June 2014.

3 *Business Day*, 8 July 2014.

4 *Business Day*, 9 July 2014.

5 *Ibid.*

6 SA Government Department of Communications: Message of 7 July 2014.

7 'Alice laughed: "There's no use trying," she said; "one can't believe impossible things." "I daresay you haven't had much practice," said the Queen. "When I was younger, I always did it for half an hour a day. Why, sometimes I've believed as many as six impossible things before breakfast."' Lewis Carroll, *Alice in Wonderland*.

Index